Praise for *Undress for Success*

"The best collection of teleworking *How-To's'* and *Why's'* that I've seen anywhere. This book is a gold mine for anyone seriously considering working from home. Whether you want to freelance, operate your own business, or stay fully employed while you work at home, you'll find dozens of hints and insights in this wonderfully entertaining and insightful book. And if you're an employer who wants to attract and retain talented people, give them a copy of this book, send them home, and reap the benefits of their productivity and motivation. They'll love you for enhancing their lives."

—**Jim Ware**, cofounder, Future of Work Program

"No one should attempt e-work until they understand how to be a competent e-worker. This unique and enlightening guide will help you open the door to e-work success—and improve every aspect of your life in the process."

—**Marcia Rhodes**, Public Relations Director, WorldatWork

"There's never been a comprehensive guide to all aspects of telecommuting, until *Undress for Success*. Whether you want to work remotely occasionally in your current job, find a full-time eWork job, or start a business that allows you to work from or at home, Lister and Harnish cover all of the bases in this comprehensive, easy-to-read guide that clearly outlines the rules of success."

—**Cali Williams Yost**, *Fast Company* expert and author,
Work+Life Fit: Finding the Fit That's Right for You

"*Undress for Success* offers the perfect balance between covering all the details and doing so in an easy-to-read and light-hearted way."

—**Bob Fortier**, President of InnoVisions Canada,
and The Canadian Telework Association

"I wish I'd had this book when I first started out—it's like having your own personal career coach. Reading this will save many new freelancers a lot of grief!"

—**Allena Tapia**, About.com: Freelance Writing Guide and
Editor of Garden Wall Publications

"If you're an old-fashioned manager who's obsessed with face time, hide this book now. There is no way your employees will commute to their cubicles Monday morning after reading this entertaining manifesto for ditching the panty hose and actually enjoying work."

—**Laura Vanderkam**, author, *Grindhopping: Build a Rewarding Career Without Paying Your Dues*

"You could spend years with focus groups, assemble cross-functional internal teams to study and recommend organizational changes, or simply read *Undress for Success* to obtain the practical knowledge necessary to better serve your customers; increase loyalty and productivity; avoid layoffs; and improve your profitability for whatever comes your way. Kate and Tom are the 'guiding hands' for self-reliant control of your future success from home!

—**Jack Heacock**, SVP and cofounder of The Telework Coalition, Washington, D.C.

UNDRESS FOR SUCCESS

UNDRESS FOR SUCCESS

The Naked Truth About Making Money at Home

Kate Lister
Tom Harnish

Foreword by Jack Nilles, internationally acclaimed telework authority

WILEY

John Wiley & Sons, Inc.

Published by John Wiley & Sons, Inc., Hoboken, New Jersey
Published simultaneously in Canada

For general information on our other products and services or for technical support, please contact our Customer Care Department within the United States at (800) 762-2974, outside the United States at (317) 572-3993 or fax (317) 572-4002.

Wiley also publishes its books in a variety of electronic formats. Some content that appears in print may not be available in electronic books. For more information about Wiley products, visit our web site at www.wiley.com

Library of Congress Cataloging-in-Publication Data:

Lister, Kate, 1959-
    Undress for success : the naked truth about making money at home / Kate Lister, Tom Harnish.
      p. cm.
    Includes bibliographical references and index.
    ISBN 978-0-470-38332-2 (cloth)
    1. Telecommuting. 2. Virtual work teams. 3. Home labor. I. Harnish, Tom, 1945-
II. Title.
    HD2336.3.L57 2009
    331.25'68–dc22   2008054164

Printed in the United States of America

10 9 8 7 6 5 4 3 2 1

For Gretchen

Contents

Foreword

One afternoon during the Vietnam War I was summoned to give a briefing the next morning to the Undersecretary of the Air Force. The subject was the status of one of our highly classified space programs. I dutifully assembled my overhead slides (the personal computer hadn't been invented yet) and boarded the "red eye" from LA to Washington, arriving bleary-eyed at 6:30 AM ready to go to the Pentagon. In the subsequent seven hours the meeting was repeatedly postponed until, at 2:00 PM, it was canceled entirely. So I caught the 5:30 flight back to Los Angeles. My foremost conclusion about the trip? This is *dumb*! This situation was especially annoying since, two floors above my office there was an encrypted color videoconference link to the Pentagon. Why couldn't I have used the TV link instead of blowing a whole day—and sleepless night—for nothing? Because only generals were authorized to use the link and I was not a general. Hence the fruitless, expensive round trip via jet.

A decade later I was busy trying to prove that it was possible to use the latest gadgetry ("dumb" terminals connected via a local minicomputer to a downtown mainframe) to avoid similar dumb trips. By then I had morphed from rocket scientist to interdisciplinary research director and, with the help of a grant from the National Science Foundation, signed up a downtown insurance company that was willing to test whether their employees could work effectively from offices nearby their residences. It *worked*! The employees didn't have to make those dumb trips to be successful at their work—their productivity even rose almost 20 percent—and the company saved operating expenses to boot. Even with technology that seems primitive by today's standards.

Another decade and the personal computer had arrived, not to mention increasing traffic congestion and its accompanying air pollution. The dumb trips were getting dumber but the technology was getting better: your office—or at least all the necessary software for it—in a box. With the proper telecommunications interfaces those boxes could be anywhere. Large organizations, like IBM, AT&T and state governments began to realize that many of those daily trips between homes and workplaces were dumb. They also discovered, among other things, that fewer people who need to be in an office meant less demand for office space; in short, reduced expenses for better output means increased profitability. Not so dumb.

By the 1990s the word began to spread around the world that many work-related trips weren't necessary and that the world could go on quite nicely, thank you, without the trips. The European Commission even funded their own research into how this was possible. The idea was spreading in the U.S. like an incoming tide. An occasional disaster, like the 1994 earthquake in Southern California, reinforced the idea that distributed work sites were very useful for ensuring rapid recovery from such calamities. The Internet became an overnight sensation. It was becoming possible to cut long distance travel costs almost to zero by moving the work over the wires—or through the ether—instead of moving the workers to and from work, wherever they or their workplaces were. The pressures from more cars on the congested roads and growing concerns about energy also helped convince employers.

As this century began there were more than 19 million mostly home-based workers in the U.S. whose employers' formal workplaces were somewhere else. On average they were working half time at home. Not getting in their cars for dumb trips. Not polluting. Not wasting energy. Having a fine time. Pretty good but not good enough. Less than half as many as the fifty plus million who *could* be doing it, given the advanced state of the available technology.

So here we are, forty-five years after that non-meeting with the Undersecretary and most of us still are making daily dumb trips. Why is this? We've repeatedly proven that it is possible, even desirable, to have successful organizations whose employees are scattered around the countryside. Technology isn't the problem (if it ever was). So why do we still stick to the old ways? Because many of us are still not sure how to get from that traditional, tense, irritable and frustrated state to a new, relaxed, pleasant and self-fulfilled existence. Change is scary.

Hence, *Undress for Success*. My strategy in the past has been to concentrate on convincing management that it is good for them and their careers to encourage qualified employees to work at a distance. My approach has been top-down. But bottom-up, grass roots also can work very well. In *Undress for Success* we have a pair of experienced authors who focus on getting the workers in shape to work anywhere, to convince their employers/clients, or even to invent their own new tele-jobs. Kate Lister and Tom Harnish have been there. They are practicing entrepreneurs. They know the problems, the terrors, and the joys, of making their own future. Unclad maybe, but this new way to work can be unmitigated success for those who work at it and are well prepared. The issues, the possibilities, the hazards, practical rules of operation and a wealth of options and how-tos are here for you to explore. Particularly if you're thinking of striking out on your own.

Absorb this book. Stop making dumb trips.

—Jack Nilles, president of JALA International and author of *Managing Telework*—The book that inspired nations to rethink the way to work.
Los Angeles, CA

Acknowledgments

No one writes a book alone. Behind the authors credited on the cover are dozens, hundreds, and even thousands of direct and indirect contributors. This book is no exception. While we can't name them all and, frankly, wouldn't want to try for fear of forgetting someone, we appreciate all who played even the tiniest part in making this book possible.

Nevertheless, we couldn't have sounded even slightly intelligent about e-work without the benefit of the smart, persistent, and diligent researchers who have investigated, prodded, and exposed the trend over the past three decades. They're the brains behind more than 300 studies that helped us understand e-work—among them, Jack Nilles, the grandfather of telework; Anne Nolan, Ann Bamesberger, Bob Fortier, Bruce Phillips, Cameron Heffernan, Carol Evans, Chai Feldblum, Christian Anderson, Chuck Wilsker, Danielle Perissi, David Fleming, Diane O'Grady, Ellen Galinsky, Eric Matthews, Fiona Gathright, Heather Casey, Jack Heacock, James Ware, Charlie Grantham, Jennifer Thomas Alcott, Joanne Pratt, Joey Ledford, Judith Casey, Julie Malveaux, John Niles, Jonathan Spira, Joseph G. Grzywacz, Joseph Romm, Joshua Feintuch, June Langhoff, Katie Corrigan, Kelly Sakai, Kerry Rice, Lee Shulmann, Lisa Dawley, Nicholas Ramfos, Patricia Kempthorne, Patricia Mokhtarian, Patrick R. Casey, Peter Conti, Ray Lane, Richard Grunberg, Scott Williams, Steve Gerritson, Susan Seitel, Susan Ann Hewlett, Theresa Noll, Todd Tanner, Tom Cahill, and lots of others.

Thanks, too, to the many organizations that fund, support, and help spread the word about e-work, including Accessible Society.org, American Consumer Institute, Babson Survey Research Group, Borrell Associates, Bureau of Labor Statistics, BusinessWeek Research, CCH, CDW, Center for Energy and Climate Solutions, Dice Holdings, Environmental Defense Fund, Evergreen Consulting Associates, *Fortune* magazine, Federal Trade Commission, GetEducated.com, Global Environment and Technology Foundation, IDC Worldwide, *Inc.* magazine, Information Technology Association of America, Intranet Dashboard, Kenexa Research

Institute, Korn/Ferry Futurestep, Manpower Inc., National Federation of Independent Business, North American Council for Online Learning and the Partnership for 21st Century Skills, Nucleus Solutions, Robert Half, Small Business Administration, Society for Human Resource Management, TalentKeepers, Tanner Group, TechLearning.com, Texas Transportation Institute, the Carnegie Foundation for Teaching, The Nielsen Company, the Reason Foundation, the Taylor Research Group, ThinkEquity Partners, TransitCenter, Trendwatching.com, *Working Mother* magazine, U.S. Census Bureau, the Yankee Group, and many, many more.

What we've learned as a nation about e-work—how to make it work, and why we need it—comes from the continuing hard work of organizations such as the Center for Work-Life Policy, Commuter Challenge, Commuter Connections, Georgetown University's Workplace Flexibility 2010, InnoVisions Canada, MidAtlantic Telework Advisory Council, Sloan Work and Family Research Network, Telecommute Connecticut, Telework Arizona, Telework Coalition, Telework Exchange, Telework.gov, TeleworkVA, Twiga Foundation, Wellness Corporate Solutions LLC, WFC Resources, WorldatWork, and many more who have joined the cause.

Our clothes are off to the corporate pioneers who took the arrows in their backs and made e-work jobs available—and, best of all, aren't afraid to admit they've undressed for success: Access Outsource Solutions, Alpine Access, American Fidelity Assurance, ARO Outsourcing, Avaya, b5media, Best Buy, Booz Allen Hamilton, Cisco Systems, Dow Chemical, eBay, Exclusively RNs, ExpressJet, FedEx Office, Goldman Sachs, KPMG, IBM, LiveOps Inc., McKesson Health Solutions, MySQL, Nortel, Occurrence Teleservices, OSI Business Services, Principal Financial Group, Qualcomm, RTW Inc., S. C. Johnson & Sons, Shared Technologies, Smarthinking.com, SupportSpace.com, Sun Microsystems, Team Double-Click, Time Communications, Triangle Concierge, Troy Research, Tutor.com, VIPdesk, West at Home, Writers Research Group, Florida Virtual Schools, Yahoo!, and many more.

We're indebted to the e-workers who invited us into their spare bedrooms and gave us a peek at the naked truth of what they do there. Thanks to Anne, Ben, Bob, Dan, Eric, Jessica, Laura, Lesley, Lisa, Lois, Martha, Mary, Melissa, Nick, Patricia, Phil, Rhianna, Sue, T. Scot, Tamara, Vickie, Moo, and others whose names have been changed to protect the naked.

Many thanks to the entrepreneurs who toil to weed the Web of the scum-sucking lowlifes who prey on the dreams of others and make it easier for the rest of us to find legitimate e-work, including Allison O'Kelly, Chris Durst, Ian Ippolito, Jenny Krengel, Michael Haaren, Michael Turner, Sara Fell, Sol Levine, Karol Rose, and many others.

We're grateful for the freelance and conventional job boards that allow us to look for work without dressing up and whose executives were willing to share their insights about the e-work trend with us: Jennifer Grasz at CareerBuilder, Susan MacTavish Best at Craigslist, Cathy Siciliano and Emily Call Borders at Elance, Inder Guglani and Bethany Fricker at Guru, Lauren McDonald at Monster, Josh Breinlinger and Orie Zaklad at oDesk, Ian Ippolito at Rent A Coder, Lauren Meller at Yahoo! HotJobs, Dick Bolles at JobHuntersBible.com, Peter Weddle at Weddles.com, and Susan Joyce at Job-Hunt.org. Kudos, too, to networking sites such as Facebook, MySpace, LinkedIn, Bebo, Plaxo, SecondLife, and others for showing us a whole new way to connect with others. They're the beginning of a new social model that we believe will define the boardrooms, watercoolers, and playgrounds of tomorrow.

Thank you for your insights to Cali Ressler and Jody Thompson (*Why Work Sucks and How to Fix It*), Cali Williams-Yost (*Work+Life Fit*), Chris Anderson (*The Long Tail*), Collis Ta'eed (FreelanceSwitch.com), Daniel Pink (*Free Agent Nation*), Scott Allen (*The Virtual Handshake*), Danielle Babb (*How to Make Money Teaching Online*), Jeremy Wright (b5media.com), John Halamka (GeekDoctor.blogspot.com), Marshall Brain (*How Stuff Works* and WebKew.com), Michael Gerber (*E-Myth*), Timothy Ferriss (*The Four-Hour Workweek*), and Tom Malone (*The Future of Work*).

Hugs and kisses to friends and families for putting up with our lack of availability, short tempers, whining, glassy eyes, boring drafts, and missed birthdays.

Thanks to Gretchen, Chelsea, Sarah, Mom, and Dad for ferreting out the spelling, grammar, passive voice, and the lazy word *get* in our manuscript.

A virtual hug for our agent Bob Diforio who responded enthusiastically to our book proposal minutes after he received it. To Shannon Vargo, our editor at Wiley, who *got it* from the very beginning—thank you for assembling a terrific team and making this possible.

Most of all, thanks to you for buying this book. If you liked it, please tell your friends, family, neighbors, and even total strangers that they will, too. A glowing review on Amazon and other bookseller sites would be peachy. We wouldn't be respectable entreprenuers if we didn't ask for the business, now, would we?

Introduction

A re you sick of the rat race? Do you feel like your life is out of control? Are you tired of the time and money you waste commuting?

You're not alone. The majority of U.S. employees would eagerly trade their business suits for sweat suits if they could find a way to work from home. But already, for about 26 million Americans, work is what they do, not where they go.

Way back in 1970 Alvin Toffler understood the problem. In *Future Shock* he wrote, "In a country that has been moaning about low productivity and searching for new ways to increase it, the single most anti-productive thing we can do is ship millions of workers back and forth across the landscape every morning and evening."[1]

Does dressing up and going to an office make you any smarter? Speaking for myself, I can almost feel my I.Q. go down as I pull my pantyhose up. And what's with neckties? Who decided a tourniquet around an executive's brainstem was a good idea?

Does sitting in an office with a gaggle of people make you more productive? Between the obligatory coffee-corner blather, interminable meetings, two-hour lunches, football pools, birthday parties, and cubicle gossip, it's a wonder anything gets done.

To be fair, some folks enjoy the social aspects of office life. They're content with life on the cubicle farm. They like being corralled by the nine-to-five routine and enjoy the time away from home. But if, like me, you're happy to hammer away at your keyboard in solitude, you're eager to shed your business duds, and you yearn for more control over your life, this book is for you.

I remember the polished feeling as I greeted each day in my tailored suit—and the punished feeling after ten hours in Philadelphia's summer swelter. I remember the intrigued feeling as I set out for important meetings—and the fatigued feeling that followed the blah, blah, blah that ensued. I remember the "I've arrived" feeling when I bought my first

Mercedes—and the "I'm gonna die!" feeling as I navigated the SureKill Expressway on the way to work.

A keen sense of the obvious told me the conventional job scene was not for me, so I set out on my own. Over the past 25 years, I've run several successful businesses from the comfort of my own home, and couldn't be happier.

The last 16 of those years, Tom and I owned and operated a vintage airplane ride business, mostly from home. We had seven historic aircraft, 25 pilots, and three virtual staffers. We chose to run the business, for the most part, in our underwear. A reporter once asked: "So what inspired you to start *this* business?" My answer—on live TV—was, "Panty hose. I can't stand 'em."

We sold that business in 2006, and while initially retirement beckoned, we quickly burned out on life in the slow lane. So we set our computers in search of something that would allow us to continue to work, if not *au naturel*, at least in comfy clothes. Google didn't disappoint. It found 1.6 million work-at-home opportunities and another 2.2 million home business ideas. Gulp—we'd be eligible for social security before we'd make a dent in the list.

We engaged our b.s. detectors and quickly realized that finding legitimate at-home work is akin to hunting for lost pirate treasure. You've heard there's booty out there, but you don't know exactly where it is, you're not the only one after it, and all manner of ne'er-do-wells are out to hornswoggle you along the way.

Those who do manage to secure a home-based living still face an uphill battle. They often find that people don't take them seriously because they don't dress up for work.

We encountered the work-at-home prejudice on several occasions as we interviewed people for this book. Though virtual employers themselves, they refused to be quoted because of the title of the book. One virtual accounting firm owner said he didn't think the image of his bookkeepers wearing nothing but a pencil behind their ear would be good for business. "It's not like they're meeting clients in their jammies, so who cares?" says 75-year-old Jack Nilles, who coined the word *telework* over three decades ago.

Another stigma home-based employees and business owners face is that folks think they have it easy. Their co-workers, neighbors, and even families picture them sitting around eating bon-bons while they giggle at reruns of *The Office*. The fact is, successful pajama professionals work every bit as hard as, and often harder than, their dressed-for-success colleagues. Indeed, overworking is a common problem—having the office right there makes it very hard to turn work off at the end of the day.

Troy Research is an all-virtual market research company with seven full-time employees and about 50 contractors. The owner found that not having a "real" office added an unusual hiring challenge. It seems he made a woman a job offer, but her husband insisted she visit the office first. The job just sounded too good to be true, and he figured it was yet another in a long line of rip-offs.

It's been three decades since forward thinkers saw that telework had the potential to unclog the nation's highways, clean up the air, and improve worker morale. Until recently, the anticipated wildfire of change has simply smoldered. Now the high cost of gasoline, labor shortages, environmental worries, and commuter gridlock are adding fuel to the fire. Technologies that weren't available even a decade ago are fanning the flame. In spite of the many obstacles, the at-home workforce is growing by about 10 percent each year.[2]

There's never been a better time to undress for success. Over half of all U.S. employers have tested the waters,[3] and many have found telework the cure for all sorts of business maladies. Venture capital is pouring into companies with remote-work business models. Politicians are calling for laws that support and even require it.

A trip to the bookstore finally pushed us to write *this* book. While we found plenty of titles that claimed to offer expert work-at-home advice, most were stuck in the days when June and Ward Cleaver were the American idols. They touted treasures in antiques, cash from crafts, and fortunes from cookies. Few mentioned the concept of having a *job* you could do from home. Most seemed to assume that only mommies care about spending time with their families. More to the point, none of the books really showed their readers a way home.

What we've tried to do here is deliver the naked truth on how to earn a living at home as an employee, a freelancer, or a business owner. Since most people long for more control in their lives, we've organized this into six sections that you can read in whatever order you darn well please.

Part One, "Bare Essentials," offers a peek at the who, what, why, and how of working from home; the good, the bad, and the ugly; the skills and traits you'll need to succeed; and how to keep from losing your shirt as you attempt to undress for success.

Part Two, "Pajama Paychecks," focuses on how to get a job that allows you to work at home. It includes advice on how to pitch your boss on the concept; the jobs that are best suited for the unsuited; the best-bet virtual and traditional employers (who aren't too prudish to admit they employ people who may be working in their skivvies); and how to use the Web to find a home-based job.

Part Three, "Freelance in Your Frillies," is essential reading if you want to earn a living selling yourself—or at least your skills. It includes details about how to price your services, use the Web to find work, develop professional bids and contracts, manage your workload, and make sure you're paid.

Part Four, "Bedroom Businesses," is for prospective home-based business owners and freelancers. It includes information about the motivations, personality, talents, and resources you'll need; the best home businesses; and the naked truth about what it's like to sleep where you work.

Part Five, "Does It Come with Batteries?" offers a roundup of the technologies you'll need to succeed as a home-based professional.

Part Six, "What If Everybody Did It?" shows why, as a nation, we should make the road less traveled our way to work.

In 1973, a colleague teased Nilles, a former rocket scientist, "now that you've put a man on the moon, why don't you figure out how to eliminate traffic jams?" So, he set out to do just that. Originally referred to as the "telecommunications–transportation trade-off," the concept cried for a more media-friendly moniker. Thus, the terms *telework* and *telecommuting* were born. Nilles defined telework as any form of substitution of information technologies (such as telecommunications and computers) for work-related travel. A teleworker was someone who worked remotely—on the road, at an off-site office, in some other country, or at home. Nilles defined telecommuting as periodic (one or more days per week) work out of a principal office, at a client's site, in a telework center, or at home. To make the difference clear, he points out that, "All telecommuters are teleworkers but not vice versa." Over the years, these terms have become somewhat interchangeable. Related labels include *home-based worker*, *home-based professional*, *home-based employee*, *home-based business owner*, *home-based freelancer*, *remote worker*, *virtual worker*, and *road warrior*. Clever marketers have even created monikers such as *solopreneur*, *mompreneur*, *dadpreneur*, *seniorpreneur*, *ecopreneur*, and *adventurepreneur* to further define the audience.

Still, neither term quite serves our purpose. The focus of this book is work that offers a full-time income and can be done *at* home. Plumbers may work *from* home, for example, but they can't RotoRooter© your drain without leaving their house. To make the distinction between working *from* home and working *at* home, we've decided to use the term *e-work*—a popular term in Europe—throughout this book to describe jobs and businesses that will allow you to undress for success.

To avoid confusing you by switching back and forth between authors' viewpoints, Kate takes the well-deserved spotlight, although we sat within arm's length and worked on the book together. Some names have been changed to protect the naked. No animals were injured in the making of this book, although we came close a couple of times. We accept no responsibility for lost wages, bad investments, or earthquakes over magnitude 3.0.

While the e-work movement has grown steadily over the past decade, for all the reasons you'll read in the pages ahead, we're convinced it's reached a tipping point. As a result, work-at-home jobs, businesses, and resources are changing rapidly. To save you the frustration of typing in long URLs only to find they've since moved, links to all the resources mentioned in this book—and lots more—are available on our web site along with special book-buyer-only bonus material. Visit us at Undress-ForSuccessOnline.com.

1

E-work, the Bare Essentials

1

Who E-works and What Do They Do?

Imagine organizations in which bosses give employees enormous freedom to decide what to do and when to do it. Imagine electing your own bosses and voting directly on important company decisions. Imagine organizations in which most workers aren't employees at all, but electronically connected freelancers living wherever they want to. And imagine that all this freedom in business lets people get more of whatever they really want in life—money, interesting work, the chance to help others, or time with their families.[1]
—Thomas W. Malone, *The Future of Work*

About 14 million people run home-based businesses or freelance in their frillies.[2] In addition, depending on who you ask and how they count, somewhere between 5 million[3] and 12 million[4] Americans hold jobs that allow them to work at home in various states of undress.

The counting problem isn't because no one has bothered to study the work-at-home population. The IRS, Bureau of Census, Bureau of Labor Statistics, Small Business Administration, and a number of private researchers all collect data about people who work from home. But they all come at it with their own needs and biases. Some researchers count small businesses, others don't. Some surveys include people who work from home as little as one day a year, while others focus on people who primarily work from home. Some fail to distinguish between paid and unpaid work. None separate out those employees and business owners who work *at* home from those who work *from* home.

Bruce Phillips, a researcher for the National Federation of Independent Business, described during an interview the task of trying to find the real work-at-home numbers as "a statistical Vietnam—the data goes in, but you can't get it out." As a result, studying the work-at-home population is a little like trying to study meteoroids. We know there are a lot of them and we know they're important, but we don't know where they all are and not everyone agrees on which ones to count. Still, based on what we *do* know, we can begin to develop a model that's helpful.

E-work by the Numbers

While it's true that figures lie and liars figure, statistics do offer a useful insight into the nature of e-workers. Surveys show that men outnumber women e-workers five to three.[5] Four out of five e-workers are married or cohabitating,[6] and three-quarters are college grads.[7] Fifteen percent are over age 55.[8] Forty percent have a household income over $75,000 a year,[9] and only about a third of those who work at home for an employer have been with the company for less than two years.[10]

So a forty-year-old, college-educated, married man, who's been with his employer for five years is a shoo-in right? No, not really. There are lots of thirty-year-old, high-school educated, single women who e-work too.

The Nature of E-work

A program called *Workplace Flexibility 2010* was started by Georgetown University to help policy makers and corporate leaders understand the need for more flexible work environments. They examined the jobs that

Table 1.1   Best E-work Jobs Involve These Processes

Analysis	Editing
Auditing	E-mail correspondence
Budget preparation	Evaluations
Calculating	Graphics
Computer	Internet research
programming	Planning
Conceptual work	Project management
Contract administration	Reading
Concept development	Record keeping
Data entry	Transcribing dictation
Database maintenance	Telephone contacts
Design work	Thinking
Dictating	Word processing
Drafting	Writing

Table 1.2 Best Job Categories

Professional	20%
Sales	17%
Technical	16%
Manager	12%
Clerical	9%
Supervisor	7%
Service	6%
Executive/senior manager	4%
Crafts/skills trades	3%
Operative	3%
Laborers	2%
Other	2%

offer the best fit for home-based work. Table 1.1 is a summary of their findings.[11]

You'll note that many of these skills are common to professional, technical, or sales functions. In fact, those types of jobs account for over half of all e-work. Table 1.2 summarizes the best job categories for e-working.[12]

If you look at the industries where those skills are dominant, as Table 1.3 demonstrates, business services accounts for the highest percentage.[13]

Table 1.3 Best Industries for E-work

Business services	12.3%
Health care services	9.1%
Electronics and computer manufacturing	7.9%
Government/public administration	6.9%
Retail/wholesale	6.4%
Communication services	5.9%
Other/farming/forestry	5.9%
Heavy manufacturing	4.9%
Education	4.4%
Transportation services	4.2%
Construction/engineering	3.9%
Light manufacturing	2.9%
Health care products	2.9%
Food industry	2.7%
Banking services	2.2%
Accounting legal	2.2%
Other financial (insurance and real estate)	1.2%
Restaurant	0.2%
Other personal services	0.2%
Hotel services	0.1%

As we mentioned earlier, some of these industries, such as construction and real estate, don't truly offer the opportunity to work at home—that just happens to be where they're based.

The Trade-offs

Landing an e-work job or starting a home-based business may require retraining, and even a change in lifestyle. For many, the desire to work from home is worth the effort.

Robert is a registered nurse specializing in pediatric care. He wanted to work at home so he could be there if his wheelchair-bound father needed him. He found e-work as a telenurse. It meant a cut in pay, but being available for his father was more important.

Eleanor had a good job as a corporate bookkeeper but decided to freelance so she could spend more time with her kids. It meant a less stable income, but she says the move has really improved their quality of life.

Jim, an at-home legal transcriptionist, has a law degree but frequently moves because of his wife's military career. He doesn't practice law anymore, but he *can* take his job with him wherever she goes.

In the chapters that follow, you'll read how millions of others have made the road less traveled their way to work, and how you can too.

2

What's in It for Me?

When we started writing this book we made a habit of asking people whether they'd like to work from home. Their answers were either something like, "Wow, would I ever" or, "No way; I could never work at home." Since you're reading this book, you're probably one of the former, and a member of a majority. Almost two-thirds of people surveyed by CDW-G, a leading provider of information technology, said they want to work from home.[1] Why? Probably for all the same reasons you do: to ditch the commute, to create a better balance between work and life, and to save money.[2]

Taken from studies of workers around the globe, here's why folks are eager to undress for success.

Save Time

Would you like to add six productive years to your life without giving up red meat or working up a sweat? Sound like an infomercial? It's not. By not commuting, that's how much time a New York City worker would save over the course of a 40-year career.[3]

While not all cities are as hellish for commuters as New York, even the average U.S. worker wastes almost four years of their life on the trek to and from their job.[4] By avoiding the commute, home-based workers have more time for family, friends, exercise, hobbies, or even work.

Achieve a Better Work/Life Balance

The most obvious benefit of e-work, aside from being able to work in various states of undress, is increased flexibility. Need to drop the kids at school at 9:00? No problem. Have to meet the refrigerator repairman between the convenient hours of 8 AM and 4 PM? You'll be there. Want to make sure your Mom takes her medicine? Checking on her is easy. Work better late at night? Bring on the Red Bull.

A whopping 90 percent of e-workers say they are happier with the balance in their lives because they work at home.[5]

Susan, a 32-year-old home-based customer service agent began e-working so she could spend more time with her children. "If I have to, I can schedule my work around my family. Now I can go to the grocery store, make real meals, take the kids to the doctor, meet with teachers, and tuck them in at night. It's even been good for my marriage. I'm not exhausted at the end of the day anymore."

"Being at home and part of my kids' life helps make up for the three days I'm on the road," says T. Scot, a technology manager for FedEx Office and Print Centers. "All said and done, even on a bad day, I have a pretty cool gig."

Be More Productive

Research shows that successful e-workers are more productive than their office counterparts.[6] Sheldon, a news reporter, used to work in the traditional bull-pen-style newsroom. "I was beginning to think I'd never make it as a reporter. I was always missing deadlines. I just couldn't block out the frenzy that was all around me. Since I started working from home, my stories are not only on time, they're often early."

In fact, about 40 percent of e-workers surveyed report being more productive at home.[7]

Save Money

You probably won't make more money as an e-worker, but the money you'll save will substantially increase what's left in your bank account at the end of the week (see Table 2.1 for some examples). And we're not talking chump change here. A typical e-worker can save between $7,000 and $17,000 a year.[8]

Table 2.1 Estimated Annual Savings If You E-work

Expense Item	Office Average	Office High
Parking	$0	$10
Morning latte	$2.50	$2.50
Lunch	$6.00	$15.00
Afternoon soda	$1.25	$1.25
Transportation	$14.55	$29.10
Wardrobe	$2.78	$8.62
$ Saved/day	$27.08	$66.47
$ Saved/year	**$6,770.00**	**$16,617.50**

Lisa, a home-based call center agent for LiveOps (you'll read more about her in Chapter 11) lives so far from civilization that a FedEx driver once asked if she was in a witness protection program. She quit her job as an assistant manager with WalMart when she realized her take-home pay (based on a $40,000/year salary) was less than $12/hour. The cost of commuting and day care took its toll. With LiveOps, she arranges her call schedule so she doesn't need day care, so she can tend to her pet cow, and so she can dress for success in overalls.

Some professionals find e-work allows them to live in more affordable places. As urban and suburban home prices climb out of sight, e-work can allow people to live in more remote, less expensive places. For each $50,000 reduction in housing cost, a family saves about $3,000 a year in mortgage payments.[9]

Paul and Gerry run a graphic design business from their home. In spite of their $100,000-plus combined incomes, making ends meet in suburban Baltimore was a challenge. So they packed their bags and headed for a beach in North Carolina. While their new home is substantially larger, they were able to buy it for $155,000 less than the one they sold. That saves them $9,000 a year in mortgage costs. And because the cost of living in the area is lower, every time they go to the grocery store, movies, or out for a night on the town they save money, too.

The IRS may even reward your work-at-home lifestyle with a home office deduction. The average deduction is about $2,000/year. The rules are strict, but you'll qualify if you run a business from home or are an employee who does not have an office to go to, and if you have space in your home that is used "regularly and exclusively" for business.

Finally, consider what you'll save in dry cleaning, lunchtime shopping sprees, bad office football pool bets, obligatory birthday and holiday presents, all the stuff your co-workers peddle on behalf of their children, and after-work drinks with the gang.

Better Health

Stress is considered a trigger in 85 percent of chronic diseases.[10] E-workers avoid the tension of traffic jams, angst over being late for work, concerns about the family left behind, and the biggest stress of all— at least for me—clothes that pinch, bind, chafe, and constrict.

Then there's the comfort of being surrounded by things familiar— your cat, your favorite chair, and music you enjoy instead of that hideous stuff the punk-junkie in the cubicle next door played so loud you could hear it through his earbuds.

Want to lose 10 pounds of ugly fat? Go virtual and watch the pounds melt away like a Hershey bar on a hot laptop. Speaking for myself and other e-workers I know, working at home allows you to eat healthier. No more pastry stash in the coffee room, cheesy double-double with large fries at lunch, afternoon frappachino, M&Ms from the bowl on the skinny guy's desk, or dinner based on what you can fix in less than 10 minutes. A thousand calories here, a thousand calories there, pretty soon they add up. E-workers also report they're able to exercise more frequently because of the time they save commuting and because their schedule is more flexible.

Finally, while I haven't seen a study on the subject, common sense suggests that e-workers suffer from fewer colds, flu, and other sicknesses, simply because they're exposed to fewer bugs. The conventional work-place is a veritable petri dish. In fact, concern about the spread of contagious diseases is at the root of Federal policy that requires that all eligible employees be allowed to work from home on a regular basis.[11]

Greater Job Satisfaction

Over a thousand workers were asked how satisfied they were with their jobs. E-workers who said "very satisfied" far outnumbered those who worked in offices.[12] In fact, over 40 percent of workers who have the option to e-work are "very satisfied" with their jobs compared to only 27 percent of those who are stuck in the office.

Tony liked his job as a computer programmer, but hated all that went along with working in an office. "My high school guidance counselor was the first person to tell me I was best suited for solitary work. That's part of the reason I went into programming. I finally worked up the nerve to ask my boss if I could work from home. Long story short, he went for it. Before I moved home I liked my job; now I love it."

Level the Playing Field

Have you ever met someone you've only known by phone or e-mail? Chances are, they weren't like you imagined.

"Gee, I thought he was taller."

"I didn't know she was in a wheelchair."

"Boy, his e-mails are hysterical, but he's kind of a wallflower in real life."

"She's a lot older than I would have guessed."

"Was that a safety pin in his eyebrow?"

Fortunately, virtual interaction is the great equalizer. It doesn't matter if you're loud or quiet, skinny or fat, tall or short, young or old, handsome or homely. In the virtual world, what you *do* is what counts.

Live Longer

If you've ever suffered through the daily commute in a big city, you know that driving, particularly at rush hour, can be hazardous to your health. Over 1.5 million people are involved in car accidents every year as they travel to and from work. Forty-four percent of those accidents involve injury or fatality.[13]

Since the most dangerous part of a worker's day is the time he spends in the car, an e-worker may live longer than his commuter friends.[14] Perhaps e-work is a survival strategy.

3

Expose Yourself—Are You Right for E-work?

You wouldn't choose to be a nature photographer unless, in addition to being a shutterbug, you have a good eye, extraordinary patience, and the willingness to travel to places where there are no Holiday Inns. Likewise, you shouldn't choose to work at home unless, in addition to wanting to avoid the commute, you have a supportive family, understand the social and career issues involved, get along with technology, and are highly motivated.

Not everyone is cut out for e-work. There are no hard-and-fast rules about who is or isn't, but a number of studies suggest some common success factors that are worth noting. Table 3.1 lists the skills and traits that are common to successful e-workers.

The absence of any one or even several of these traits isn't necessarily a showstopper if you're determined to undress for success. While I've been successfully working from home for over 20 years, my personality and skills aren't a perfect fit.

Were I less of a loner, I'd be more successful; recognizing that, I make an extra effort to connect with people. I'm also not much of a techie; but Tom is, so on-site tech support is available 24/7.

If you're motivated and willing to work, you're more than halfway there. As you read more about what makes e-workers successful, take an honest look at where your strengths and weaknesses lie, and give some thought to how you can improve your e-work potential.

Table 3.1 Traits of a Successful E-worker

Has a supportive family.
Does not care for young children during working hours.
Has a quiet, secluded area in the home in which to work.
Has moderate need for social contact.
Is able to connect with people nonvisually.
Has strong communications skills.
Is a self-starter and self-sufficient.
Has a strong work ethic.
Is as effective time manager.
Is goal-oriented.
Is a perfectionist.
Likes what he/she does.
Is dependable.
Is organized.
Is good at multitasking.
Is results-oriented.
Is comfortable with technology.
Is a problem solver.
Is computer proficient.
Has a strong desire to work from home.
Climbing the corporate ladder is not a priority.

Support Network

The cooperation of family and friends is an important factor in e-worker success. If the bumper sticker "Piss Your Kids Off, Work at Home"[1] feels like a fit, someone will need a serious attitude adjustment.

Scot preempted any family issues by involving his family from the outset. He, his wife, and their three children worked together to turn their guest bedroom into his new office. They even crayoned a set of ground rules for the office door.

"You have to establish expectations for the kids," he says. "They understand that if I'm in my office, I'm working. If the door is open, I'm not doing anything that will suffer from minor interruptions and it's okay to ask for help with something. But if the door's closed, that means you can't bang on it and expect an answer except in an emergency." After a few minor incidents, they found they needed to clarify the word *emergency*.

Actual emergencies
- The toilet is overflowing.
- The dog's head is stuck in the cat door.
- Kenzie swallowed Nemo.

Non-emergencies
- You're hungry.
- You're bored.
- Bailey's flight simulator plane crashed.

People often hope that e-work will allow them to forego day care. That's not realistic unless your work schedule is very flexible.

Even in families with older children, working at home can require some serious reprogramming. "When I first started working at home, my husband and teenage kids expected their dinner to be ready when they got home. They wondered why they had to help with the housework when I was at home all day," says Helen, a home-based graphic artist.

Friends may need to be educated as well. They may think your home-based position will give you time for coffee in the morning or golf in the afternoon. They may even take advantage of your seeming availability by asking you to meet their appliance repairman or pick up their kids at school. "It'll only take you a few minutes, and I can't get away from work," they'll say.

The problem was so bad for Chelsea, a telenurse, she resorted to posting a sign on the front door (see Figure 3.1).

The neighbors took the hint, but Chelsea didn't receive any Miss Congeniality votes. Oddly, when she spent the same hours working in the intensive care unit at a hospital (plus additional time commuting), her friends admired her dedication.

DO NOT DISTURB
9 a.m. to 5 p.m.
This means you!

Figure 3.1 Do Not Disturb

Office Issues

Most people find that a designated workspace for e-work is a must. "Personally, I've found a door to be an essential work tool," says Eric, a home-based animator. "It helps keeps the distractions out and me in. It allows me to close the door and 'go home' at the end of the day."

Madison, a work-at-home programmer, makes up for what she lacks in office space with an extraordinary ability to concentrate. She manages to twiddle bits from a laptop on her dining room table amidst the chaos of three children, two dogs, and a hamster called Houdini (because he regularly escapes from his cage). To make sure everyone knows when she isn't available, she wears a tiara when she's "at work."

Social Issues

For some, going to the office offers a respite from the battles on the home front. It gives them a chance to spend time with big people—ones who speak in full sentences and rarely wet their pants. It fulfills social needs.

Anne Fisher, a senior writer for *Fortune* magazine, admits, "Every now and then it gets a little lonely—you do miss out on the watercooler buzz and camaraderie of working with colleagues in an office—but, for me at least, the advantages outweigh the disadvantages."

Some e-workers get their social fix along with their morning latte. Doug Novak owns La Costa Coffee Roasting in Carlsbad, California. He says he's seen a dramatic change in his business because of e-work. "We're social beings. People who work at home often come here to work because they seek other people. Not necessarily to talk, just to have them around." His shop was one of the pioneers of free Wi-Fi access in San Diego. It's become so popular among e-workers that he's renovated twice to install more electrical outlets for laptop users.

Others find they're able to replicate the social aspect of work with technology. "You'd be amazed at all the friends I've never seen," says Martha, a home-based call center agent for Alpine Access. She's constantly chatting with co-workers via instant messaging. "It's like popping your head up over the cubicle and saying, 'Hey, does anyone know how to handle this problem?' Someone's always there to help."

OSI Business Services, a 25-person home-based bookkeeping and accounting business, conducts weekly teleconferences to bring its nationwide staff together. Through the company's intranet, employees create virtual friendships and even have virtual birthday parties. Instant chat keeps them constantly in touch.

In organizations where some people e-work and others don't, jealousy can be a problem. Your old buddies may feel cheated: "Why do you get to work at home and I don't? Of course you're more productive—I'm stuck taking care of all the stuff that comes up around here." Others may not believe you're actually working while you're at home: "Finally here to do some real work, eh, Bill?" "Nice tan, Susan. All those extra hours on the golf course, eh?"

For some e-workers, these snipes and jabs can become so demoralizing that they throw in the bunny slippers and head back to the office.

Loners and introverts don't make the best e-workers, either. Left to their own devices, they have a tendency to become even more withdrawn, causing folks at the office to wonder if anyone's home.

Successful e-workers need to communicate with colleagues frequently. It's up to you to keep co-workers and managers informed about what you're working on, what you've accomplished, and what you're thinking about. Set a goal for daily interactions with your manager, and stick to it, no matter how busy you are. Don't let them wonder what you're up to.

Communication Skills

How well e-workers communicate is just as important as how much. Even a seemingly innocuous e-mail can mushroom into a full-blown incident.

Skip, a proctologist, was eager to launch his new ad campaign. He sent Chuck, a home-based graphic artist, what he thought was a light-hearted email, one that would gently urge him on without creating a stink:

> Dear Chuck:
> Do you have those proofs for me? I'm running out of patients.
> Skip

Chuck, already feeling the schedule pressure, neglected to note the spelling of "patients" and replied:

> Skip:
> I told you they'd be ready later this week. Don't get your bowels in an uproar.
> Chuck

E-mail, instant chat, and even telephone communications are very low fidelity. Had Skip been standing in front of Chuck, the turned-up corners of his mouth would have likely explained the joke. Even if it hadn't, Skip would have instantly noticed Chuck's reaction and explained the funny. No dwelling, no swelling. It would have been a nonissue.

Another problem with virtual communications is that silence is often misinterpreted. "Gee, I haven't heard from Brandon all week. I wonder if he's angry about the comments I made on his proposal. I was only trying to help him make it stronger. See if I help *him* out again." Meanwhile, Brandon earnestly pounds away at the proposal, incorporating the much-appreciated suggestions.

Given the ineffectiveness of some electronic media, the best e-workers are good communicators. In the absence of face time, you have to be extra careful that the message sent (or not sent) is the message you intended.

Organizational Skills

As an e-worker, you are the master of your own day, your own schedule, and your own little world. If you don't get to that important project, you have only yourself to blame. If you don't meet your goals, either they were poorly set (for which you are at least partly to blame) or you didn't do a very good job of staying on task.

Sure, office workers have to prioritize, organize, and generally keep themselves on track, too. But the additional oversight and peer pressure in an office environment can help them stay organized.

When you work at home, the boss isn't likely to stop by to see how you're progressing. You're not going to be roused from your stupor by colleagues asking you if you want to go to lunch.

There's been many a day that the setting sun reminded me it was time for dinner. If it wasn't for to do lists, pop-up calendars, and my tummy alarm, I'd be lost.

You have to organize more than your work, too. As an e-worker you'll wear many hats. Even simple things, such as the lack of a company supply cabinet, can sap your productivity if you're not careful.

Phil Plait quit his office job to run BadAstronomy.com full-time. Being the logical, rocket-scientist kind of guy that he is, he knew that working from home would take some getting used to. Still, things he didn't anticipate surprised him:

> I was going through some stuff, and printed out some papers. I
> needed to staple them, so I open the desk drawer. Hmm, no
> stapler there. How about the cabinet? Nope. Shelves? Other
> shelves? Kitchen? Nope, nope, nope.
>
> How can I not have a stapler? How can anyone not have a stapler?
>
> Then I remembered: you idiot, you have to go out and buy one.
> I don't have a job to give me supplies anymore!
>
> Wow. Nothing brings home the fact that you made a major change
> in your life like realizing you need to go out and buy a stapler.[2]

Anyone who's worked at home can probably identify with Phil
Plait's plight. When you realize that somebody used the last ream
of paper, printer cartridge, or box of staples, remember that same somebody is going to have to drop what they're doing to go get more supplies.

Discipline

While research shows that more than half of e-workers feel they were
more productive at home (and only 5 percent felt less productive), almost
a third of non–e-workers worried that productivity would go down if they
worked at home.[3]

Let's face it, most of us would rather play than work, but some
people are more easily swayed than others. No one's going to look over
your shoulder to monitor your progress. You'll need to find a way to
ignore the distractions and separate what you need to do (work) from
what you want to do . . .

> I really should paint that railing.
>
> Oh goody, FedEx just delivered that new racing game.
>
> Those petunias really need to be deadheaded.
>
> I wonder if the DVR caught the last episode of *CSI* last night?

Despite all the hype about working where you want, when you want,
most successful e-workers find they have to settle into a routine.

'Holic Tendencies

Hi, I'm Kate and I'm a workaholic.

If, as an office worker, you frequently take work home and carry your
Crackberry wherever you go, be forewarned that having the office right

there, in the next room 24/7, can be a problem. Your boss may be impressed with how productive you are, but your family may not. "I'll be there in a minute, Honey. I just need to answer one last e-mail." Two hours later, when you emerge, Honey may not be so sweet.

Scot says, "The three-minute commute, including a stop for coffee, is awesome. But instead of reading the paper at Starbucks, I invariably sit down to review endless e-mails. And because I'm responsible for stores in three time zones, they have a head start on me, so it's not uncommon to find myself in the shower after work. After the kids are down at night, I'm often in the office again reading e-mail. Makes for a long day."

"You really have to wrestle with working too much," says Sue LaPointe, owner of Triumph Communications. "It's by far a bigger challenge than staying motivated." Another woman we talked to told us she'd left the hospital with a urinary catheter because of a complication, but she really loved it—said it saved all that time she used to waste going to the bathroom!

Common sense suggests that working at home, away from the watchful eye of society, will exaggerate any other 'holic tendencies you may have. If food, alcohol, drugs, or other indulgences are a problem for you, e-work may not be a healthy choice.

Technology Skills

Computers, software, faxes, modems, telephones, printers, scanners, and copiers are essential elements of the work-at-home world. Being able to work with technology, particularly when it's not cooperating, is an essential skill for e-workers. Whether it's the Microsoft Windows blue screen of death, a computer virus, a backup glitch, a firewall issue, or a cable or DSL modem failure, you need to be able to diagnose and fix the problem quickly.

Fortunately, companies with experience in e-work understand that not having the IT department down the hall is a problem for remote workers. A 2008 survey showed that three-quarters of e-work employers provide some type of remote technology support—a substantial increase from the less than half that offered it the year before. Of those that provide support, almost all offer telephone help, two-thirds offer online help, and half employ technologies that allow them to troubleshoot and fix your computer just as if a techie was sitting in front of it.[4]

If the company where you e-work doesn't offer tech support, or if you're planning to freelance or run a home business, consider that even a mild case of technophobia can mean trouble, so give some thought to how you're going to manage it. You could take a computer course, for example, or subscribe to a remote tech support service. Whatever you do, don't pretend it won't be a problem. When your computer flips a bit as you're rushing to meet a deadline, flipping your lid isn't going to help.

Chapter 34 offers a rundown of the major types of e-work technologies and our favorite providers of them.

Advancement Issues

Over 60 percent of executives surveyed by Futurestep (a subsidiary of Korn/Ferry International, one of the premier talent hunters in the world) felt that e-workers missed out on advancement opportunities. Indeed, e-workers often report suffering an out-of-sight, out-of-mind bias. They feel that when organizational opportunities arise, those with the most face time win out.

As e-work evolves, standout performers will be recognized for what they do, not where they do it, but corporate America has a long way to go in this regard. For now, if you want to climb the corporate ladder while you e-work, frequent proactive communications are essential. Use the telephone, e-mail, instant messaging, webcams, video conferencing, and even regular office visits to solidify your relationships and maintain your presence. Don't be a virtual wallflower.

4

Dirty Underwear—Uncovering the Scams

Our research shows that the ratio of scams to legitimate home-based opportunities is almost 20 to 1. The problem is so bad that even the Federal Trade Commission (FTC) has its hackles up.

"Bogus business opportunities trample on Americans' dreams of financial independence," said FTC Chairman Deborah Platt Majoras. "If a business opportunity promises no risk, little effort, and big profits, it almost certainly is a scam. These scams offer only a money pit, where no matter how much time and money is invested, consumers never achieve the riches and financial freedom promised."[1]

Scam Busting

Determined to remedy the situation, in December 2006 the FTC announced Project FAL$E HOPE$, a federal and state law enforcement sweep targeting bogus business opportunities and work-at-home scams. The crackdown involved more than 100 law enforcement actions by the FTC, the Department of Justice, the United States Postal Inspection Service, and law enforcement agencies in 11 states.[2]

Peter D. Keisler, former Assistant Attorney General for the Justice Department's Civil Division, says the sweep eventually led to sentencing 25 defendants to a total of over 160 years imprisonment for causing $86 million in consumer losses. Project FAL$E HOPE$ is a good start, but given the number of scams out there, it's a bit like putting a BandAid over a spurting artery. What's really needed is a tourniquet on the flow of money that supports these miscreants. As long as people fall for their schemes, they'll continue to exist. So the trick is to separate the wheat from the crap, the dough from the dung, the headlines from the horse-pucky. Keep reading and we'll show you how.

Sniffing Out Cons

New Web-based swindles are launched every day, but they're mostly variations on old themes. Here are the most common among them.

The Bait and Switch

A web site offers you free access to job listings. They'll even e-mail you new listings as they're added. Of course, the listings don't disclose who the employers are, and the only way to apply for the job is to sign up for the web site's resume distribution services. For just $29.99, they'll allow you to apply for as many jobs as you want for three months. Or choose their $59.99 premium service and they'll forward your resume to their phantom employers for a full year. Best of all, their $199.99 super-duper service offers to e-mail your resume to thousands of employers (who aren't hiring).

I followed one of the more prominent bait-and-switch web sites to see where it led. The first thing that happened was I received this e-mail:

> Hi Kate:
>
> When you first signed up with us you were taken to a special page that gave you the opportunity to apply for work directly with us. However, our support desk has recently been getting emails from people who missed that link. So, in case you missed it . . . here it is again:

When I clicked on the link provided, it took me to a full page of ads for other bait-and-switch sites. At the bottom of the page was a line that offered a link to the many jobs they themselves were offering "as a result of overwhelming growth." There were so many they had to assemble them into categories. Feeling geeky, I chose the programming category. Click, blink, and I'm on a page with more ads for bait-and-switch job links and, as always, lots of links to sites that offered salvation from scams: Data Entry Jobs Exposed, Avoid Work-at-Home Scams, They're All Scams, I Was Scammed 101 Times, and so on.

This entire site and all the sites it links to have one purpose—to get you to click on the ads so they make money. Even their scam warnings were linked to scams!

Send Us Money and . . .

We'll send you a list of employers, we'll share our secrets for how you can make millions, we'll enroll you in our exclusive club . . . we'll take you to the cleaners.

Sounds Too Good to Be True

Make $50/hour. No education, training, experience necessary. Make $100,000 part-time. Make a fortune while you sleep. In your dreams.

Hide 'n' Seek

Our opportunity is so fabulous that we have a whole web site dedicated to not telling you what it is. Send money, and we'll enlighten you. Or not.

Super-Colossal Sites

Marketing experts have identified a number of words that supposedly stimulate a Pavlovian response among unwary consumers. Scamsters seem to subscribe to the more-is-better theory, and their sites are littered with words and phrases such as *Free, Colossal, Premium, Guaranteed, Top Rated, Proven Winner, Top 10, No Risk, Limited Time Offer, Act Now, Big Money $Fast$, Quick and Easy!!!!!* (They're especially fond of exclamation points!)

Capital-Letter Sites

Many of the web scammers apparently use the same keyboard. You can tell because the caps lock is obviously stuck in the "on" position. These sites are usually infested with phrases like BUY NOW, LIMITED TIME OFFER, and ONLY 10 TERRITORIES LEFT. They're so excited by your visit that they flash, dance, jiggle, pop over, pop under, play music, or otherwise scream for attention.

As Seen on TV

Or not. Don't believe everything you see. Just because a web site says they've been featured in the *New York Times*, in *USA Today*, or on CNN

Figure 4.1   "As Seen on TV" Logos

doesn't mean they have. (See examples in Figure 4.1.) Unless they actually provide links to the relevant articles or features, they probably haven't.

100 Percent Legitimate Scam-Free Listings

Just because it says their job posts are fully researched or scam-free or 100 percent legitimate, don't believe it. Almost all of the scam sites we visit offer advice on how to avoid scams.

Bogus Seals of Approval

Don't assume that a seal of approval means anything. All three shown in Figure 4.2 appeared on an at-home job scam site. The first obviously is supposed to make you think they're approved by the Better Business Bureau, but the BBB has no record that the site owners are members. The second is a seal from a company that says in its web site's fine print, "The Better Internet Bureau does not monitor or regulate businesses. Our sole purpose is to monitor Internet sites for content that may be useful to our members." They offer no oversight of member companies (aside from whether they pay their $45 to join). And the third seal isn't related to any company or service at all. What's more, the site's fine print specifically says, "No Refunds."

Figure 4.2   Bogus Seals of Approval

All Dressed Up and Nowhere to Go

Be very skeptical of companies that imply that there are thousands of employers waiting to hire you, but don't say who they are unless you pay to join. Typically, all you'll receive for your money is a list of companies you could have found yourself. Many such sites also offer training—for a fee, of course. But employers may not recognize their training program, and your expensive diploma won't be worth the paper it's printed on.

Big Deposit, No Returns

Don't buy anything that doesn't offer some kind of return policy. And don't count on getting your money back even then. Remember, if it walks like a scam, and it quacks like a scam. . . .

Certified by Me

One of the more common scams is to offer certification or accreditation for work that doesn't require certification. One scammer in the virtual assistant field offers certification, for example, but none is required.

Located in Scenic Downtown Nowhere

If a web site doesn't offer a legitimate company address or any way to reach them, it's probably a scam. If their address is 1000 Harvard Way, Princeton, Florida, crank up Google Maps, and make sure that such a place exists. Call the office, and see if you get a real human. Ask them to mail you materials. If they won't, it's probably because they know it's a Federal offense to use the U.S. mail for fraudulent purposes.

Resume Snatchers

If you post your resume on job boards, even legitimate ones, don't be surprised if you receive bogus invitations to work, such as this one:

> Dear Kate,
>
> We saw your resume on Monster.com, and believe you are a perfect fit for our company.
>
> Please fill out the attached application, and be sure to include your social security number for identification purposes.

Using a technique called *spoofing*, the sender's e-mail may even look like it came from Monster.com, but don't believe it. These shysters are identity thieves, and all they want is your social security number.

Business Opportunities

The FTC has rules about what information must be provided to a prospective business opportunity buyer when the price of admission is over $500. If the marketing materials or ads include an income claim, the seller must disclose the percentage of buyers who achieve that level of income. In addition, they must give the names of 10 prior purchasers as references. If the promoter doesn't offer this information, assume it's a scam.

E-mail Miners

Some sites' whole purpose is to obtain your e-mail address so they can sell it to other scammers. Here's a letter I received after posting my resume on a job board:

> From: brianna@nvidia.com
>
> Subject: No fee required to work with us
>
> Date: November 27, 2007 11:31:54 PM PST
>
> We are looking for partners worldwide. The position is home-based. Our Company Head Office is located in UK with branches all over the world. We are looking for talented, honest, reliable representatives from different regions. The ideal candidate will be an intelligent person, someone who can work autonomously with a high degree of enthusiasm. Our Company offers a very competitive salary to the successful candidate, along with an unrivalled career progression opportunity.
>
> If you would like to work with our active, dynamic team, we invite you to apply for employment. Preference will be given to applicants with knowledge of multiple languages. Please send the following information to LnorPeryZX@gmail.com . . .
>
> Thank you. We look forward to working with you.

The giveaway, of course, is their request that I respond to a different e-mail address than the apparently legitimate one at the top of the e-mail. NVIDIA is a very respectable company, but this e-mail ain't from them.

One way to fend off e-mail spam is to use disposable e-mail addresses (DEAs). Yahoo and other web-based mail servers allow you to set up custom addresses that you can throw away if they start receiving spam. If your regular address is PajamaProfessional@yahoo.com, you can set up other addresses such as PjProf-jobs@yahoo.com, PjProf-monster@yahoo.com, PjProf-craigslist@yahoo.com, and so on. DEAs can be a handy way to filter your e-mail as well. For example, if you want to send all the Craigslist responses to one folder, just set up a filter to recognize your custom e-mail address when it comes in.

What You See Is *Not* What You Get

It's amazing how many ways scammers have found to exploit the Web. They've even found ways to hijack you away from legitimate sites. They create Doorway, Bridge, Portal, and Zebra pages to dupe you into coming to their sites. They hack, scrape, and cloak legitimate web sites to draw you into their web. And when the search engines get wise to their techniques, they quickly conjure up new ones.

Call This 1-900 Number

A 900 number is the opposite of an 800 number: The caller pays. But the insidious part is that the call rate is set by the scammer—it's not a standard long distance call rate. You can be out $20 to $30 before you realize that the number you've called is bogus. The really nasty scammers are adept at stringing you along with seductive messages, imploring you to please stay on the line. Of course, the whole time, you're paying an outrageous rate for the privilege of being on hold.

Top Scams

Some work-at-home and business opportunity scams are more prevalent than others. According to the FTC, the top ones involve medical billing, envelope stuffing, and craft assembly. Here are more details about each from the FTC:[3]

Medical Billing
Ads for prepackaged businesses—known as billing centers— are in newspapers, on television, and on the Internet. If you respond, you'll get a sales pitch that may sound something like

this: There's "a crisis" in the health care system, due partly to the overwhelming task of processing paper claims. The solution is electronic claim processing. Because only a small percentage of claims are transmitted electronically, the market for billing centers is wide open.

The promoter may also tell you that many doctors who process claims electronically want to *outsource* or contract out their billing services to save money. Promoters will promise that you can earn a substantial income working full- or part-time, providing services like billing, accounts receivable, electronic insurance claim processing, and practice management to doctors and dentists. They may also assure you that no experience is required, that they will provide clients eager to buy your services, or that their qualified salespeople will find clients for you.

The promoter will follow up by sending you materials that typically include a brochure, application, sample diskettes, a contract (licensing agreement), disclosure document, and, in some cases, testimonial letters, videocassettes, and reference lists. For your investment of $2,000 to $8,000, a promoter will promise software, training, and technical support. And the company will encourage you to call its references.

Few consumers who purchase a medical billing business opportunity are able to find clients, start a business, and generate revenues—let alone recover their investment and earn a substantial income.

Envelope Stuffing

Promoters usually advertise that, for a "small fee," they'll tell you how to earn money stuffing envelopes at home (or doing its modern variation, processing e-mail). Later, when it's too late, you find out that the promoter never had any employment to offer. Instead, for your fee, you're likely to get a letter telling you to place the same envelope-stuffing ad in newspapers or magazines, or to send the ad to friends and relatives.

Assembly or Craft Work

These programs often require you to invest hundreds of dollars in equipment or supplies. Or they require you to spend many hours producing goods for a company that has supposedly promised to buy them.

For example, you might have to buy a sewing or sign-making machine from the company, or materials to make items like aprons, baby shoes, or plastic signs. However, after you've purchased the supplies or equipment and performed the work, the fraudulent operators won't pay you. In fact, many consumers have had companies refuse to pay for their work, already delivered, simply because it didn't meet undefined "quality standards."

Curiously, no work is ever up to standard, leaving workers with relatively expensive equipment and supplies—and no income.

Other Scams

Other common scams involve (1) pyramid schemes, a type of multilevel marketing that relies on you to recruit other sales agents instead of selling actual products; (2) chain letters and e-mails; (3) paid surveys; (4) mystery shopping; and (5) refund recovery agents who supposedly help assist UPS and FedEx customers to obtain refunds.

Do Your Homework

Aside from keeping a cynical eye to the Web (and elsewhere), here are some ways you can protect yourself from bogus work-at-home opportunities.

Check to see if your local consumer protection agency or state attorney general's office has any complaints on file about the company. Try the Better Business Bureau and see what they can tell you. Also be sure to check the same agencies in the state and county where the business's home office is located. Don't, however, take a lack of complaints as a green light. Many unscrupulous promoters regularly change their name and location to avoid detection.

Ask the following questions before you get involved in any work-at-home programs, and get the answers in writing, preferably by U.S. mail:

- What specific tasks will I perform?
- Will I be paid a salary or will my pay be based on commission?

- If commission, what will it be based on?
- Who will pay me?
- How will I be paid?
- When will I get my first paycheck?
- What costs will I incur (application fees, training, supplies, equipment, software, direct deposit fees, phone/fax/Internet installation and usage, other)?
- If I'm purchasing equipment or materials, exactly what will I receive for my money? Will you send me a sample?
- What is your return policy? Can I have it writing?

Then do a Google search on the company name(s) and executives' names along with the word *scam* or *complaint* and see what you turn up. Even a phone number and the word *scam* can provide interesting results.

If equipment purchases are involved, search eBay to see if people are trying to dump what they bought after being scammed.

Ask for references and check them out thoroughly. If they won't supply any, run. If they do, make sure they're legitimate and not from shills, insiders pretending to be unbiased.

Never provide your social security number, driver's license number, or bank information over the Internet—this goes for listing it in your online resume as well. Legitimate job sites and prospective employers will offer a way to keep this information private.

Never enter private information on a pop-up form or any web page that does not provide a secure connection—a URL that starts with "https."

Copy a couple of unique phrases or sentences off the web site you're interested in, and paste them into Google's search box. If a number of identical-looking sites come up, it may be a scam.

Check out all business and job opportunities on Ripoff Report (http://www.ripoffreport.com). It's an online watchdog that offers scam victims a place to vent their spleen.

Get Even

If you're stung in a business opportunity or home-based job scam, don't just get mad, get even. Click on the "I've been scammed" link on our web site (UndressForSuccessOnline.com) and we'll show you how.

2

Pajama Paychecks: Jobs You Can Do in Your Jammies

5

Who's Paid to Work at Home and What Do They Do?

If you want to work from home, but aren't the freelancing or entrepreneurial type, you have three options:

1. If you've already established yourself with a traditional office job, your best bet for becoming an e-worker may be to approach your boss regarding a work-from-home plan. Chapters 6 through 9 offer plenty of advice for how to get to yes.
2. If you're up for a career change, jobs that offer pure e-work are becoming commonplace. These include call center agents, virtual assistants, transcriptionists, educators, technical support specialists, writers, and even medical professionals. Chapters 10 through 17 offer details about these professionals and the companies that employ them.
3. Finally, you can search for a job with a company that's known to embrace e-work. Once you've established your credibility with them, you can approach your boss about working from home some or all of the time. Chapters 18 through 21 will help you find and approach these employers.

In 2006, the American Community Survey (U.S. Census Bureau's interim census) asked respondents to state their primary place of work. About 5.4 million employees, or about 4 percent of the population, said they mostly worked from home.[1] Almost a third of them do so full-time.[2]

When you consider that estimates suggest about 40 percent of employees hold jobs that could be performed at home (about 50 million people),[3] you can see that corporate America has a long way to go on the road to e-work.

Still, there are many indications that times are changing, and rapidly. The International Telework Association and Council (ITAC) reports that 62 percent of companies now offer e-work as a means to attract and retain employees.[4]

6

Take Your Job and Love It

I f you love your job but long for the many advantages of working from home, this chapter will help you see things from your employer's perspective. Keep reading and we'll help you convince them it's a good idea—assuming, of course, that you have the right job and the right boss. Just as not all individuals are suited for e-work, not all managers or organizations are comfortable with the concept of their employees working in their tighty-whiteys.

Company Assessment

In the process of researching this book, we analyzed over 250 studies on e-work and related topics. We interviewed many of the top researchers and advocates in the field. And we interviewed dozens of successful and not so successful e-workers and managers. Here's what we've found.

The most successful e-work companies:

- Enthusiastically support the concept throughout the organization.
- Measure performance based on results.
- Trust their employees.
- Provide e-work training and technology for both managers and employees.
- Are flexible.
- Understand work-life issues.

The companies that can most easily make the e-work transition:

- Use technology to access and retrieve company information.
- Have data security policies and procedures in place.
- Offer collaborative online technologies.
- Offer remote technology support.
- Are quick to integrate new technologies.
- Are competitive.
- Are innovative.

The employees most likely to be chosen for e-work:

- Are above-average performers.
- Have substantial experience in their jobs.
- Are dependable.
- Have good relationships with co-workers and managers.
- Understand and embrace the company's culture.
- Are familiar with available company resources.
- Understand the company's policies, procedures, and technologies.

If you work for a company or individual whose managerial mind-set is stuck in the days of sweatshops and typing pools, chances are that even an expertly crafted e-work proposal won't convince them to let you work untethered. So let's start out by seeing if your work situation is suitable.

Corporate Culture

While some organizations talk the talk when it comes to e-work, they still don't walk the walk. For example, in spite of a federal mandate that requires government employees to e-work as much as possible, almost two-thirds of federal government managers felt their agencies did not support the practice.[1] As a result, less than a half of federal workers who are eligible to e-work actually do.[2]

While you may not be able to do much to fix your organization's culture, you need to be aware of how it can sabotage your e-work attempts. Major corporate obstacles include:

- Failure to measure product, not process.
- Senior management's lack of, or inconsistent, support for the concept.

- Failure to adequately gain the support of middle managers.
- Lack of training on how to manage e-workers.
- Failure to prepare employees for the special issues they'll face working from home.

Grace is a division manager for a large insurance company. In 2005, her company set up an e-work program with a goal of having half their staff e-work by 2007. Her division exceeded that goal and everyone seemed happy with the results of the program. But in 2008, Grace found herself with a new boss who felt employees should not be trusted to work from home. While existing e-workers continued to do so, no new hires were given that option. This sort of on-again, off-again commitment wreaks havoc with morale and program results.

For e-work to succeed, managers at every level need to be enthusiastic supporters. They need to have the resources to make it happen. They need to understand the special issues involved in managing a cyber staff. And they need to learn from the many other organizations that have already been down this road. Managers who fail to believe in the work method, or fail to share their vision downstream, set their e-work programs up for failure and rob their companies of the many rewards these programs offer.

Not surprisingly, those managers who are e-workers themselves are far more likely to see the advantages for their employees. While a little over half of federal managers who did not manage e-workers support the concept, over three-quarters of those who were themselves e-workers do favor it.[3]

Assuming your boss, her boss, and her boss's boss aren't Neanderthal in their attitudes, the next step toward convincing them to let you e-work is to see things from their perspective.

7

The Naked Truth about Your Boss

If you want to convince employers to allow you to e-work, you have to think like them. You need to make sure your e-work proposal addresses their concerns and explains how they're going to benefit. While your proposal may only deal with your own e-work, it will be stronger if you can document the broader impact it could have on the organization. Fortunately, there is a lot of research and plenty of outstanding resources to help you make your case.

Jack Nilles's book, *Managing Telework: Strategies for Managing the Virtual Workforce* (Wiley, 1998), though written more than a decade ago, continues to be one of the most insightful books about e-work on the market today. If you're serious about e-work, this is a must-read for both you and your employer.

Nilles laments: "The biggest barrier to telework continues to be fear; managers are afraid that employees won't work unless they're watching over them." He once argued with management guru Tom Peters about Peter's theory of management-by-walking-around. "That's fine for crumby organizations where managers don't trust their employees," said Nilles, "but if managers establish goals and criteria for meeting those goals, they can show employees what they want, how to do it, and then get out of their way."[1]

Beyond the issue of trust, other top misconceptions among managers, in spite of evidence to the contrary, are that e-work will reduce productivity (cited by 63 percent of managers) and increase security risks (cited by 43 percent of managers).[2] Their other concerns are that e-work will reduce face time, foster animosity among co-workers, require operational and organizational changes, and increase costs.

Let's look at each of your employer's potential concerns in more detail.

The Boss Worries That E-work Will Reduce Control and Productivity

Based on a recent survey, while nearly three-quarters of managers believed remote employees were more productive—and 9 out of 10 said they trusted their remote workers—a third also confessed to wanting to monitor their employees closely just to make sure.[3]

From Peter Drucker's introduction of Management by Objectives in the mid-1950s, to Six Sigma, which was popularized by General Electric's Jack Welch in the 1990s, setting and measuring goals has long been held as the key to good management.

"Work isn't a place you go—it's something you do," says Cali Ressler, author of *Why Work Sucks and How to Fix It*. "When individuals and organizations embrace this idea, it frees people up to do their best work." She should know. She and co-author Jody Thompson conceived and implemented the revolutionary Results-Only Work Environment (ROWE) that transformed retail giant Best Buy into a company where employees do "whatever they want whenever they want as long as business objectives are achieved. They get paid for a chunk of work, not a chunk of time."[4] The results, in terms of employee satisfaction, retention, and productivity, were so impressive that the program made the cover of *BusinessWeek*. More important, Ressler and Thompson's company, CultureRx, is swamped by requests from Fortune 1000 companies looking to repeat Best Buy's success, according to John Larson, a spokesman for CultureRx.

The Boss Worries That E-work Will Reduce Face Time

If you think about it, remote management is not new. In large companies, several floors or thousands of miles may separate employees. Business travel may keep managers apart from their staff for weeks or even months at a time. Still, more than half of all managers see the lack of face-to-face contact as a disadvantage to e-work.[5]

While a supporter of e-work in theory, Futurestep's Robert McNabb admits that he wants his people near him, particularly in a crisis. "There's no technology that can replicate the 'energy in the room' when a crisis occurs," says McNabb.

Managers also worry that without face-to-face contact, e-workers will miss the subtle grooming that traditional offices provide in things like how to dress, how to speak, what to say, what not to say, and how to act under pressure.

When you approach your boss about e-work, remember what we said in Chapter 3 about the need for constant communications. Tell him how and how often you intend to stay in touch. Assure him that you can stay connected via instant chat, e-mail, telephone contact, and other means.

Boel Larsen, director of human resources for MySQL, has found some unique ways of keeping her worldwide virtual employees connected. They hold events such as Global Sports Day and Global Culture Day. Everyone is reimbursed for an activity on the same day, and they're all encouraged to post photos on the company intranet of the fun they had.

Robert Stephens, founder of Geek Squad—the computer repair company now part of retail giant Best Buy—once told his deputy director for counterintelligence (company titles follow a military/law enforcement theme) that he was worried about their "agents" in Anchorage, Alaska, staying connected. The reply: "Oh, I talk to them all the time. We play Battlefield 2 online together several times a week." While not exactly your conventional approach to corporate communications, it does the trick.

For Bill Gerber, managing director of OSI Business Services, not only does technology makes it possible for him to monitor every key-stroke, every memo, every chat, every e-mail, and every document that passes among his 25 remote bookkeepers, he's constantly in touch with them throughout the week. They each have their own assigned clients, know what they have to do, and can call on him if they need help.

As bandwidth continues to increase and new technologies evolve, the line between *being* there and being *virtually* there will continue to fade. Already, younger workers who grew up in a virtual world are far more comfortable with remote work.

The Boss Worries That E-work Will Foster Animosity

As we wrote earlier, people who don't e-work sometimes resent those who do. Rather than backpedaling after feathers are ruffled, smart companies set up standards for who can e-work. Employees should see e-work as a benefit that is earned rather than given, or, better yet, a strategic work method. Not everyone will make the cut. "Allowing office slackers to work from home won't make them any more productive. In fact, it will probably have the opposite effect," says Jerry, a senior Federal Aviation Administration official who manages e-workers.

If someone isn't allowed to e-work, they need to understand why. If it's because of performance issues, they need to know that. If they weren't chosen because of the nature of their job, they need to understand that as well.

As you approach your boss about working from home, keep in mind that your request can't be considered in a vacuum. How it will affect others is a concern you'll have to address. You can help do that by offering concrete, measurable reasons why you think you should be allowed to e-work. If nothing else, propose yourself as a test case. This will encourage your co-workers to support your efforts rather than resent them.

The Boss Worries That E-work Will Require Change

Most people would rather cling to what they know than venture into unknown territory. But when the world around you is changing, that can be a dangerous attitude. "If you always do what you have always done, you'll always get what you always got," according to Linda Casey, director of operations support for McKesson, a pioneer in home-based medical triage. Newer, more agile competitors will replace businesses that fail to adapt.

Your e-work proposal should highlight how the many advantages of e-work will help your company stay ahead of the pack.

The Boss Worries That E-work Will Increase Costs

Some companies blindly focus on the cost of establishing an e-work program. The fact is the majority of companies that have put keyboard to spreadsheet, or have actually tried e-work, agree the savings outweigh the costs. Both NCR and Lucent Technologies found the savings to be more than double the e-work program costs.[6]

"While saving money was not the impetus for e-work, it's definitely been a side benefit," says Barbara Wankoff, director of workplace solutions for KMPG, one of the nation's largest accounting firms.

In Chapter 8 we'll look at the many ways e-work saves companies money, but when most employers mention the costs involved, they're generally referring to the computers and other home office equipment.

Research shows that the average first-year cost per e-worker is just over $1,000, and subsequent year costs can be as low as $300.[7]

That said, many employers spend nothing at all. Only about a third of federal agencies, for example, pay for home office equipment. Of those that do, the majority pay only a portion of the costs.[8]

Admittedly, companies new to e-work may incur additional overhead from labor associated with policy development and program implementation, technology assessment, systems configuration, employee manual revisions, and tech support solutions. However, these costs need to be balanced against the benefits, both financial and nonfinancial, of a successful e-work program.

The Boss Worries That E-work Will Increase Security Risks

Some employers' fear or naivete about security issues can curb their enthusiasm for e-work.

In 2006, for example, a Veterans Administration laptop was stolen. The loss threatened to expose private data, including social security numbers, for 18,000 veterans. While the publicity in the case aroused new concerns about e-work, the loss did not, in fact, involve a formal e-worker—it was just someone taking work home.

Security breaches are a very real concern, but the issues are not specific to e-work; they're organization-wide. They're not even specific to technology. They happen when employees carry paper files to their homes. Security breaches can even occur while chatting in an elevator, in a bar, or at a coffee shop.

While e-working at Starbucks one morning, we overheard a fellow at the next table talking on his cell phone—loudly—to someone about his strategy for dealing with the person he was waiting to meet. "Yeah, I won't bring that up unless he does . . . " It was obvious from the conversation that the person he was meeting was a potential investor for his company. "I'm willing to go as high as forty percent ownership, but I'll start out much lower," he said.

As we listened, so did the man who was sitting behind him—with rapt attention. You guessed it; he was the mystery investor. When he finally introduced himself, the chatty business owner was apparently none the wiser. We didn't stick around, but it's a pretty good guess that the meeting didn't exactly go as the owner had planned.

In reality, over 90 percent of those charged with security in large organizations feel that e-work is not a security concern. In fact, they're more concerned with the occasional work that's taken out of the office by traditional employees because they lack the training, tools, and technologies that are part of the e-work model.[9]

The Boss Worries That E-work Will Increase Technology Support Problems

Employers know that their employees' technical problems are their problems, too. While support issues, software version control, and viruses are not new to most organizations, how they deal with them when their employees are off-site may require a change in procedures. As you make your pitch to management, make sure they know that you're not going to call the IT department's VoIP desk when the DSL on your PC won't connect to the VPN using Wi-Fi so you can FTP in your BVDs. Rather, be able to tell them you've thought about these issues; you have a full suite of firewall, virus, and malware software; and you're eager to work with the IT department to ensure everything goes smoothly.

8

What's in It for Your Employer?

The philosophy of enlightened self-interest suggests that if you act to further the interests of others, you ultimately will serve your own. If you're trying to convince your boss that you should be allowed to work at home, keep that idea in mind.

James Ware, cofounder of the Future of Work program and lead author of *The Search for Digital Excellence*, suggests that "many companies have become prisoners of their outdated business practices and their assumptions about how work gets done. Most organizations find themselves losing ground to competitors who were not even on the map a decade ago. They've become victims, rather than beneficiaries, of advances in information technology. And at a time when the attraction and retention of qualified, engaged employees has become an even more critical factor in a business's success or failure, they find themselves out of touch with a workforce that has undergone a dizzying transformation in attitudes, abilities, and ambitions."[1]

E-work Increases Employee Satisfaction

Smart employers understand that a happy employee is a loyal one. "When employers offer the option of flexible hours and telecommuting, they help employees maintain balance in other parts of their lives. That, in turn, fosters satisfaction, loyalty and retention," says Robert McNabb, vice president of Korn/Ferry (and CEO of its subsidiary, Futurestep).[2]

Over 80 percent of employees consider working from home a perk of the job.[3] In a recent study, over a third of the people surveyed said they'd prefer the option to work from home over the holy grail, a pay raise.[4] In another poll of 1,500 technology professionals, 37 percent said they'd take a pay cut of 10 percent if they could work from home.[5]

E-work Increases Access to Qualified Employees

MySQL is the world's most popular open source database. The company has e-workers on every continent except Antarctica. "I can't imagine that we'd be nearly as successful at finding the talent we need if working from an office was a requirement," says Boel Larsen, their senior director of human resources.

Over 40 percent of employers report feeling a labor pinch.[6] Three out of 10 are concerned over the loss of intellectual capital as baby boomers approach retirement age.[7]

The first of the boomers will turn 65 in 2011, and there aren't enough new employees to replace them. Worse, three out of four employees plan to retire before the age of 60.[8] "Too many employers haven't thought [the growing labor shortage] through, saying they'll worry about it when it happens. If they do, they'll be caught flat-footed. The time to plan is now; they can't do it overnight," says Justin Heet, a former consultant with the Hudson Institute.[9]

Fortunately, while most retiring boomers will be looking for a more flexible lifestyle, nearly 75 percent of retirees want to continue some kind of work after retirement even if they have enough money to live comfortably for the rest of their lives.[10] Tired of the rat race and ready for a work situation that allows them to enjoy their golden years, this pool of seasoned citizens may find e-work to be just the ticket.

High fuel prices also threaten the talent pool. BusinessWeek Research Services found that almost two-thirds of the people they surveyed would take another job to ease the commute. More than 70 percent say the availability of telecommuting will affect their next job move.[11]

Home-based staffing offers local employers access to people all over the country, even the world. Because a substantial majority of employees would prefer to work from home, a company that allows e-work is a step ahead of its competitors in luring talent. E-work could also help employers gain access to the 52 million Americans who aren't currently working and the 26 million who only work part-time.[12]

These include people who want or need to be at home to care for children or aging parents, or have health conditions that prevent them from working in an office. Only 75 percent of women (still the traditional primary caregivers) age 25 to 54 participate in the labor force, compared to 90 percent of men.[13] Almost a quarter of women work part-time (16.5 million), compared to 10 percent of men.[14]

Additional talent available to pajama-savvy employers includes the more than 12 percent of the working age population that's disabled. A full three-quarters of unemployed workers with disabilities cite discrimination in the workplace and lack of transportation as major factors that prevent them from working.[15]

E-work programs also enable employers to retain staff that might otherwise have to quit because of a relocating spouse—a problem particularly common to military families.

E-work allows companies to reach beyond their local populations for employees. This can be extremely helpful to companies based in places that are hard to reach or demographically mismatched with the kind of people they're trying to hire. E-work allows fast-growing employers a way to continue to expand beyond the local talent pool. And it offers an innovative solution to a number of unique hiring problems.

J. Crew, a clothing retailer with stores throughout the United States, wants its telephone sales agents to live near a store so they can touch, feel, and see the clothing they're selling, and to relate to customers as neighbors. E-workers are the perfect fit.

A multistate mortgage brokerage found its customers preferred to deal with someone local, too. By employing e-workers, they can hire for the specific neighborhoods they serve. The telephone workforce sounds like they are calling from around the corner—because they are.

A Korn/Ferry client had a very specific person in mind. They wanted a PhD from MIT with a background in ballistics. Only a handful of people in the country fit the bill, and none of them wanted to live where the job was offered. So Korn/Ferry suggested the employer take a shot at hiring someone by offering the job on an e-work basis. Bull's-eye.

A West Coast investment broker was having trouble staffing its 6 AM telephone shift. East Coast home-based traders solved the problem.

E-work Increases Productivity

There's a big difference between being at work and *working*. It's estimated that American businesses lose around $600 billion a year due to workplace distractions.[16] Many an hour is lost:

- Jawing around the coffee pot.

- Listening to stories about Joe's trout-fishing trip, his teenage daughter's transgressions, his son's amazing batting average, and his spastic colon.
- Traipsing to and from the bathroom (especially Joe).
- Waiting in line at lunch.
- Breaking for this birthday party, that going-away party, and so on.

And the problem extends beyond the interruptions themselves. It may take another 15 to 30 minutes to recover from the hiatus and get your head back in the game.

All that misplaced energy, together with what's lost on the drive to and from work, is what allows e-workers to be more productive than their bricks-and-mortar associates. Ann Bamesberger, a vice president with Sun Microsystems, says employees who take part in their e-work program give 60 percent of their saved commute time back to the company.[17]

While management and employees differ about the extent of productivity improvements that come from e-work, the consensus points to increases of 30 to 40 percent. At the five-year mark, Best Buy has seen a 30 percent increase in productivity and a dramatic reduction in attrition thanks to their Results-Only Work Environment (ROWE).[18] Their success isn't unusual. British Telecom and Dow Chemical both measured a productivity increase of more than 30 percent.[19] A survey sponsored by AT&T showed that nearly 60 percent of Fortune 1000 managers found that e-work increased productivity.[20]

Finally, e-workers are four times more likely to work while on vacation. Once the tools to work remotely are in place, it's sometimes hard to turn it off.[21]

E-work Saves Money

If the way to a man's heart is through his stomach, the way to a business owner's heart is through her bank account. While saving money isn't the primary driver for companies that adopt e-work programs, it certainly sweetens the pot. Here are some of the ways e-work can save companies money—lots of it.

Real Estate Savings

Real estate costs employers an average of $10,000 per employee per year.[22] IBM, another e-work early adopter, was able to slash its real estate costs by $50 million a year by allowing its people to work remotely.[23] Sun Microsystems estimates that they save $70 million a year in real estate alone.[24] McKesson saves $2 million a year by using home-based telephone staff.[25]

Even companies that practice partial e-work find they can save money in office-related costs. About 40 percent of KPMG's staff works at home and on the road. When e-work auditors do need time in a real office, they can log on to the company's office-hoteling program and reserve one, along with whatever equipment they need, at one of the local KPMG sites—just like booking a room at the Four Seasons, except there's no champagne waiting in the room when they arrive.

Administrative Savings

The savings go well beyond the cost of real estate. E-work programs save companies money in office furniture, equipment and supplies, utilities, janitorial service, security, maintenance, paper goods, coffee and water service, and leased parking spaces.

Dow Chemical was able to lop off a third of its non–real estate administrative costs by inviting its workers to go home.[26]

Labor Savings

Some companies find their e-work staff easier to manage.[27] "Thanks to Alpine Access's home-based call center agents, I can manage the entire 250-person call center with just one person—and he has other duties as well," says Trish Winebrenner, vice president of marketing for Express-Jet, a regional airline that operates almost 300 aircraft.

Relocation Savings

For companies that need to relocate staff, the costs can be enormous. Nortel estimates that it can cost up to $100,000 to move an employee from one city to another. Even a move from one cubicle to another can cost $2,500.[28] E-work eliminates those costs.

Absenteeism Savings

Nortel, a communications technology company, found that the entire cost to outfit and equip an e-worker can be made up in the first year if only 3.5 days can be saved in absenteeism.[29]

ADA Compliance Savings

E-work enables compliance with the Americans with Disabilities Act (ADA) at a significant savings. The ADA requires employers with 15 or more employees to provide reasonable accommodation for employees with disabilities.[30] By using home-based employees' already ADA-compliant home offices, a company can save thousands of dollars by not having to retrofit its workplace. There are even grants available to train and outfit disabled home workers.

E-work Improves Disaster Preparedness

Almost three-quarters of e-workers say they could continue to work in the event of a disaster; this compares to just 17 percent of non–e-workers.[31]

Concerns about terrorism, together with worries over what would happen in the event of a flu pandemic, places e-work at the cornerstone of U.S. government agencies' disaster response plan. Disaster preparedness is a hot topic with private employers as well.

In 2003, an angry tobacco farmer blasted military exercise cadences from the tractor he'd parked in the reflecting pool near the Washington Monument. His threat to detonate 82 pounds of explosives caused road and office closures for two days.

In 2004, the General Services Administration building in Boston was closed for nearly a week because of security issues at the neighboring Democratic National Convention.

In 2005, a New York City transit strike halted subway and bus service and left millions of commuters without a ride to work.

In 2006, a record-breaking snowstorm walloped the East Coast, forcing many employees to simply pull the blankets over their heads.

In 2007, a stretch of highway near the San Francisco–Oakland Bay Bridge collapsed, leaving hundreds of thousands of commuters without a way to reach their workplace.

In 2008, Midwest floods closed hundreds of businesses and essentially shut down the entire city of Cedar Rapids, Iowa.

Whether it's a cataclysmic event or a tractor-wielding psychopath, e-work is key to maintaining a stable workforce in unstable times.

E-work Reduces Attrition

TalentKeepers, Inc., a global leader in employee retention research, estimates the cost of losing a customer service person ranges from

$10,000 to $20,000; and nearly 40 percent of the companies they surveyed estimated that the cost of losing a salesperson can exceed $35,000.[32] It pays to keep good people on board. E-work is one way to do that.

The call center industry was an early adopter of the move from office to home. The agents love it and it shows. At McKesson Health Solutions, a health care call center, attrition among e-work operators is just 20 percent, compared to 38 percent for the same company's on-site staff.[33]

WorldatWork, a global association of human resource professionals, found that almost half of its members, representing 95 percent of Fortune 500 companies, say e-work has had a high impact on employee retention.[34]

E-work Reduces Absenteeism and Tardiness

A study by Harris Interactive and CCH.com, a leading provider of business law software solutions, showed that unscheduled absences cost employers an average of $1,800 per employee per year.[35] Only a third of the people who call in sick actually are—the balance do so because of family issues, personal needs, entitlement mentality, and stress.[36,37] For the nation's largest employers, the cost of unscheduled absences can run in the millions, and even more when the effects on productivity, revenue, and morale are considered. A study by Hewitt Associates showed that alternative work arrangements, and specifically telecommuting, were the most successful work-life programs for reducing unscheduled absences.[38] That's because folks who e-work:

- Avoid colds and flu that lurk wherever people gather.
- Are less stressed.
- Return to their at-home desks quicker following birth, surgery, heart attack, illness, or those of family members.
- Put in a full day in spite of crippling storms.
- Take care of doctor's appointments, house maintenance issues, or child/parent emergencies without taking a whole day off.

A study of over 3,000 employees showed that people with flexible schedules were less likely to have health problems that affect their job performance.[39]

E-work Distributes Risk

Not having all your eggs in one basket, or in this case all your employees in one location, mitigates business interruption risks.

A decentralized workforce also means that there is no World Trade Center or Pentagon-like target to attack. If an attack does occur, fewer people will be affected, economic stability will be more easily maintained, and continuity of operations will be assured.

E-work Forces Better Goal Setting

According to Robert McNabb, CEO of Futurestep, "Performance that is measured can be managed. Performance that isn't measured can't be managed."

As we've said before, e-work forces supervisors and employees to focus on product, not process, and on productivity, not presence. The result is people who understand what's expected of them. That, in turn, leads to higher job satisfaction.

E-work Improves Staffing Options and Reduces Redundancies

The uncertainty of who may or may not show up for work forces many companies to build redundancy into their workforce—just in case. Others overstaff to deal with unpredictable peaks in volume. And many are forced to pay overtime, even double-time, when they're suddenly faced with a staffing shortage.

"I went into this whole home-based operator thing kicking and screaming. I didn't see how it would work" said ExpressJet's Wine-brenner. But, she admits, "I was delighted to be proven wrong. Now when we're suddenly inundated with calls because another airline runs a sale, we send a quick e-mail to all off-duty call agents. The first time it happened I didn't believe anyone would be just sitting there at their computer, much less willing to jump on the phones for a half hour or so. But within a few minutes, we had another thirty agents on the phones. When the rush was over, the extra agents just logged off and went back to whatever they were doing."

The flower industry offers another example of a business with extreme peaks and troughs. The Valentine's Day sales of 1–800-Flowers far outpace those of the rest of the year. That's why you'll probably be talking to someone in their jammies when you suddenly wake up and realize that you have nothing for your snookums. Without the home-based agents, the company would need to maintain a back-up staff of holiday employees and provide the phones, desks, and other infra-structure to support them.

Lots of businesses, including those that need to accommodate customers in different time zones, those that need to ramp up quickly in response to a news event, and those that face unpredictable spikes in activity find home-based staffing much more flexible and economical than traditional staffing.

E-work Equalizes Personalities and Reduces Discrimination

Some e-workers are hired sight unseen. They interview virtually, operate virtually, and are managed virtually. For employers, this reduces discrim-ination risks and it gives them access to voices they might not have otherwise heard. In the sight-unseen world, the loudest voice doesn't always dominate the thought pool.

E-work Cuts Down on Wasted Meetings

As you might guess, e-workers attend fewer meetings than their office cohorts. When a virtual conference or rare live meeting *is* called, people tend to arrive more prepared and are less apt to wander off the subject. As a result, based on what the e-workers we've interviewed tell us, meetings are shorter and more meaningful, and they're back to work as soon as the teleconference ends, often earlier.

E-work Increases Empowerment

Being on your own is empowering. Just as you learn survival skills after the loss of a loved one, e-workers learn how to fend for themselves when they're not surrounded by easy outs. When popping over to the next cubicle for a solution or bumping it up the chain of command is no longer an option, e-workers become more self-sufficient. The result is fewer interruptions for co-workers and fewer trivial problems for managers.

E-work Increases Collaboration Options

In a virtual workplace, the world's top authorities can be brought together to work on a problem. Once solved, they can go about spreading their genius elsewhere. E-workers can easily and quickly form virtual teams. This distance-independent collaboration allows management to put the best people, both their own and those outside the organization, to work on critical issues more quickly and economically than if they had to rely on planes, trains, and automobiles to bring them together.

E-work Makes Working Easier

The systems that support e-work also help those employees and managers who don't work at home. Once the company's programs, files, and documents are securely available in cyberspace, employees can work anywhere, and many will; on the plane, on vacation, even in the bathroom.

It's Green

Seventy percent of employees report that they would see their company in a more favorable light if their company helped employees lower their carbon emissions. Almost a quarter say they'd take a 10 percent pay cut to help the environment.[40]

We're finally waking up to the need for a kindlier, gentler approach to our planet. Environmentally conscious companies create goodwill with consumers, employers, and shareholders. Polluters, by contrast, expose themselves to the wrath of environmental activists and the negative press that results.

Stricter environmental laws are on the way. As federal and state governments develop their own plans to reduce pollution, companies will be held accountable for doing their part. E-work offers an inexpensive approach for complying with such measures.

E-work Offers the Possibility of Grants and Incentives

Some states offer companies a not-so-subtle shove toward e-work. Incentives as high as $3,500 per employee are available to Virginia employers. Georgia and Oregon also offer financial incentives, and other states are considering such programs. Many others, including Arizona, Vermont, and Connecticut, offer free assistance for prospective e-work employers. Our web site has links to all the active state and local programs in the country.

9

Making Your E-work Pitch

"If your first reaction when you think about teleworking is 'Oh, my boss will never go for it,' you aren't alone," Cali Williams Yost told us. She's a work-life flexibility consultant and author of *Work + Life: Finding the Fit That's Right for You* (Riverhead/Penguin Group, 2005). "In fact, I've helped tens of thousands of people use flexibility to find their work-life fit, and the top fear they all express is the fear that the answer to their proposal is going to be no. How do you get past this very common fear? Ask yourself, what's the worst thing that can happen? The worst thing that can happen is that the answer is no. Then where are you? You are no worse off than when you started. And from my experience, nine times out of ten, if you are a good employee, the answer is going to be yes to some version of your well thought out plan for at least a trial period. So what do you have to lose?"[1]

So let's work on that well thought out plan. Before you start to actually write, spend at least a couple of weeks cataloging what you do on a daily basis. The more specific you can be, the better. For example:

7:00 Left for work.

8:00 Arrived at work.

8:20 Arrived at desk after getting coffee.

8:40 Finished checking voice mail.

10:00 Checked and responded to e-mail until George stopped by with gossip about the merger.

10:30 George left and I went back to e-mail.

And so on. You may want to change the names to protect the guilty, or better yet, create categories for how you spend your time, but the point here is to gain a clear picture of how much of what you do could be done from home. Along the way, you'll find some office time wasters that may help your pitch as well.

Next, you want to show management that you understand they may have a concern about not being able to monitor your activity. If your company already embraces results-based management, you'll have a head start. Look at your job description and compare it with the work log you've been keeping. Indicate the extent to which each of your job activities can be done remotely.

Finally, list a measurable result next to each element of your job. You and your boss will want to finalize these jointly. For example, an auditor might be measured on completed audits:

- No more than five errors per month are found on audits.
- For at least 10 weeks per year, no audits are more than 30 days old.

A salesperson might be measured on quotes and proposals:

- Ten calls made, resulting in four meetings and two requests for proposal.
- Proposals are submitted within two days.

A technical support person might be measured on client satisfaction:

- Calls answered within 45 seconds.
- Case settled, on average, within six minutes.
- Customer satisfaction score of at least 9.0.

Armed with clear understanding of your job, and how your performance can be measured, you can start to pull together a proposal for your manager. Remember: Think about things from his or her perspective, and don't forget to deal with the company-wide picture.

An e-work proposal template is available on our web site. It includes a summary of the pros and cons and supporting data covered in this chapter. All you have to do is customize it for your situation.

Here are the broad issues your proposal should cover:

- Your reasons for wanting/needing to e-work.
- The benefits for your company, your manager, your co-workers, and your customers.

- Any challenges or concerns you anticipate from your manager, co-workers, and customers.
- Specific strategies for how you will address or resolve the issues. Be realistic—saying there won't be any issues is naive.
- An explanation of why you're a good candidate for e-work, taken from what you learned in Chapter 3.
- A time frame for when you would like to start e-working, how often you want to do it, and how long you would like the arrangement to last. (Proposing a test period offers employers a safety net.)
- Specifics about how and when you propose to have the success of your e-work trial measured and under what conditions the arrangement can be terminated prematurely.
- A schedule you plan to keep, and what your manager and co-workers can expect in terms of your availability.
- Details about how and how often you'll stay in contact with your manager and co-workers.
- A description of your home office—it's not unreasonable for your employer to want to pay a visit.
- Details about what equipment, software, technologies, and office supplies you'll need and who you expect to supply them.
- Details about how your home computer will be safeguarded and backed up.
- Specifics about how you propose to deal with data security and privacy issues.
- A plan for how you will handle technology problems.
- A plan for how you will access company information systems, hard copy files, and internal and external mail.
- If you have small children at home, a plan for how you will keep them from interrupting your work.
- Information about whether you will be available for on-site meetings or an emergency and what notice you'll need if you're wanted in the office.
- An understanding about work-related travel expenses. If you expect to be reimbursed for the times you come into the office, be sure to discuss that.
- A discussion of any labor union issues that may apply.
- A checklist for compliance with safety- and/or OSHA-related issues.
- An understanding of who's responsible for at-home injuries. (Some e-workers have sued their employers for nonwork injuries: A

neighbor assaulted one when she opened the front door for him; another claimed injuries she sustained on the way to the lunchroom—her kitchen. Both lost in court, but they add a new worry for e-work employers.)

- A statement about how you intend to comply with company policies, rules, and procedures while e-working. Federal labor laws apply to home-based staff as well. Believe it or not, even an employee's after-hours use of a Blackberry can violate federal overtime laws.

About two-thirds of companies that offer e-work have written policies in place to govern the arrangement.[2] If your company already has one, chances are they'll also have a written agreement that governs the relationship between you and the company. If not, once you and your manager agree to an e-work arrangement, take a lesson from the experience of others and set the parameters down in writing (links to a variety of sample e-work agreements are available on our web site). Even if your boss is your best friend, who knows what tomorrow will bring—a new boss? New ownership? A formal agreement is your best protection against future unknowns.

10

Best-Bet E-work Employers

According to Marcia Rhodes, spokesperson for WorldatWork, "Telework has become a staple of the total rewards mix."[1] For all the reasons we pointed out in Chapter 8, employers are beginning to see the light when it comes to the benefits of e-work. If you prefer the assurance of a weekly paycheck and your current employer doesn't share your enthusiasm for e-work, maybe you need a new employer.

The federal government is actually leading the way home—40 percent of federal employees are considered eligible to e-work and about 17 percent do so.[2,3] In the private sector, 36 percent of employees work for companies that allow e-work and 14 percent participate in it.[4] What follows is information about some of the best-bet government and private e-work employers. With e-work growing at a rate of 10 percent a year,[5] a printed list of companies is stale the minute the ink hits the paper, so check our web site regularly for updates and links to good sources of jobs.

Uncle Sam for E-work

As we've mentioned, the federal government has been actively promoting e-work for its workforce for almost a decade. As we go to press, a meatier federal e-work mandate is garnering bipartisan support. During the past year, both the House and Senate have voted for more oversight and stricter enforcement of existing e-work policies. Rather than allowing federal managers to determine who's eligible to e-work and who isn't, the proposed mandate would assume everyone is eligible. The onus then

Table 10.1   Percent of Federal Employees Eligible for E-work by Agency

U.S. Government Agency	Percent
U.S. Access Board	100%
Nuclear Waste Technical Review Board	93%
Consumer Product Safety Division	54%
Pension Benefit Guaranty Corporation	43%
Equal Employment Opportunity Commission	42%
National Council on Disability	42%
Overseas Private Investment Corporation	42%
Committee for Purchase from the Blind or Severely Disabled	38%
National Endowment for the Arts	37%
Department of Commerce	34%
Department of Education	33%
Railroad Retirement Board	33%
Inter-American Foundation	32%
National Mediation Board	31%
Selective Service System	30%
Securities and Exchange Commission	29%

would be on managers to allow their workers to e-work or document why they can't.

Because the goal of the federal e-work program is to be sure that employees are equipped, trained, and capable of working at home in the event of a disaster or pandemic, full-time e-work is not the goal. While some federal agencies report that over half their staff works remotely, they are the exception.[6] Roughly 77 percent of federal employees who e-work do so one day a week or less, and only 6 percent e-work full-time.[7]

Table 10.1 shows those federal agencies with the highest percent of *eligible* e-workers. Table 10.2 shows those with the highest *number* of e-workers (although, due to the size of those agencies, they may not represent a very high percentage of workers).[8]

Companies That Offer E-work as an Employee Benefit

A job with a company that offers e-work does not guarantee you'll be working from home. As we've said, so far most employers consider e-work a benefit—something that's earned by proving yourself on the job. Working on-site for a period allows an employer to see you in action. It helps ensure that you understand their corporate culture. It gives you a

Table 10.2   Federal Agencies with the Largest Number of E-workers

Federal Agency	Number	Percent
Department of Defense	34,000	6%
Department of Treasury	20,000	19%
Department of Interior	12,000	17%
Department of Commerce	12,000	34%
Health and Human Services	6,000	10%
Department of Agriculture	5,000	7%

chance to meet your co-workers and become familiar with the resources that are available within the company. This makes it easier for you to be successful from home if you earn that chance later on.

WorldatWork reports that almost two-thirds of employers have begun offering e-work as an employee benefit.[9] CareerBuilder's annual survey indicates that a third of companies plan to expand their e-work programs over the next year.[10] And in 2008, over 80 percent of *Fortune* magazine's "100 Best Companies to Work For" allowed their employees to e-work at least once a week.[11]

Full-time e-work is more common for corporate employees than federal workers. An encouraging 30 percent of company e-workers do so full-time, though a larger number—35 percent—e-work one day a week or less.[12]

Some companies embrace e-work in a big way. All of the more than 200 people who answer the phones for JetBlue Airlines work from home in locations all over the country, as they have from day one. At MySQL (a subsidiary of Sun Microsystems), 70 percent of the workforce is home-based. Tutor.com, a venture capital–backed company, employs over 2,000 home-based tutors. LiveOps's 16,000 call center agents field everything from restaurant takeout orders to insurance questions, all from the comfort of their homes.

The best source of e-work-friendly companies we've found for men or women is *Working Mother* magazine's annual roundup of the "100 Best Companies" for working parents. In addition to those that allow e-work, the list includes details about other flexible work and family-friendly programs offered by each. We've extracted the e-work employers from their "100 Best" and made them available at UndressForSuccessOnline.com along with links to other good sources of e-work employers. *Working Mother*'s full updated list is available on their web site at WorkingMother.com. Keep in mind that the city listed with each entry is their main office; many offer jobs throughout the country.

When approaching these companies for a job, keep in mind that, just as you wouldn't want to give an employer the impression that their vacation policy is your biggest concern, it's not a good idea to waltz into your first interview demanding e-work. That's not how it works. Also keep in mind that some may allow it only part of the time. Others will want you to be available to attend regular on-site meetings, so you'll have to be nearby.

Companies That Are All about E-work

While most employers who allow e-work do so as a benefit, some have embraced it wholeheartedly for all or part of their staff. The biggest opportunities for pure e-work are in the following fields: call centers, virtual assistants and virtual concierges, transcription, teaching, remote tech support, writing, and medicine. The following chapters offer an overview of each as well as details about hiring, training, scheduling, compensation, and technology issues.

Visit our web site, UndressForSuccessOnline.com, for an up-to-date list of employers in each of these fields as well as links to other scam-proofed resources that can help you find your way home.

11

Work as a Call Center Agent

The call center industry was an early adopter of home-based employees. Most of the 2.2 million call center jobs in the United States are with insurance companies, banks and credit unions, employment agencies, and retail businesses. About a quarter of these call center operators, or 672,000 of them, work from home.[1]

The technology analysis firm IDC expects exponential growth in home-based call center jobs through the rest of the decade as *homeshoring*, a term they coined, all but replaces the offshore call center trend.[2]

Customer care agents with English as a second language have become fodder for Jay Leno—and a great source of frustration for American consumers. "Companies that wanted to save money by sending call center work offshore were disappointed in the quality of those calls, and are now finding home-based agents an excellent alternative to offshoring," says David Pleiss, vice president at West Corporation, where 20 percent of their 7,500 agents are home-based.

ExpressJet's Trish Winebrenner, says that since they outsourced their calls to home-based Alpine Access, they actually receive letters complimenting the professionalism, courtesy, and kindness of their agents. "I just can't tell you how unusual that is in the traditional call center business," says Winebrenner.

Almost a quarter of call center agents in the United States and Canada are now home-based, and the trend is expected to increase because the benefits of home-based call center staffing go beyond the financial ones.[3,4] Our interviews with the top five home-based call center employers revealed that some of the many benefits of the at-home business model are reduced turnover, the ability to draw from a larger population (including rural and disabled workers), and access to better educated and more motivated staff.

"Oddly, the impressions we form about a company are usually based on our interactions with their lowest paid people," says Christopher M. Carrington, CEO of Alpine Access. When you call to place an order for that great new candy bar deep fryer, you expect the person who answers your call to be informed, enthusiastic, understandable, capable, and efficient. If they aren't, you may have second thoughts about that $29.95 purchase, regardless of the free glass knives with no tinny-metallic taste that come with it. That's bad for business, and every company that deals with the public worries about it (okay, some less than others).

Established in 1997, ARO, Inc., is one of the oldest virtual call centers in the business. Michael Amigoni, their chief operations officer, said the virtual model came out of sheer desperation—they simply couldn't recruit or hire a good workforce.

Traditional call center employees don't typically last long. The places are noisy, the work is stressful, and the pay is low. "How are you supposed to deliver excellent customer service with people who hate their jobs?" says Carrington. By contrast, attrition among Alpine Access's home-based staff is half that of traditional call centers. "Productivity is higher, average sales are higher, and the people are eager to work," says Carrington.

Another reason for the movement toward home-based agents is cost. Building and staffing a traditional call center is expensive. Finding motivated, enthusiastic, intelligent people who will sit in a noisy room talking to angry customers is darn near impossible. Faced with attrition rates of 40 to 80 percent, many traditional centers were forced to move to a different town every few years because they'd exhausted their local populations.

What Call Center Agents Do

Call center jobs typically involve:

- Order taking for companies such as 1-800-Flowers, J. Crew, 1-800 Contacts, Walgreens, and even McDonald's—do you want fries with that?
- Ticketing for companies such as American Airlines, ExpressJet, JetBlue, and Virgin Airlines.

- Customer service for banks, insurance companies, leasing companies, and even the IRS.
- Dispatch and scheduling for auto clubs, repair agents, and even pizza delivery.
- Technical support for computers, DVD players, and home appliances.
- Medical triage.
- Outbound sales and telemarketing.
- Employment recruiting.

In addition to telephone help, some companies are beginning to use remote agents to support customers via live chat and by e-mail.

But first a word of caution. Many outbound telemarketing companies that conduct aggressive telephone sales, telemarketing, and lead generation services make extraordinary claims about what their operators can earn. Many of the jobs are on a 100 percent commission basis. If you don't sell or produce leads, you don't make money. In some cases, the company provides qualified sales leads. The word *qualified*, however, may need to be qualified. If, while shopping for a new pair of snow boots, you stop to fill out a sweepstakes card for a trip to Tahiti, you may be a qualified lead on some poor telemarketer's "vacation condo buyers" lead list. If you answered "yes" on the pop-up window that offered free long-distance service—mostly just to get it off your screen—you may look like a meal ticket to a telemarketer. If that health care survey you took indicated an interest in cheaper health insurance . . . well, you get the idea.

Is it true that some people make good money in telephone sales? We'll answer with a guarded "yes." Just because we never actually met one doesn't mean they don't exist. What we do know is that there are lots of people who wouldn't be reading this book if that home-based telemarketing gig they signed up for had produced the fortunes it promised.

The Business Model

Some companies choose to outsource their telephone answering to professional call centers that answer phones for a wide variety of clients. Others run their own call centers. While home-based positions are common to both, we found independent call centers more committed to the virtual model.

Within the large inbound call center model, there are two very distinct types of home-based agent opportunities. One offers the standard employee/employer relationship. In this scenario, you, the agent, are paid either hourly or by the call, and you are entitled to benefits like paid health care, vacation pay, and 401(k) participation (if you work a minimum number of hours). Your employer pays a portion of your taxes and deducts the employee share from each paycheck.

The other model is more entrepreneurial. You establish yourself as a business (typically as a sole proprietor, although one company requires that you form a corporation) and the call center hires you as an independent contractor to answer phones. We look at the some of the issues of self-employment in Part 4, but the biggest disadvantages are having to pay both the employee and employer share of taxes (totaling an extra 9 percent or more over what you'd have paid as an employee); having to file quarterly estimated taxes with the IRS; and not receiving medical, vacation, sick leave, or other benefits. On the upside, you are free to work for other companies and you can deduct your start-up and operating expenses on your tax returns.

What to Expect

Unlike the traditional call center business, the number of job applicants for home-based positions far exceeds the number of jobs available. LiveOps, a call center service with over 16,000 agents, got its start with the infomercial industry. They receive over 150,000 job applications a year—less than 3 percent are hired. Other virtual call centers report similar numbers.

We asked Tim Whipple, vice president of agent services for Live-Ops, with so many applications, what makes the difference in who makes the cut. He and others told us that a large majority of applicants drop out of the hiring process on their own. "A lot of people apply for these jobs because they think it's going to be easy money. It's not," says Tim. Martha, an Alpine Access call agent whose disabled daughter also works for the company, told us, "There's no real magic to getting a job here, you just have to act professional and show you're committed to doing a good job."

Some call centers require prior customer service or sales experience; others do not. All require basic familiarity with a PC, the ability to work independently, flexibility, and a good telephone presence. Attention to detail plus fast and accurate keyboard skills are also essential. While none of the companies we researched required a college education, most reported that the majority of their agents had at least attended some college.

In terms of the hiring process, you'll start out by completing a job application on the call center's web site. If your application is approved, some companies will conduct pre-interview screening, while others will move right to technical skills testing, personality testing, and a voice audition. Some will follow up with a telephone interview to give them a chance to get to know you better. Links to some sample tests are available on our web site at UndressForSuccessOnline.com.

Assuming you receive a job offer, most call center employers will require a full background and criminal history check (for which they legitimately charge $35 to $50, nonrefundable). Some will also conduct a credit check and drug test.

Training

Large call center companies offer online training once you've been hired; some may require on-site training, and a few even require a period of on-site call work before you're allowed to work from home. About half of the companies we interviewed compensate agents for their training time or offer reimbursement as a bonus on completion. None of the legitimate companies charge for training.

Some call centers conduct scheduled classes, while others offer self-paced instruction. Scheduled classes are generally offered at a variety of times to accommodate participants in different time zones. Scheduled training requires 100 percent participation, no excuses. Here's where you get a chance to prove, or disprove, your dependability. Initial training generally takes a week or two.

Testing is conducted throughout the training. While the operators we spoke to reported the training is not particularly hard, a large percentage of trainees quit because they simply don't like the work or they find it too tedious or stressful.

Most agent positions answer phones for more than one company. Additional training is required as you take on new accounts.

Free computer training and job placement for disabled persons and military spouses is available from several sources. Additional information about them and Internet links are available on our web site.

Scheduling

Most, though not all, call centers require agents to work a minimum of 20 to 25 hours a week. This helps maintain proficiency. Some allow scheduling in increments as short as 15 minutes. Some also require an agent's work schedule to include weekend and holiday hours. Dependability is critical in this business, so once you sign up for a time slot, you'd better be there. If you're not, you may find yourself out of a job after just one missed session.

The nuances of call center priorities are interesting because they conflict. The companies you answer calls for want their calls handled professionally, of course, and that takes time. However, your employer, the call center operator, also wants throughput. If you talk too long, that limits the number of calls you can take and therefore increases the per call expense.

In a telemarketing call center, the metrics are even more complicated. Both your employer and the end client want to convert callers to customers, so your conversion rate and your ability to up-sell are important: "Do you want bunny slippers with that bathrobe?" All of those factors go into a formula that determines not only which operators do the best overall job, but also which products they're best at selling. One operator may find it easy to up-sell a high-end flower arrangement but impossible to peddle a John Grisham novel even to a courtroom drama fan.

The call center digests all the data and assigns calls based on agent performance. In other words, the better you are, the more calls you receive. When you're paid by the call or by the minute, and especially when you can earn up-sell commissions, this is important. Of course, if the routing programs were *too* strict, newbies wouldn't stand a chance against seasoned veterans, so accommodations are made in the beginning.

The time slot you choose can also be a significant factor in how much you make. The graveyard shift is when many infomercials run. Holiday hours can be lucrative, too. Martha, the call agent for Alpine Access, lays in a supply of what she calls "ramp food" or ramp-up vittles in preparation for Valentine's Day and Mother's Day, much like a runner preparing for a marathon. Once the flower orders start, "There's no time for lunch. Everyone is scrambling for a last-minute gift. I keep a bag of Cheerios handy for when my blood sugar peters out."

Compensation and Advancement

The people we interviewed who work for large call centers described a wide variety of compensation models. Some pay by the call. Some pay by the minute. Some pay by the hour. Some offer a combination of all three. Many offer incentives for productivity, sales, and unpopular shifts.

Some even offer their operators discounts on the products they represent. Broadly, the range of pay works out to $7 to $15/hour for nontechnical jobs. Those that require special training or experience in medicine, technology, or repair pay more. In May 2006, median earnings for a telephone call center operator (not including outbound sales) was $10.29/hour.[5]

Advancement for at-home call center agents is somewhat limited, but exceptional agents are sometimes able to move up to supervisory and training positions.

Office Essentials

Home call center agents are typically, though not always, required to supply their own equipment. Technology requirements are a moving target, but you'll probably make the grade if you have a PC with a fairly new processor, the latest operating system, a reasonable amount of RAM memory, and the latest spyware, anti-virus, and firewall safeguards. None of the companies we spoke to were Mac-compatible.

In addition, most call center jobs require their home-based agents to have the following special equipment:

- A soundcard with speakers or a headset, and an extra USB port (V2).
- Cable high-speed Internet (preferably digital cable, but in some cases DSL is okay).
- A separate land line with a corded handset. (Voice over Internet Protocol, or VoIP, as well as cellular, cable, or satellite phones are not allowed.) Some companies require that the phone be exclusive to their operation, and some also require agents to have an unlimited long-distance calling plan.
- A corded noise-canceling telephone (not computer) headset.

In addition, agents must have a quiet room or area of the home (with a lockable door) that can be dedicated to their at-home job.

From the Horse's Mouth

Martha has been a home-based call center agent for Alpine Access for five years and was recently promoted into a coaching position. She's a grandma and lives in Aurora, Colorado, with her husband, a disabled veteran. Martha has worked as an emergency care clinical coordinator and a paramedic, and she's lectured nationwide on the topic of managing change. After being downsized in her prior job, she decided to give Alpine a try.

Martha answers phones for 1-800-Flowers, a client of Alpine Access. Here's what she told us about her job:

> I did about 40 hours of training with 1-800-Flowers before I started taking their calls. I was scared to death for the first few, but I knew there were plenty of people out there (virtually) to help me if I had any questions. Turns out I was a natural at it. If you need lots of direction, it's not for you. You need to be empathetic. You need to quickly tease out how you can help the person on the other end of the line. You need to be independent—even a little driven.
>
> For the most part callers are happy (when they order flowers), but there are funerals and things like that that can really choke you up. Still, it makes me feel good when I can help people figure out just the right thing to say on a card.
>
> Since I'm near the home office, I've attended a couple of company functions. It's always a little weird to meet people I've only known virtually—like when you listen to a DJ on the radio and then you see him in person.
>
> At one of the company meetings I found out that several other agents live right around the corner from me. Now we get together for lunch once in a while and swap stories. It's amazing to hear their backgrounds. It's a really diverse bunch.

Lisa has been a call center agent with LiveOps for two years. She's 40-something years old, married, with three sons (ages 12, 9, and 6) and a pet cow, Moo. With LiveOps she can work in coveralls, tend to Moo and the horses she boards, and arrange her call schedule to eliminate the need for day care.

The majority of the calls Lisa answers are for infomercials and insurance companies. She found the application and training process amazingly easy.

Having stumbled across every scam in the book, Lisa was skeptical about LiveOps. "It sounded too good to be true, so I gave it a try on a very part-time basis. Before long, I was making an extra $150 to $200 per week, so I quit Wal-Mart and went at it full-time. The great thing about it is that it's totally performance-based. It doesn't matter what I wear, what I look like, what car I drive, or how my hair looks. I bragged about the job to my sister-in-law, and now she's working for LiveOps too."

Lisa says she makes as much as $18/hour around the holidays. On a slow day, she might make half that, but the average falls somewhere in the middle. When the kids are home, Lisa only works in one-hour increments. "It's not for everyone, but I love it. Last week, in between my scheduled hours, I helped deliver a foal. So while I'm still as knee-deep in manure as I was in my corporate days, now it only comes from the animals I love," says Lisa. You can read more about Lisa on her web site at http://www.crazycowcountryfarm.com.

Worth Knowing

You're not paranoid if someone really is watching you, and when you're a call center agent, they will be. The same computer system that routes calls, provides caller information, offers scripted answers, allows you to chat with other agents, and offers help from supervisors when you need it also monitors your calls and keyboard activity. If that spooks you, get over it. Without the ability to listen in on calls and record them for training and evaluation, these e-work jobs wouldn't be possible. Such monitoring is commonplace in traditional call centers anyway.

Interactive computer systems are becoming increasingly common as a way for companies to manage office-based and remote resources. They allow companies to keep software up-to-date, detect viruses, monitor quality, measure results, verify sales, and protect themselves from liability. Some call center systems even use sophisticated speech recognition tools to detect and deal with problems much more quickly than if they had to wait for a supervisor's daily reports. If the words *broken leg* start appearing in caller conversations, a doll company may have a manufacturing and product warranty problem on its hands. If so, they can quickly deliver scripts on how to help agents advise callers and also make sure manufacturing corrects the problem.

Best Fit

Call center jobs are a good fit for at-home caregivers who can manage their hours around the needs of their loved ones. Disabled workers also find home-based call center work a good career option.

The best call center candidates are naturally pleasant and have exceptional listening, communications, and problem-solving skills. Basic computer skills are necessary, but successful operators do not have to have advanced technical skills (unless, of course, they're fielding technical calls). Bilingual skills are a big plus. The average age of a call center agent is 35 to 40. About three-quarters have taken college courses, three-quarters are women, and most have been in the workforce for 10 years or more.

Major Employers

Call centers that will hire you to work for them as an employee (not as a contractor) include Alpine Access, ARO, Inc., Convergys, O'Currance Teleservices (requires initial on-site work), and West Corporation. Live-Ops and Working Solutions will hire you as a contractor.

The Rat Race Rebellion web site offers details about over 60 other call center jobs. You can find a link to them as well as other information, links, and details about call center jobs on our web site.

12

Work as a Virtual Assistant

The term *virtual assistant* (VA) became popular in the 1990s. Virtual assistants are the cyber equivalent of the personal assistant, administrative assistant, executive assistant, right-hand man, or, going way back, gal Friday. Like their traditional counterparts, some specialize in services such as event planning, real estate marketing, and bookkeeping, while others are generalists.

According to the U.S. Department of Labor, administrative assistants held approximately 2.3 million jobs in 2006, mostly in offices. The need for executive assistants is expected to grow by 9 percent over the next 10 years—faster than the overall job market. The greatest growth is expected in the health care and social assistance industries. The best opportunities will be for those with extensive knowledge of software applications and strong communications skills. Virtual assistant educational requirements will continue to increase.[1]

Recessionary pressures and the need for cost containment as well as the trend toward homeshoring should allow VAs to grab a disproportionate share of job growth.

What Virtual Assistants Do

Harried business owners, sole proprietors, and home-based business owners are a VA's bread and butter. In short, their job is to do whatever it takes to make their clients look good and help them succeed. Think concierge meets executive secretary.

Typical clients include real estate agents, speakers, authors, business coaches, insurance agents, mortgage brokers, and lawyers. These and other professionals with billable rates that can run several hundred dollars an hour—or whose average sale can run into the thousands of dollars—can't afford to be bogged down in minutiae. Nor can they afford to lose an important sale because they dropped the ball.

A VA might be asked to do data entry, maintain mailing lists, proofread documents, prepare presentation slides, plan events and trips, perform research, buy gifts, prepare newsletters, screen calls and e-mail, manage receipts, schedule appointments and meetings, follow up with customers/employees, send thank you notes, add content to a blog, coordinate webinars and seminars, package and ship products, do online errands, bill clients, pay bills, and even bug slow-paying customers.

Jane Anne is a company president with an important presentation to make to a prospective client in Pittsburgh next week. She needs someone to make sure her airline, hotel, and limo reservations are made. She needs to know that a conference room is reserved and, when the time comes, that the projector has been set up and tested. She needs to impress her prospect with prompt and professional follow-through even while she's on the road. She needs someone else to remember that the prospect's wife is expecting and to take the initiative of sending a personalized Teddy-Gram when the baby is born. She needs someone to make sure the bills are paid while she's in Europe next month. She even needs someone to remind her that next Tuesday is her husband's birthday, and have reservations made at his favorite restaurant.

Real estate VAs are worth a special mention because that industry uses virtual assistants more than any other. Licensing laws are very specific about what a real estate VA can and can't do, and they vary significantly from one state to the next. In general, they're aimed at keeping an unlicensed person from advising buyers or sellers. Of particular importance, real estate VAs may not hold themselves out as licensed professionals. To keep them from crossing over into Realtor territory, most states strictly forbid commission-based payment for VAs. The laws are so specific that they even cover whether a VA may copy a key on behalf of a real estate agent. Fortunately, the list of things a VA can do is plenty long enough to keep you busy. Here are some of the specialty tasks a real estate VA can expect to perform:

- Maintain contact information.
- Process mailings to potential buyers or sellers.
- Post fliers on message boards.

- Coordinate e-mail, social networking, and other online marketing efforts.
- Manage pay-per-click advertising campaigns.
- Make outbound telemarketing calls.
- Prepare newsletters.
- Plan events.
- Arrange seminars, teleseminars, or webinars.
- Answer incoming calls for the client.
- Return phone calls on behalf of the client.
- Research and screen potential sellers.
- Work with spreadsheets to organize data.
- Create mail-merge documents and process mailings.
- Compile mailing lists for expired MLS listings.
- Prepare legal documents for house closings.
- Assist with closing papers.
- Edit and post listing photos.
- List properties for sale.
- Maintain and update web site.
- Make travel arrangements for the client.
- Confirm appointments with buyers and sellers.
- Arrange home showings.
- Obtain contractor quotes.
- Schedule contractor work and monitor the job.
- Call to have utilities discontinued or set up on behalf of the client.
- Call for quotes for other services (such as rental cars, moving vans, etc.).
- Arrange for pest and other home inspections.
- Send tenant or tenant buyer applications to potential tenants.
- Screen potential tenants.
- Correspond with tenants regarding payments and late fees.

The Business Model

The majority of VAs are self-employed owner/operators. Virtual assistants generally have just a handful of clients at any one time to ensure they can deliver the executive handling that makes a VA valuable. Some operators, however, expand by adding helpers or affiliating with other VAs.

One company, Team Double-Click, has trained and certified over 45,000 VAs. Each operates as an independent contractor, but Team Double-Click provides the sales, training, and backroom support that allows the VAs to do what they're best at: helping weary business owners and executives.

"We're the human resources, IT, marketing, bookkeeping, and training department for our contract VAs," says Gayle Buske, president and founder of Team Double-Click. "Billable hours are the lifeblood of an independent professional service provider. But, in addition to doing what they do, an independent VA has to manage their own business and keep a constant lookout for new clients. As a result, an independent VA may find they had a mere thirty billable hours in the sixty hours they worked. We set out to remedy that when we started Team Double Click in 2000," says Buske.

Whether you choose to work with a company like Team Double-Click or you go it alone, if you want to be successful as a VA, you need to think of yourself as an entrepreneur and treat your operation like a business.

What to Expect

Team Double-Click is the only company we found that offers nationwide home-based VA positions on any large-scale basis. Here's how you go about working as one of their contract VAs.

Open their web site (teamdoubleclick.com) and follow the "I Want To Work" link. Once you've entered your basic information, you'll be given a choice of which type of VA positions you'd like to qualify for (e.g., public relations, real estate, customer service, translator, or generalist). Next you'll be presented with a series of timed tests that determine whether you have the basic computer skills necessary for the position. The primary software programs they test for are Microsoft Word, Excel, and Outlook. You'll also be tested in basic math, money management, Internet and e-mail skills. More specialized VA positions may require proficiency in ACT! (contact management software), Top Producer or SharperAgent (programs used by real estate VAs), PowerPoint, Photoshop, Illustrator, Microsoft Money, Quicken, QuickBooks, and other specialty software.

Tests are scored automatically, so you'll know whether you passed or failed as soon as you finish. You only get one chance to take the tests, so be sure you bone up on your skills before you begin. You'll find links to free tutorials you can use to practice on our web site at UndressForSuccessOnline.com.

When you've completed the testing, you can request a pre-interview questionnaire. Expect to receive that in 10 days or less. Your answers to this questionnaire will be evaluated within three to four weeks. If you're approved, you'll download the VA orientation package, study up, and take an orientation quiz. This must be done within three days of its receipt. Following that, you'll be scheduled for a telephone interview with a real live human. Assuming you don't blow it at this point, you'll be an official member of Team Double-Click. If your skills are in high demand, you may receive work as quickly as the next day. In some cases, it can take substantially longer.

Success rate, beginning to end, is about 30 percent, says Jim Buske, CFO for Team Double-Click (with conjugal rights to the CEO). "Most people drop out of the process either because they don't have the skills or because they really don't want to work. They think this is going to be an easy income, and it isn't," says Buske.

Training

Most VAs will already have experience as an executive assistant or secretary, and they'll have substantial knowledge in their particular specialty.

Team Double-Click provides free training for new VAs in the form of a very thorough 200-page manual. It includes a wealth of advice on everything from where to order a dancing gorilla-gram to how to convince your family and friends that your work-at-home job is a real career. It's also full of links to VA must-haves, such as telephone follow-me technology, a free incoming fax service, free conference call providers, and much more. Quite frankly, the manual is worth the trouble of going through the approval process all by itself.

Other training is available for a fee from the International Virtual Assistants Association. If you happen to be a military spouse, you may qualify for free training through a special program run by Staffcentrix.com.

Scheduling

As a virtual assistant, you set your own hours. But because the rest of the world largely marches to the beat of a nine-to-five routine, you'll need to fall into step with their parade to some degree. Phone calls, e-mails, and faxes will have to take place on their schedules, but provided you can meet their deadlines, the actual work can be completed according to your own schedule—especially if you have time zone differences working in your favor.

That said, the tricky part for a busy VA is time management. Imagine having a dozen bosses of equal rank. How are you supposed to know who to suck up to when they all weigh equally on the performance review you won't be receiving? And just to complicate things, you can pretty much count on the fact that when it rains, it pours. Everyone will suddenly need everything at the same time, and right away. Being able to prioritize is an essential skill for a VA. That goes for knowing when to say no, as well. Jim Buske suggests that if VAs "underpromise and overdeliver," they can't go wrong.

Compensation and Advancement

Independent virtual assistants currently charge between $25 and $55 per hour. When significant availability is required, some VAs will charge a retainer. Team Double-Click VAs earn between $10 and $25 per hour; but remember, more of their time is billable because Team Double-Click handles the marketing, sales, and administrative functions. Given the cost of commuting, clothing, day care, and so on, on a net hourly basis, home-based VAs earn more than their bricks-and-mortar counterparts, who typically earn between $12 and $26 per hour.[2]

Virtual assistants need to carefully track their time and document their work. An independent VA will invoice the end client for services rendered. Team Double-Click VAs invoice Team Double-Click, who, in turn, invoices the client.

Office Essentials

Office requirements are similar to those of home-based call center agents. All hardware and software is typically provided by the VA. Where specialty software is required, the client may bear the cost. Provided that software compatibility is not an issue, Mac computers may be an option. Additional items a VA may want to invest in include:

- Webcam.
- Computer speakers.

- USB noise-canceling headset.
- Offsite backup software and storage.
- Fax or online fax capability—preferably color.
- High-speed multipage scanner.
- Copy machine.
- Postage meter.
- Digital camera and/or video camera.
- Separate phone line with follow-me technology, voice mail, and free long distance.
- Personal digital assistant (i.e., iPhone, Blackberry, Palm).
- Web programming and blogging software.
- Locking file drawers.

From the Horse's Mouth

Lois has been a VA with Team Double-Click for six years. She and her husband live in Merrimac, Wisconsin, in the heart of cheese country (population 300). A liver and kidney transplant seven years ago gave Lois a new perspective on life. Before that, she'd been working 65-hour weeks as the typesetting manager of the state's largest newspaper. Lois told us:

> Looking back on it now, I can't believe how much I allowed my job to run my life. Newspaper publishing is a very demanding business. The news just had to get out, no matter what. I was never really off. Even when I took a few vacation days, they wouldn't leave me alone. Once my boss even demanded I cancel the rest of my vacation and come home to help him get things sorted out. We didn't have a social life because more times than not, there'd be some crisis, and I'd have to cancel at the last minute. I don't know which was the final straw, my boss's desperate calls while I was still in a morphine-induced stupor following my surgery, or the day I had to tell my husband I couldn't leave the office when his mother died.

Lois's life as a VA couldn't be more different. "About a month into the new role, it was like I woke up from a bad dream. Suddenly I realized, wow, there's a whole life out there that I've been missing." Still a hard worker, being able to do it on her terms makes all the difference.

My clients work regular hours so I have to be available to them during the day, but at the end of the day, I can turn it off. If I want to go on a hiking trip with my husband, I just call Team Double-Click, and we figure out how to handle my client's needs while I'm gone. If I want to gussie up in my red hat and have lunch with my friends, I can. If I can't sleep in the middle of the night, I get up and work for a while. And it's billable!

Lois says she makes more money now than she did when she worked in a management position at the newspaper. Her various appointments with Team Double-Click have included three years as the right-hand woman for a real estate investment coach, a year as a lawyer's assistant, and several months as an author's assistant. Her work includes booking travel, organizing fund-raisers, writing letters, answering phones, reviewing legal documents, coordinating speaker schedules, and even, in the case of one entrepreneur, managing his business while he honeymooned in Europe.

Lois likes the Team Double-Click approach because she knows she's not in it alone. If she needs help, it's there. If a client drops off, there's another one waiting. If she wants to get away, she can. "It's like having a virtual assistant for my virtual assistant business. I'm not saying it's easy. You really have to be a hard worker to make it in this business. But that's never been a problem for me. When you love what you do, working is a joy."

Tamara, by contrast, is relatively new to the VA scene. Based in the small town of Laveen, Arizona, no one could accuse her of being a couch potato—I doubt she even knows where their sofa is. The mother of five children ranging in age from 9 months to 10 years, she owns her own cake decorating business that specializes in wedding creations, plays violin and piano, is studying to be a nurse, and puts in about 30 hours a week as a VA. And no, she doesn't pay for day care for the three little ones who aren't yet in school.

In the morning, she showers and dresses, "all the way down to shoes." She readies two of her kids for school, sets the others up for independent playtime, and works until 10 a.m. when it's the family "cars and bubbles hour," as she calls it. She puts in another hour of work before lunch and makes phone calls while the kiddos nap. Once the others are home from school, she devotes her time to them. Her husband, an aerospace engineer, helps with the evening routine, and then she goes back to work.

For Tamara, the team approach is the only way to go. There's no other way she could do all that she does while dealing with the vagaries of raising a family and running a small business. Tamara's best advice for someone who wants to be a virtual assistant: "You have to want to work. This isn't project work. It's a career as well as a small business. You have to be disciplined and have an entrepreneurial spirit. You also need a supportive family. They need to understand that what you do is real, not just a hobby."

Worth Knowing

All of the VAs we talked to mentioned the fact that they often underbill their hours. If they feel, for whatever reason, that they should have been able to finish a project more quickly than they did, they adjust the bill accordingly. Lois explains:

> Trust is all-important here. The more a client comes to trust me, the more they'll be willing to relinquish. Most small business owners aren't natural delegators. They feel they have to do everything. Once I earn their trust, they begin to let go of their need to do it all. If I'm not as productive as I feel I can be, the client shouldn't pay for the extra time I spend. In the end, my honesty will bring me more work. That's not just rhetoric—I've cashed the checks that prove it.

As in any pay-for-performance business, getting paid can be a hassle. You feel like you did what the client asked, but they don't agree. Who wins? Or suppose your client goes out of business? These are realities a VA must recognize and deal with. Successful VAs learn to establish clear communications with their clients, accurately estimate the hours a project is likely to take, and keep their clients informed of the time they're spending on a project so there are no arrhythmias when the bill comes. Regular billing and collection protect VAs from allowing their clients to fall too far behind in what they owe.

Best Fit

The best virtual assistants are energetic, enthusiastic, and willing to try new things (like running someone's business for them while they're gone). Being helpful and anticipating people's needs should come naturally.

With careful planning and client selection, a VA can manage both the job and the demands of a family.

Educational background isn't nearly as important as attitude, proficiency in a broad range of computer applications, and communication skills. Unique skills, experience, advanced education, and specialty certification offer access to higher-paying VA jobs.

Major Employers

Team Double-Click is the only major employer of virtual assistants we found. Many smaller VA companies form as one-person operations and expand. Large companies also occasionally hire home-based assistants. Chapters 18 through 21 will help you look for VA positions. Check UndressForSuccessOnline.com for useful links to VA resources.

If you decide to work as an independent VA, Part 3 on freelancing and Part 4 on home businesses will help you on your way.

13

Work as a Medical Transcriptionist

Medical transcription represents the largest portion of the transcription industry. It also employs the largest portion of home-based transcription staff—nearly 75 percent of all medical transcriptionists work at home.[1] But home-based transcription jobs in other fields are available, too.

In public safety and legal fields, transcriptions are required for court reports, depositions, legal notes, arbitration and mediation hearings, police interrogations, and witness interviews. In the academic world, transcriptions are prepared from lectures and presentations. In entertainment, movie audio is transcribed to create closed-captions, and music performances are transcribed to capture lyrics, too. In the business world, conference proceedings, surveys, focus groups, meeting notes, press briefings, teleconferences, and training sessions may require a transcript. Even webcasts, podcasts, and webinars are often transcribed.

This chapter focuses on medical transcription because that's where the majority of the home-based jobs are today.

Medical transcription is a $12 billion industry, and qualified medical transcriptionists (MTs) are in short supply.[2] One reason for the demand is our aging population. Not only do older people require more health care (which creates a greater need for transcription), but the MTs are aging, too—most are between 40 and 60 years old.[3] According to Lea Sims, spokesperson for the Association for Healthcare Documentation Integrity (AHDI), "Everyone agrees we're about to reach a crisis point. Over half of the medical transcriptionists are approaching retirement."

What Do Transcriptionists Do?

Medical transcription involves converting audio files, dictated by health care professionals, into text. The dictated recordings may include patient histories, physical exam reports, diagnostic imaging results, pre- and post-surgical tissue and lab analysis reports, referral letters, consultation reports, post-op notes, and, if things didn't go well, autopsy results.

Typically, a doctor, nurse, radiologist, pathologist, researcher, or other medical provider dictates over the phone or sends a digital audio file to a transcriptionist. Large service providers receive dictated notes sent via the Internet to a central server, where they are accessed by transcriptionists. The dictation is transcribed into a text file and transmitted back to the server, where another transcriptionist reviews it. It is then forwarded electronically to the client, or printed and mailed. This all usually happens within 24 hours—or even quicker, if the need is urgent.

An MT is a knowledge worker and, in a very real sense, a linguist and interpreter—a medical language specialist. Medical transcriptionists need to know Greek and Latin suffixes, prefixes, and roots. They also need practical knowledge of anatomy, physiology, disease processes, pharmacology, laboratory medicine, and medical report standards so they can accurately translate and type what they hear.

The Business Model

Medical transcriptionists work predominantly for an insurance or health care institution, or for a medical transcription service organization (MTSOs). A quarter of all MTs are independent contractors working for MTSOs, while the balance are employees of MTSOs.[4]

While none of the MTSOs are household names, the dozen or so big ones who handle a million or more transcribed lines per year dominate the market. Still, a lot of the transcription work is done by small MTSO companies, mom-and-pop outfits really, serving local clients.

MTSO clients include doctors, dentists, and psychiatrists; hospitals, clinics, urgent and emergency care facilities, and rehabilitation facilities; laboratory, pathology, and radiology departments; coroner and hospital morgues; and long-term and rehabilitation centers. Transcription customers also include HMOs, insurance companies, health care associations, medical libraries, government medical and research facilities, legal offices, veterinary medical schools and facilities, and chiropractors.

What to Expect

To be successful as an MT, your fingers and brain need to work fast. "If you can't type 55 words a minute accurately, you won't even be able to keep up with your training. If you can't type 100 words per minute virtually error-free, you'll have a hard time making money," say Sims.

Top MTs are able to transcribe and edit at the same time; a skill they cultivate called *prior line editing*. Like a pianist in a bar who can chat with customers and play at the same time, experienced transcriptions can let recorded dictation go in their ears and out their fingers, while their eyes and brain double-check the line they just typed.

Another key to success is being willing to acknowledge what you don't know and quickly figure it out. One MTSO tests prospective contractors with a five-minute tape that includes the names of two obscure mushrooms. Spell the names right (by looking them up online) and you pass. Make a good but incorrect guess, and you won't make the cut.

Training

There are a number of vocational schools, community colleges, and distance-learning (online) programs that offer two-year associate degrees or one-year certificate programs in medical transcription. There are also some very reputable schools, such as the Andrews School and Career Step, which offer a six-month program that will teach you what you need to know. Before you sign up for training, be sure the program is approved by the AHDI. Also rummage around MTstars.com and MTdesk.com for insider scoop from working MTs.

MT training programs include course work in anatomy, medical terminology, legal issues relating to health care documentation, and even English grammar and punctuation. If, as a nurse, emergency medical technician, or medical secretary, you're already familiar with medical terminology, you can redirect your knowledge and skills through MT courses.

As in many other fields, certification is recognized as a sign of competence, and AHDI awards Registered Medical Transcriptionist (RMT) and Certified Medical Transcriptionist (CMT) certificates. If you're a recent graduate of a medical transcription educational program, or have fewer than two years experience in acute care, you can earn an RMT certificate once you successfully pass the registered medical transcription exam. To sit for the CMT exam, you need at least two years of acute care experience working in a variety of specialties using a variety of dictation types and report formats.

In order to maintain your certification as an RMT or CMT, you'll have to earn continuing education credits every three years.

The medical books you'll need can be expensive. Check eBay and Amazon for used copies. We saw some for as low as one cent (plus $3.99 shipping). Just be sure they're the current editions before you buy them.

A word of warning: MT training scams are common. One web ad describes medical transcription something like this: "The perfect home business. Earn a six-figure income with little investment. Just send us $399 for our do-it-yourself Home Transcriptionist Kit that includes leads to thousands of potential customers, software, and a Certificate of Completion. You can soon be earning $100 an hour."

In many cases, what you'll get for your money is a list of potential customers that's nothing more than a copy of an online phone directory; a CD-ROM with software that's useless; and a Certificate of Completion that's worth less than the paper it's printed on. But they delivered what they said they would, so no one can make a case against them.

One specific rip-off is perpetrated by a company that industry insiders refer to as TransScam. Web reports about them say the scam goes something like this:

- You post your resume on one of the general job boards and mention something about typing skills or the medical profession.
- They send you a professional-looking e-mail saying how impressed they are with your background and ask if you'd be willing to take a free medical transcription test. If you pass, they say, they'll pay for your training and guarantee you a work-at-home job. All you have to do is buy their transcription software.
- They send you a tape, which you transcribe and send back to them. You ace the test (of course). They rave about your potential.
- So you fork over $400 for what turns out to be awful software and start to work on their so-called free course. When you complain about the program they up-sell you on their "professional" software and a foot pedal to make you more productive.
- But that stuff's junk, too, so you ask for a refund.
- "Read the fine print," they say. "We don't do refunds. Have a nice day."

Scheduling

Because productivity is measured on a per line basis, your schedule can be flexible as long as work units are accomplished in the time frame required by the client health care provider. Most MTSOs have on-call representatives that handle after-hours and quick-turnaround transcriptions. But make no mistake; you'll have to work a full day to earn a living as an MT.

Compensation and Advancement

As a new graduate with no experience, you'll probably have to start out as a contractor with an MTSO. But, despite the shortage of MTs, jobs for newbies can be hard to come by. Mistakes can be lethal, after all.

Like most industries, your earnings will be at the low end of the scale until you gain experience. You'll be paid, for the most part, on a per-line-transcribed basis and start at about $.06 per line. That equates to about $20,000 a year, assuming you're industrious. With experience, you can make $40,000 a year or more—but rarely over $50,000 (in spite of what the scams promise). The median income for an MT in 2007 was $32,400.[5]

With experience, you can move into a salaried position as a trainer, quality assurance specialist, editor, supervisor, or manager. Self-employed MTs generate more income by adding staff and sometimes form MTSOs of their own.

Office Essentials

Your office equipment will include a computer, a high-speed Internet connection, and word-processing software designed for transcription. ExpressScribe is one of the more popular programs and is available for free. You'll also need a USB foot pedal—the Infinity USB Foot Pedal is the de facto standard ($50 to $75) and a set of headphones ($10 and up) to keep from driving those around you nuts.

Worth Knowing

Price, turnaround time, and quality drive the industry, and quality comes first—provided it's not too expensive.

"Some MTSO's are better to work for than others," says Shyanne, an independent transcriptionist. "Early on I was stung by a company that refused to pay because they said there were too many mistakes. I've since learned this is a modus operandi for the bottom dwellers in the industry. You do the work, they get paid, but they refuse to pay you."

Slow pay is also a problem with some companies—a doubly vexing problem because the time you spend trying to collect is time you can't spend transcribing.

The trickiest issue in the industry, though, seems to be a matter of semantics. In an industry of professional nitpickers, it's no surprise that arguments over what constitutes a word, a sentence, or even a character are common. Since those are the metrics that determine the size of your paycheck, pickiness counts.

It used to be a line, any line, defined a unit of work. So

Cataract removed,
right eye.

would earn the same compensation as

Extracapsular cataract extraction, right eye,
by phacoemulsification.

As you can guess, transcriptionists liked the approach; MTSOs didn't. The battle became so heated that ADHI stepped in and suggested that 60 keystrokes should be the standard. But what is a keystroke? Is a space a keystroke? How about a capital S—is that one keystroke or two (Shift + s)? AHDI stepped in again, and recommended a standard called VBM, or visible black mark—if you can see it on a page, it counts. But that definition has drawn fire as well.

Let's say you're preparing a web-based document for a medical court case. The way you tell the web page that you want something in bold print is to type three characters, <B>, before the first word you want boldfaced, and four more </B>, after the last boldface word. These are called HTML syntax characters, and they don't show up in the finished document—so, using the VBM standard, you're not paid for them.

The battles continue, and while AHDI and others have encouraged the industry to adhere to standards, not everyone plays by the same rules. The point is, make sure you know how your employer or client defines a unit of work before you sign on.

Best Fit

Medical transcription offers a real intellectual challenge and the opportunity to make a unique contribution. The field is part of a rapidly growing health care industry, and the demand for quality documentation is on the rise. The profession provides a high level of job security, and skilled medical transcriptionists can expect to make good wages. Transcription is a highly needed, portable skill that offers convenient, flexible hours and can be done almost anywhere.

However, this is not a, "Gee, that sounds like interesting work, I think I'll become a transcriptionist" kind of job. To be successful, you'll need exceptional language and typing skills, quality training, and be able to dependably deliver quality work and great customer service.

While some newly trained MTs jump right into freelance transcription, as we wrote earlier, experience counts for a lot. AHDI advises that you first gain experience in a health care facility or transcription service organization under the direction of a qualified medical transcriptionist.

The largest medical transcription service organizations include:[6]

- Acusis
- Axolotl
- CBay
- DSG
- Encompass
- Focus Informatics
- Heartland
- MDI
- MedQuist
- MedScribe
- Spheris
- SPi/CyMed
- Sten-Tel
- Superior Global
- Transcend Services
- TransTech

Links to other employers and useful resources for future MTs are available at UndressForSuccessOnline.com.

14

Work as a Teacher or Tutor

Almost three decades ago, Benjamin Bloom proposed a revolutionary view of the relationship between time and learning: "Rather than treating time as fixed and success as variable—the usual formula in our educational system—I believe we need to initiate a reform that begins by reversing the two."[1] Technology is turning that vision into a reality.

Terms such as *virtual education*, *distributed learning*, *Web-based education*, *distance learning*, and *online degree* weren't around just 15 years ago. But web- and telephone-based training, tutoring, and education have mushroomed in recent years, and will continue to expand as educators integrate technology both within and outside of the classroom. As a result, a growing number of opportunities exist for online instructors, remote tutors, foreign language coaches, corporate trainers and coaches, online curriculum and content developers, and test preparation coaches.

According to TechLearning.com, "The iPod, the most ubiquitous student tool, is enabling college students to tap into lectures on their own time, and in the K–12 space, podcasting is opening up the classroom to parents and to the community. Up next, look for the cell phone to play a transforming role."[2]

Online training and education is quickly gaining respect. Almost 80 percent of corporate managers rated online university learning to be as good as traditional programs, up from less than 50 percent a decade earlier.[3]

K–12 Teaching Opportunities

The America's Digital Schools 2006 survey predicts that eight million students (about 15 percent of the student population) will be studying core curriculum topics online by 2011 and predicts that most online classes will be taught by adjunct faculty.

In 2006, a quarter of U.S. school districts were in the process of transitioning to a ubiquitous computing program for which every student has his own device. This trend is expected to continue and will ease the path toward virtual delivery of education.

Online programs benefit schools, especially rural schools, by allowing them to:

- Offer courses not otherwise available.
- Meet the needs of specific groups of students.
- Offer advanced-placement or college-level courses (40 percent of high schools don't offer college prep).
- Reduce scheduling conflicts for students.
- Allow students to retake failed courses.
- Reach out to a larger body of certified faculty.
- Teach students time management and self-direction skills.
- Provide opportunities to collaborate with students all over the world.

Factors that may slow the growth of online programs at primary and secondary schools include a lack of standards for course content and quality; the cost to develop or purchase programs; concerns about attendance-based funding; the need for teacher training; and federal, state, and local restrictions. As with the post-secondary programs, many teachers voice concerns about student discipline and faculty acceptance.[4]

Thirty-eight states currently have significant online learning programs or policies.[5] Public and private programs in Louisiana, Florida, Idaho, and Ohio have seen double-digit expansion in enrollment.

The Florida Virtual School, founded in 1997, was the first state-led program to be funded with per-pupil public education funding. More than 68,000 students were enrolled in the 2008 academic year, taught by 440 full-time teachers and 110 adjuncts.[6] Students determine what month of the year they want to start, what time of day, and where they want to study. They can even choose how they respond to assignments—a PowerPoint presentation, a podcast, a traditional essay, or by creating a web site.[7]

Post-Secondary, Graduate, and Doctoral Teaching Opportunities

According to the Sloan Foundation, two-thirds of American graduate schools now offer fully online programs. In 2005, over three million students were taking at least one online course—a 35 percent increase in just one year. In the four years from 2001 to 2005, the market for online higher education more than doubled in size, reaching $11 billion.[8]

Once frowned on in scholarly circles, a majority of academic leaders now consider online learning to be equal or superior to traditional methods.[9] Almost 60 percent of academic leaders consider online courses a critical part of their long-term strategy. Baccalaureate programs have been the slowest to adopt online teaching strategies, but that is beginning to change. Meanwhile, associate programs, master's and doctoral programs, and specialized certificate programs have eagerly embraced technology as a way to widen their geographic reach, reduce costs, and attract teachers.[10]

Post-secondary educators predict significant expansion of their online programs (and thus staff), but cite concerns over how to deal with the need for greater student discipline and increased teacher workload. Marking a change in attitudes, most post-secondary educators are no longer concerned about faculty acceptance, costs, and employer perceptions.[11]

Nationwide, the use of post-secondary adjunct faculty doubled in the past decade—compared to just a 17 percent increase for full-time tenured-track faculty.[12] Many of those adjuncts are filling virtual teaching roles.

Corporate

Nearly 80 percent of corporations use distributed learning, up from 4 percent in 1998. Corporate and government spending on e-learning is estimated at $18 billion.[13] International Data Corp. (IDC) predicts that the worldwide market for corporate e-learning will reach $26 billion by 2010.

While we've seen little evidence that sex discrimination classes and the like have moved out of the corporate classroom and into the bedroom office, they're definitely headed that way. Studies show that e-learning in a corporate setting produces a 60 percent faster learning curve than traditional on-the-job training. IBM's Basic Blue e-learning initiative is reputed to have produced more than a 2,000 percent return on investment. Union

Pacific Railroad was able to implement new processes using e-training 12 months sooner than with traditional training.[14]

All of which is to say, keep an eye out for home-based opportunities in the corporate training and program development markets.

Tutoring

While most tutoring is still done the old-fashioned way, the field is slowly moving Web-ward. Venture-backed Tutor.com went live in 2000. They now have 2,200 virtual tutors and 175 mentors who provide quality control and professional development for tutors. They offer online, on-demand homework help for students in grades 4 through 12. Math and science tutors are most in demand. Student and parent ratings play a big role in monitoring the quality of their tutors.

George Cigale, founder of Tutor.com, sees this as one of the key factors in their success. "Our public school system tries to educate every student, but the students are never asked for feedback about their teachers or schools." Tutor.com now serves over 100,000 students each month. Cigale expects to see that number grow into the millions as online tutoring becomes as commonplace for students as texting their friends.

Smarthinking Inc. started in 1999 with a nearly all-virtual staff. They now employ more than 700 virtual tutors and focus mostly on college-level tutoring. According to Christa Ehmann Powers, vice president of education for Smarthinking, Inc., they expect growth of more than 50 percent per year for the next five years.

What Virtual Teachers Do

Your duties as a virtual teacher will be much the same as a traditional teacher except, as an adjunct, you'll be able to sidestep most of the political overhead: no commencements to attend; few, if any, committee meetings; and no hall monitoring. Virtual teachers and tutors, however, need to develop the additional skill of being able to connect with students in a nonvisual way.

As online programs grow, demand for course developers will follow. Currently the majority of the content for primary and secondary school online programs comes from postsecondary institutions (47 percent), independent vendors (32 percent), state virtual schools (34 percent), and the schools themselves (20 percent).[15]

Lack of federal, state, and local policies for primary and secondary school online programs, how they should be paid for, and how compliance with No Child Left Behind will be measured, may slow adoption. However, no one argues that the genie is out of the bottle. If you're a teacher who wants to work from home, hang tight—your wish may soon be granted.

What to Expect

The process you'll go through once you apply for a position will vary greatly from one school to the next. As you might expect, the more ivy that adorns the walls, the more cumbersome the application process will be. At the other end of the spectrum, a nontraditional or community college may hire you after only one or two phone interviews.

According to Danielle Babb, PhD, author of *Make Money Teaching Online* (Wiley-Interscience, 2007) and a professor for several online colleges, beyond your academic qualifications, what virtual employers want most is online experience, a similar teaching philosophy, responsiveness, patience, and flexibility.

If you wow them with your *curriculum vitae* (CV) and in the interview process, the next step will be an offer. For the most part, the pay is standard, though there may be some wiggle room if your qualifications are exceptional or if the school is desperate for instructors.

Once you're hired, the process will be very different from one school to the next. The motto at the Florida Virtual School is "Anytime, anyplace, any path, any pace." If the students work on weekends and holidays, so will you. The school requires that new teachers carry a beeper for the first year. They stipulate that you must speak to your students and their parents at least once a month—that will usually be on nights and weekends. You're required to check your voice mail and e-mail three times a day.[16] Policies like these are common for primary, secondary, and post-secondary virtual teaching positions.

Some schools will assign a mentor or shadow for your first course, or even your first year. Even if they don't, someone at the school will be monitoring your communications with students for both quality and quantity. Your failure to participate actively, or too many negative student evaluations, will determine whether you're invited back the following semester.

Virtual tutors can expect to interview and test online.

Training

Most, if not all, online higher education teaching positions require at least a master's degree and work experience in your chosen subject. Many require a terminal degree. More established schools will require online teaching experience.

For post-secondary teaching positions, training can take as little as a couple of hours or as much as six weeks. The training typically covers school philosophies and policies, how to use its virtual teaching computer interface, and what's expected of you as a teacher. Most, though not necessarily all, of your training will be online. Some schools require real-time participation, others offer self-study. "Remember that you are constantly being evaluated as you train, and the job isn't yours until you're done. This is not a time for whining, complaining, or lackluster participation," advises Babb.

Surprisingly, while almost all states require their K–12 virtual instructors to have the same teaching certifications as traditional teachers (including certification in the state where you teach), only a handful of states require specialized online training. Over 60 percent of K–12 virtual teachers receive no training prior to online teaching, and almost a third receive no training in online lesson design.[17] Among those schools that do provide training, it may take as little as one day or up to 270 hours, in the case of a new teacher or a new course at the Virtual High School, a cyber school with participants in over 20 states.[18]

Some of the more rigorous schools will include training in online teaching fundamentals, asynchronous (delayed) and synchronous (real-time) communications tools and issues, assessment tools, design tools (HTML editing, web creation tools), online instructional design principles, meeting the needs of students with multiple learning styles in the online classroom, engagement and motivation in online lessons, building a community within the online classroom, maintaining proper student etiquette, meeting the needs of students with disabilities, managing groups and collaboration in the classroom, time management, identifying at-risk students, and active listening.

K–12 tutors include undergrad and grad students, teachers, and industry professionals. College-level tutors typically have a graduate degree and experience in teaching or instruction. Company-specific training, usually about two weeks long, typically includes a combination of webinars, online videos, and mock tutoring sessions. Some firms pay their tutors during training.

Scheduling

Virtual learning involves a combination of asynchronous and synchronous elements, but the former are far more prevalent. The real-time needs of your students will largely determine when you work. Some schools will require you to schedule office hours and be available by phone, e-mail, or instant chat. E-mails and voice mails generally have to be answered within 24 hours, and grading is expected three to five days after assignments are completed. Online tutors generally work evenings and weekends. The average number of hours varies with the school year. At Tutor.com, teachers work as little as 3 hours a week or as much as 30. Smarthinking.com tutors average between 6 and 20 hours per week. While most online tutors work part-time, full-time work is available.

Compensation and Opportunity for Advancement

Online adjunct faculty members can earn $1,500 to $5,000 per course. Some schools pay on a per-student basis at $150 to $300 per student. The per-student model can be dicey if you're teaching an unproven course. One online teacher we interviewed taught a whole course for two students, and earned only $400 for a whole quarter's work. She described it as a nightmare.

The same teacher was hired by another university to prepare and teach three courses for the upcoming semester. She reviewed course materials and web links for errors, obtained and read the texts and articles that would be used, developed course announcements, posted discussion questions for each week, developed and posted faculty expectations, and set up discussion forums. One week before the start of the quarter, all three courses were cancelled because of poor enrollment. She was wiser but poorer, out a whole quarter's income.

Some schools pay for developing a new course ($1,000 to $4,000), for revising a course ($500 to $2,000), and for being a faculty lead (an additional $2,000 to $10,000 per year—the higher end representing a lead for multiple courses). Other influences on pay include the prestige of the school, the demand for the program, the level of the course, and your credentials. In some cases, a premium is paid for large classes.

A school that offers entirely asynchronous communication, automatically grades exams, and expects students to be self-directed may require only a three to four hour per week commitment.[19] In that case, an

$1,800 course fee might work out to $60 an hour. Conversely, a higher-paying course with lots of administrative overhead might yield less than $15 an hour. Babb suggests one way to reduce overhead is to teach the same course twice in the same semester, rather than teaching two different courses.

Online tutors earn between $12 and $15 per hour. Some firms pay by the minute, others pay for the time a tutor is available, regardless of the number or length of sessions.

No matter how you slice it, the reality is that the compensation for virtual teachers compares miserably to that of their traditional counterparts, where the national average salary for faculty members on 9- and 10-month contracts is $68,514, and adjunct faculty earn $53,011.[20] It's likely that as the penetration of online courses increases, supply and demand pressures will help close the compensation gap.

Office Essentials

Companies that employ tutors generally use a combination of instant chat and proprietary work tools. Blackboard Inc. is the leading supplier of virtual classroom software. Its programs are used by almost 30 percent of the post-secondary online education market. Instructors and students access their courseware, discussions, assignments, and messaging options from a web browser. Some schools, including MIT, Stanford, and many others, are adopting open-source products such as Moodle, Angel, and Sakai. Other platforms you may encounter include WebCT (now owned by Blackboard, but still supported separately), Desire2Learn, Campus Edition, eCollege, and a variety of school-specific proprietary systems. Even Facebook, MySpace, and SecondLife are beginning to adapt their social networking platforms to education.

While experience with a platform may give you a head start, each school will have its own way of using the system, so don't expect to play hooky during the training.

From the Horse's Mouth

Dr. Patricia Deubel has over 30 years experience as a secondary and university-level educator in both traditional and online education settings. Her primary focus is mathematics and computing technology in education. In addition to developing and teaching online master's and doctoral programs for almost 10 years, Duebel's experienced the other end of online learning as a virtual doctoral student at Nova Southeastern University in Florida.

Deubel described a recent experience she had teaching two 10-week online graduate and doctoral courses:

> There were a total of thirty-seven students between the two classes. In response to fifteen graded topics and twenty-seven course discussion threads, there were 2,855 student posts—all of which I read. I sent over thirteen hundred messages consisting of instructional or facilitative discussion posts, individual feedback to graded discussions, responses to email, and individual feedback on course projects. There were also periodic communications via email or phone with the department chair. Plus, there were a number of proactive emails to at-risk students with additional communications to alert the university. Add time for reading course materials, troubleshooting errors in posted content, and record keeping, and you can see that these two courses were a nearly full-time commitment.[21]

Babb advises prospective online teachers to investigate the workload before they sign up at a new school. "Discussion forums can be very time consuming, as you need to monitor a whole class of contributors and add value. Some schools require a response to each student's post. This can eat up a lot of time. Consider a class of thirty-five students with three assignments a week. That's over a hundred items to grade. It's not unusual to spend thirty hours a week on a single course at one of the more demanding schools."

Worth Knowing

Babb advises that online teaching requires a great deal of perceptiveness. "There are no visual or auditory cues to provide feedback on whether or not you're getting through to the student. While sixty percent of people are visual learners, thirty percent are auditory and ten percent are kinesthetic. As a virtual teacher, you need to find new ways to figure out who's who, and then develop ways to facilitate their needs," says Babb.

Babb also advises that it's a good idea to work for more than one school at a time, though some of the more august schools may frown on it. "The problem is that as an adjunct, you have no job security. You can be let go at any time. My best advice is to think of yourself as an entrepreneur who's running a business that serves students. Through numerous customers, the schools, your aim is to maximize income per workload," said Babb.

Given all the ambiguities in online teaching, be sure you have a contract in hand before you go to work developing or teaching a course. Even some good universities get poor grades for the way they treat their online adjuncts.

Best Fit

The best virtual teachers and tutors are computer literate, have the patience and aptitude for technical troubleshooting, can communicate effectively without body language, are comfortable working asynchronously, have the ability to motivate students, understand and can show people how to be self-disciplined and effective time managers, and know and love their subjects.

Major Employers

For K–12, virtual teaching and course development opportunities exist with state-managed virtual schools, private and charter schools, and public schools that offer hybrid teaching approaches. Many have found it easier to hire experienced online faculty over retraining existing staff.

Not all online degrees are created equal, nor are all online teaching gigs. In the United States, colleges and universities are accredited by one of 19 recognized institutional accrediting organizations. Specialty programs are accredited by one of approximately 60 organizations that are recognized by the Council for Higher Education Accreditation (CHEA) or the United States Department of Education (USDE). "Sad to say, there are more nonaccredited online programs than there are accredited ones," says Babb. "If a school isn't accredited, its degree is of little value and teaching for them can soil your reputation."

Traditional not-for-profit universities have been the slowest to adopt online teaching. Tenured faculty and their edifice complex make them slow to change. Nontraditional schools such as Capella and Walden, and for-profit universities such as University of Phoenix and Baker College, offer a wider choice of online teaching programs.

"While I might recommend taking a job with a nonaccredited school as a last resort, or to gain some online teaching experience, you never, *ever* want to work for a diploma mill. Programs that essentially sell their degrees are scams, and you don't want your name associated with them," says Babb. "If all they need to enroll a student in a degree program is a credit card, run."

Top virtual tutoring employers include Tutor.com, Smarthinking.com, and Tutorvista.com. Check out our web site for links to other virtual education employers and other useful resources.

15

Work as a Remote Tech

If you're good with technology, have excellent communications skills, enjoy helping people, and have a great deal of patience, a job as a remote geek might be your ticket home.

In the old days, the on/off switch was the only thing between consumers and all kinds of electronic fun. Nowadays, for many, powering up is just the start of their troubles. Televisions, cell phones, DVD players, remote controllers, and all kinds of devices that are supposed to simplify our lives, don't. And it's not just about toys. As you've read in other sections of this book, the ability to provide remote technical support is a significant problem for companies with a home-based workforce.

Responding to the market need, a number of companies have created online support centers to help frantic consumers and employees with their technology problems. Not all of them are home-based (yet) but many are.

What a Remote Tech Support Person Does

You don't have to be an expert in everything digital to qualify for a job as a remote support agent. A specialist might focus on one or two areas such as Windows XP and Vista, or system tune-ups. And there are a lot of niches you could focus on including Microsoft Office, Apple products, e-mail, backups, networking issues, security, printers, viruses, digital cameras, MP3 players, video and webcams, malware/spyware removal, or other specific products and programs.

"Job one is fix the customer, job two is fix the problem," says Jason, a freelance geek. "You not only have to be a competent tech, you have to be able to make a customer with a fried hard drive happy they called."

Remote techs solve problems using a combination of talk therapy and tools that allow them to control a customer's computer from their own. Patience and the ability to communicate with people of all skill levels are essential. Jason once had a customer who couldn't get his laptop powered up. The caller explained that nothing happened when he hit the power button. Starting with the basics, Jason asked if the power unit was plugged in. When the customer asked, "How can I tell?" Jason knew he was in for a long session.

The flip side is the customer who acts like the expert, but clearly doesn't have a clue. "In some ways, they're even harder to deal with because they refuse to listen," says Jason. Conversely, knowing what you *don't* know as a tech, and being willing to admit it, is an important job skill too. "There's nothing more frustrating than trying to get help from a support person who knows less about the problem than you do."

Of course, not all calls are as easy to diagnose as the guy who complained that he couldn't get the cup holder closed—he meant the DVD tray. "Many of the problems involve several programs that don't play well together," says Jason. "You really have to know your systems backward and forward."

The Business Model

When you call tech support at Apple, Epson, Microsoft, and the other big technology companies, you're probably talking to an office-based employee. But for all the reasons that led call centers to embrace the home-based model, those jobs are beginning to move home, too. Third-party support direct to consumers promises a new crop of work-at-home jobs.

SupportSpace, for example, offers consumer tech support services for PCs and peripherals through a network of independent providers. Its web site allows customers to select whom they want to work with based on the provider's biography, areas of expertise, and user ratings. Using SupportSpace's remote control software, its home-based independent agents help customers solve problems via chat or telephone.

Applications, Training, and Scheduling

Remote tech support employers look for experienced techs, but you don't necessarily need a computer science degree. Many freelancers are self-taught. One freelancer we talked with started out providing class-room support for his high school and grew from there.

Formal certifications such as Microsoft's Certified Desktop Support Technician (MCDST) certificate and Help Desk Institute (HDI) Desktop Support Technician certificate can help you land a job. A college degree isn't required but most employers prefer it. While the typical 16-year-old may know more about computers than many 60-year-olds, for legal reasons tech support agents must be at least 18 years old.

After filling out an online job application, if you look like a promising candidate you'll be scheduled for a telephone interview. Assuming you aren't tongue-tied, you'll move on to skills testing and a background check. Don't be surprised if your interviewer is, well, difficult. It could be part of the interview process and it's certainly a reality of the job.

Once you're hired, remote tech companies will provide training in how their systems and tools work, their company policies, and their job expectations.

Perhaps the most attractive aspect of working as a remote tech, at least with SupportSpace, is that your schedule can be whatever you want it to be. You simply log on to their web site and start taking calls based on your expertise. Log off, and you've effectively put out the cat, pulled down the shade, and locked the door on your shop.

Compensation and Opportunity for Advancement

Pay varies from company to company, but generally you're paid either by the minute (or fraction of an hour) or by the session. SupportSpace agents are independent contractors and are free to set their own rates. The company's fee for providing the calls and infrastructure is 25 percent of what you earn. A full-time, hardworking tech with plenty of experience and a good repeat customer ratio can average $30 to $40 an hour, although $18 to $20 per hour is more typical. Keep in mind these are clock hours, not billable hours. You might be logged in and available, but not working with a customer. As a result, while your advertised rate may be $75 per hour, you may only be billing an average of 20 minutes for every clock hour.

Office Essentials

If you're enough of a geek to be good at remote tech support, you no doubt already have high-speed Internet, a cool headset, and all the hardware and software you need to be successful. Any proprietary or specialty software will be provided by your employer or the company you work through.

From the Horse's Mouth

Nick, a college sophomore, works for SupportSpace. He rolls out of bed and logs in while the coffee's brewing. "I have 45 seconds to respond to a customer connection, so I can't wander off. But I can work for a couple hours, and make a quick forty bucks. That's pretty cool," says Nick.

Nick characterized his typical customer as a befuddled senior citizen who really appreciates a sympathetic, patient, helping hand. "But they aren't all old folks," he said. "I had a kid call in a panic yesterday. He'd been using his Mom's laptop and managed to infect it with a virus. He said his mother would kill him if he didn't get it fixed before she came home." While Nick was discrete about the nature of the issue, our guess is that the caller's real problem was that he'd picked up the nasty virus on a visit to a virtual red-light district.

Worth Knowing

As you might expect, customers often are upset when they call. Worse, you may not be the first person they've talked to about their problem. In fact, they may be paying to talk to you because of the abysmal customer support they received from the hardware or software vendor. To succeed you need to be part shrink, part teacher, and part tech guru.

Major Employers

The largest remote tech support employer with home-based techs we found is SupportSpace. Their unique approach has attracted venture capital investment. We expect that as their model proves itself, many of the office-based technical support providers will join the e-work trend. Other remote tech employers include Apple, SpeakWithAGeek.com, AskDrTech.com, and Arise, a company that provides tech support for Fortune 500 companies.

Links to other employers and useful resources for rent-a-geeks are available at UndressForSuccessOnline.com.

16

Work as a Writer

Few occupations are better suited to working anywhere than writing. Even before the advent of the Internet, a writer equipped with a typewriter and a mailbox or a courier service could click out a living from home. Newspaper journalists, after all, delivered breaking news to their editors from remote locations by telephone or wire services as far back as the 1920s.

It's odd, then, that most full-time salaried writers still work in offices. For example, the old bullpen scene where dozens of busy journalists bang out their stories alongside frantic colleagues is still played out today at virtually every newspaper (albeit in front of a computer monitor instead of a typewriter). If you're lucky enough to work at one of those office-based writing jobs and want to work from home, be sure to read Chapter 9 for ideas about how to approach your boss about e-work.

What Writers Do

About 300,000 people in the United States earn their living by writing.[1] Over 80 percent of them write or edit fiction or nonfiction books, newspapers, magazines, trade journals, newsletters, radio and television programs, stage productions and movies, advertisements, web sites, and blogs. Technical writers and editors, representing about 16 percent of the market, develop product documentation, operating and maintenance manuals, assembly instructions, technical specifications, project proposals, business plans, and white papers.

Writers with special creative or persuasive skills write speeches, advertising copy, press releases, catalogs, greeting cards, songs, and even cereal box copy. After all, somebody was paid to come up with "I'm Cuckoo for Cocoa Puffs." Others with special language skills work as proofreaders and translators.

A full one-third of writers and the large majority of those who are home-based are self-employed freelancers.[2]

What to Expect

In salaried writing positions, new writers typically start out doing research, fact-checking, or copyediting before they move on to byline positions.

Unless you write for a large organization, you can expect to do your own research, schedule and conduct your own interviews, fact-check your work, and deliver error-free finished copy to your editor.

Increasingly, writers are also expected to be multimedia content developers, using a combination of words, images, and sounds to convey the story. This requires an understanding of—and talent for—graphic design, page layout, photography, videography, web editing, and blogging.

If you freelance, expect that it will take time to build up a reliable pipeline of work. You'll need experience and sample work to show prospective employers. Fortunately, it's easy to get your name in print. Small newspapers and magazines are hungry for inexpensive—read *free*—content.

At the time of the savings and loan crisis of the late 1980s, I'd recently left my job as a commercial lender and had started my own consulting firm to help business owners find financing. I started writing topical articles and submitted them to local and regional newspapers. With those as clippings, I was able to find work with some of the major business magazines.

Then I landed a full-page article in the *Wall Street Journal*'s *National Business Employment Weekly*. That led to a *Wall Street Journal* radio interview, which caused an editor from Wiley to pick up the phone and ask if I'd like to write a book about venture capital. It wasn't that I was a great writer—it was just a matter of knowing my subject and being able to put words on paper in a way that, at least, was clear.

But understand that there's a big difference between writing a few articles and making a living as a writer. Unless you're very good *and* a little lucky, developing a steady stream of work will take time. The problem with freelance writing for a living—and, for that matter, any freelance income—is that as soon as you finish a project, you're unemployed again.

Good writers will spend at least as much time chasing work as they do words. Eventually, you may get to a point where you've built up enough of a reputation and enough relationships that new work will find you, but even that can be tricky.

"I've been working as a freelance writer for twelve years now, and while I earn a decent living, the work is never steady," says Jessica. "It never fails: I'll be working on a rush article for one editor and another one will call with an equally time-sensitive job. I can't do them both so I have to pass on the second one. The following week, it's like the whole literary world is on sabbatical."

Training

Most, but certainly not all writers have a college education. Employers will generally look for a broad liberal arts background, or a degree in communications or journalism. Specialty training and/or experience is required for technical writers.

For self-employed writers, academic achievement carries less weight than experience, publication history, and the authority of the writer. What you studied in college won't matter as much as whether you're a recognized expert in your field.

You might be surprised to learn that becoming a recognized expert isn't as hard as you may think. First, find out who the experts are, digest their work, join relevant organizations, attend conferences, and read everything you can find on the subject. At some point, you'll likely begin to see opportunities to synthesize what you've learned or see a way to approach the topic in a manner that no one else has. If you've done a good job of connecting with the experts, you can solicit their opinions of your conclusions. Then you can establish a web site or blog and build an audience. You can write articles and send out press releases about your work, offer yourself to the media, do your own studies, give speeches, and write a book.

Scheduling

Unless you work for a daily newspaper, freelance writing really can be a wherever/whenever occupation. Four months before the deadline on this book, a bush pilot friend of ours asked Tom (a pilot for over 40 years) if he wanted to come up to Alaska for the month of July and fly sightseeing tours in a rare and famous 1929 floatplane. We decided it was one of those chance-of-a-lifetime opportunities, so several of these chapters were hammered out in a log cabin and at the Washboard (the local coin-operated laundry) in Homer.

Most writers discover a particular time of day and setting when and where they are most productive. For me, I don't actually start producing until about 1 PM Provided I'm not interrupted, and my back doesn't start to spasm, I typically work until about 7 PM For a long time I fought my natural rhythm. I was determined to start writing first thing in the morning. Finally I gave up. Now, rather than fighting with myself, I use the morning hours for e-mail, research, interviews, blogging, web maintenance, and marketing.

We like to tell people the nice thing about being self-employed is you only have to work half days—the question is which 12 hours.

Compensation and Opportunity for Advancement

Sadly, though some writers manage to achieve a degree of fame, fortune rarely follows. The average writer earns about $49,000 per year. The lowest 10 percent earn less than $25,000. Editors' incomes aren't much better. Technical writers fare slightly better, earning about $10,000 a year more than other writers.[3]

Advancement for freelance writers comes not in the form of pro-motions but as steady work with well-paying organizations. While it's not entirely true that the larger, more august publications pay better than smaller ones, it's certainly true for the majority of them. Rates range from $.10 to $5.00 a word, making a 1,000-word article worth anywhere between $100 and $5,000. A number of excellent resources are available to help you determine where you can get the biggest purse for your verse. Visit UndressForSuccessOnline.com for web links.

You might think that with the proliferation of blogs, writers would be in short supply and, as a result, compensation would be good. Sorry to say, while demand is up, pay is down. Bloggers are among the lowest-paid writers. Many, in fact, write for free. Those who are paid often settle for an income that's based on the number of people who visit the blog. The approach is intended to encourage the writer to promote the site.

According to Jeremy Wright, founder and president of b5media, the largest blog network on the Web, "Most of our bloggers aren't doing it primarily for the money. They're just passionate about their topic and happy to make some extra spending money doing something they love."

The majority of independent bloggers make less than $100 a month. That said, some of the top bloggers, such as Darren Rouse of Problogger .net, report a six-figure income. People don't actually pay to read his blog. His income, and that of other independent bloggers, comes from blog-site advertising, subscriptions, and product sales. To make money as a blogger, you need exceptional online marketing skills and content that draws a lot of readers.

Marshall Brain, founder of HowStuffWorks, does a web marketing blog called WebKEW. He's calculated that to earn more than $1,000 a month, you need about 50,000 unique monthly visitors who each view 10 pages or so per visit. At 100,000 visitors, you can start to earn a full-time living from ads and click-through income.[4]

Office Essentials

Your technology needs as a writer are minimal. A basic computer system, high-speed Internet access for research, reliable off-site backup, and maybe a noise-canceling mic and headset for interviews is all you need. That said, for me, having two large computer screens that allow us to surf the Web while I write is nearly as essential as caffeine.

From the Horse's Mouth

Writer Laura Vanderkam never really had to escape the corporate grind. Her first and only "real" job was the one she took fresh out of college—a one-year internship at *USA Today*. Then she decided to move to New York City to try the freelance life.

"I got some lucky breaks," she says. Educational philanthropists Jan and Bob Davidson read one of her columns and hired her to co-write a book called *Genius Denied: How to Stop Wasting Our Brightest Young Minds*. Simon & Schuster published *Genius Denied* in early 2004. While continuing to write regularly for *USA Today*, she added other clients including *Reader's Digest*, *The American*, *Scientific American, and others*. For fun (and exposure) she blogs at the *Huffington Post*. In 2006, she wrote her own book, *Grindhopping: Build a Rewarding Career Without Paying Your Dues* (McGraw-Hill, 2006).

On a typical day, Vanderkam wakes up around 7 AM, "when Jasper [her three-year-old] starts making noises." She or her husband walks him to his day care/preschool two blocks from their apartment, and then she puts in a full day at the home office. She creates lists of weekly priorities—write a column, pitch a feature, prepare for a speech, interview three people for another article that's in the pipeline. She tries to use the morning for work that requires lots of thinking (e.g., cranking out drafts). Then she goes for a run around noon, and spends her afternoons researching, interviewing, and pitching. She picks Jasper up around 5 PM, makes dinner, and catches up on e-mails throughout the evening.

To come up with story ideas, Vanderkam reads two newspapers most days and at least a dozen magazines a month. "I am always looking for trends," she says. "Three related items can be pieced together to make a story." She tries to juggle at least one book proposal or project, a column, and two to three other pieces at any given time. Over the years, she has resigned herself to the feast-or-famine nature of freelance writing. "My first year, there was one month where I made $400, followed by a month that I made $10,000," she says. "You learn to build up savings and to track down clients who don't pay quickly."

Because working in a home office can occasionally be isolating, Vanderkam makes sure to get out from time to time. She sings in a choir on Tuesday nights. She enjoys the music but also the people. "I've even interviewed some for articles. When you run your own business, every-thing becomes a networking opportunity."

Allena Tapia's story is quite different. She planned to earn an English degree but didn't plan to become a freelance writer. "I thought I'd teach high school English or journalism. But by the time I finished my degree I was in my late twenties and tired of the school scene. I wasn't keen to spend yet another year on a teaching certificate," says Tapia. She tried her hand at a couple of writing and editing jobs, but found they weren't for her. "I'd become accustomed to pursuing my own ideas, having a lot of freedom, and getting my work done at a time that was convenient for me."

So she struck out on her own, building her freelance writing business slowly and steadily. "I didn't have a business plan, and honestly, I kind of thought of freelancing as something I would do in between jobs, while I figured out what kind of balance I needed in life." But the gigs kept rolling in, and Tapia realized she'd found her niche. "I took it very seriously from then on. I've always had the attitude that this was *mine*, something for which I was personally responsible, and it was my intent to build my business well."

Her lucky break was becoming a Guide with About.com. "The About.com gig offered me the stability of an ongoing, reliable source of income. Right now About.com provides about a third of my income needs," says Tapia. She looks to the rest of her work as a way to meet her need for variety. "Although I do have a couple of other ongoing clients, I find my 'filler' clients to be my most exciting. I have a short attention span. I always want something new."

Tapia's typical day starts at 7:30 when she sees her kids and husband off and empties the house. Since she's found she's most productive in the morning, she prepares her to-do list the night before. "Otherwise I'll pilfer my morning time trying to figure out where I left off," she says. She looks for work every day, no matter how busy she is. "I believe this is the only secret to beating the freelancer feast-or-famine cycle."

Since she only has six hours per day of dedicated work time, she avoids interruptions at all cost. "I'm so busy most of the time, I hate to even break away from my desk. One interruption could mean I'll be working late into the night," say Tapia.

Once the children arrive back home around 4 PM, work is suspended until later that night. "We do the usual soccer, PTA, dinner thing," she says. After the children are off to bed, she and her husband settle in front of the TV with their laptops. "We always make fun of how romantic we are, with our matching laptops in front of Letterman!" From then until around midnight she does what she considers to be the easier tasks such as invoices, research, personal blog posts, and online networking. "It's the only time of day I really have any contact with the world beyond my front lawn," says Tapia.

Worth Knowing

- Don't quit your day job for a career as a freelance writer unless you can afford to go without an income, or you have an established record of accomplishment and connections as a writer.
- Spend more time marketing yourself than you do writing. You need to keep the pipeline full.
- Be open to all sorts of work. The key is to keep working.
- Write for a variety of publications and industries. That way if one goes south you still have an income. Just like any business, you never want all your checks in one basket.
- Become acquainted with more than one editor of the publications you write for. Editor turnover is high, and you don't want to be lost in the shuffle if your only contact moves on.

While we can't call them scams, many of the writing jobs you'll see posted around the Web are looking for slave labor: "Write 50 articles for $50." Yet you'll see ads proclaiming, "Unlimited Income Potential"—provided you do the marketing. If these weren't freelance "opportunities," the minimum wage police would have a field day.

Best Fit

In addition to being able to communicate clearly, the best writers are adept at cutting to the heart of a matter. They're curious about a wide range of subjects, creative, self-motivated, highly disciplined, and versatile. Writers must have the confidence and perseverance to deal with frequent rejections, grumpy editors' feedback, and public criticism. The ability to concentrate and work under the pressure of deadlines is important as well. As in most fields today, being computer savvy is increasingly important.

Major Employers

Most writers who work from home are either freelancers or established magazine staff writers. While our research failed to find any companies that hire large numbers of home-based writers, we did run across a couple of smaller ones.

Writers Research Group, founded in 2000 by Lori Packwood and Karen Tingle, is a full-service writing, editing, and research firm with over 500 contract writers. They specialize in writing Internet articles and search engine optimization copy. Their home-based positions include writers, editors, researchers, and data entry specialists. "It's hard work. Out of ten hires, only about four stick. The rest aren't self-disciplined enough to hack it," says co-owner Karen Tingle.

ProofreadNow.com contracts work out to over a hundred home-based proofreaders and copy editors. Pay is by the page, and the rate depends on experience and skill. Candidates are required to have a minimum of five years experience in proofreading and copyediting.

Some of the best paying blogger jobs are with About.com, b5media.com, and LifeWire.com. Compensation is generally a mix of base pay and revenue sharing (where you are paid based on traffic and ad click-throughs). Traffic bonuses of $1 to $2 per thousand readers are typical. Average bloggers make between $250 and $750 per month with these organizations. Competition for these jobs is fierce, and few who have them give them up. B5media's Wright says they receive more than 5,000 applications from new bloggers each month, but only a handful of their 350 writers ever quit.

Links to writing gigs and other useful resources are available at UndressForSuccessOnline.com

17

Work In Telemedicine

A joint U.S.–UK study of over 1,700 patient care cases estimated that 45 percent of U.S. patient care could be handled via telemedicine.[1]

Telemedicine includes fields such as telenursing, teletriage, teleradiology, and telehealthcare. While these fields haven't yet become mainstream health care approaches, some major companies are eyeing telemedicine as a remedy for tired doctors, talent shortages, and shrinking profit margins. A traditional home health care nurse, for example, might visit five or six patients a day, while a telenurse using video conferencing or the Internet can visit two or three times that number.

Telephone health services evolved to enhance access to medical care, act as a gateway to traditional health care providers, reduce insurance costs, offer disease management and chronic care advice, provide around-the-clock access to qualified health advice, and reduce costs by preventing worried patients from seeking more expensive, and often unnecessary, face-to-face care. They've been particularly helpful in providing access to mainstream health care in rural areas.

McKesson Health Solutions, a Colorado-based Fortune 500 company, pioneered its e-work program in 2003. "Many companies are reluctant to venture into telework, but once they do, there's no turning back," says Linda Casey, director of operations support for McKesson. Home-based positions now account for 98 percent of the company's medical call center jobs.

Home-based teletriage nurses allowed San Diego–based KP OnCall to quickly ramp up for the overload of calls that accompanied the 2007 wildfire outbreak. Some nurses who themselves were evacuees were able to move in with friends and quickly return to the phones so they could help others.

What Do They Do?

Insurance companies hire telenurses to field calls from anxious patients and recommend whether they need to see a doctor. Doctors hire them to attend to callers whose medical needs are not urgent and to provide after-hours access to advice. Worker's compensation and other insurance providers hire telenurses as case managers to oversee the intake, care, and rehabilitation of injured workers. They help ensure patients receive proper care and return to work as soon as medically feasible.

Teleradiologists work remotely to interpret digital X-rays, CT scans, and MRIs. Such services are particularly helpful in filling health care gaps in small and remote hospitals that may not have access to an on-staff radiologist.

Pharmacists, behavioral management specialists, social workers, and medical case managers also fill gaps in health coverage by providing telephone-based advice.

Even doctors are in on the virtual act. A company called Hello Health recently introduced a platform that it describes as Geek Squad meets Netflix. Through their subscription-based service, you may soon be able to reach your doctor without leaving your hot water bottle.

What to Expect

Nurses and other medical providers who offer advice to patients are required to be licensed in the state where they practice. One to three years of clinical nursing experience is required for telenurses.

Strong communications skills and computer skills are necessary. Experience in case management, disability management, occupational health, and workers' compensation is required for some positions.

For the most part, the job application and interview process for at-home medical positions is conducted online and over the phone. Nicole Baker, a Solution Care Manager at RTW, Inc., says they look for people who are self-motivated, self-directed, and have professional communication skills. Most importantly, they have to be good at building relationships with patients and medical providers. As you might expect, competition for these positions is tough, but the industry is still very young. Future opportunities are likely to be more plentiful.

Training

Medical training and experience are prerequisites for telemedicine employment. Any legitimate employer provides call management, software, privacy, and other company-specific training free of charge.

Where and how the training is conducted varies by the company and the position. At McKesson, the training lasts six weeks and is provided via the Internet. RTW, Inc. requires a week of on-site training in its Minnesota headquarters, followed by on-the-job training with a virtual shadow.

Scheduling

Teletriage and telenursing agents are most in demand when other health care services are unavailable—on weekends, at night, and on holidays. Other telemedicine positions allow more flexible scheduling.

Compensation and Advancement

Home-based telenurses earn between $24 and $27 per hour—about 12 percent less than office-based telenurses. Compensation in other home-based telemedicine positions is competitive with that of traditional health care providers.

Office Essentials

The office needs in this field are similar to those of a call center agent. Some employers provide computer or *dumb terminal* setups for their telenursing staff.

From the Horse's Mouth

"We offer a caring and compassionate voice even if it's 2 AM," says telenurse Anne Afshari. She and Laura Hagler founded Exclusively RNs in 2002 to specialize in obstetric/gynecological teletriage. "A mother-to-be might call because she's worried about something as simple as whether tuna fish is safe for her unborn baby, or as frightening as her water broke and she's home alone," says Afshari. "One of our telenurses even answered a call from a pregnant mom who got herself stuck in a chair."

Afshari and Hagler find that their callers are often more willing to open up to them than to their doctor. "Somehow it's less intimidating to ask a nurse what feels like a stupid question," says Hagler.

But it can be stressful work. Jaydn is a telenurse for a health insurance provider. "Your first call of the day might be someone with heart palpitations, and your last might be someone who's contemplating suicide. Some days I'm wrung out at the end of a shift," says Jaydn. Still, she prefers her virtual nursing position to the 12-hour night shifts she used to pull as a critical care nurse.

Vicki Orth is a Solution Case Manager with RTW, Inc. From her home in Sioux Falls, South Dakota, she and her husband, a paramedic, are raising three boys, ages 6, 8, and 14. Vicki spent 25 years as a nurse specializing in critical care and emergency room nursing. When she and her husband started a family, the long nights and odd shift work took its toll. She moved into case management 10 years ago, but still felt guilty about the time she spent away from her family. "Two years ago when I spotted an ad for RTW's home-based positions, I jumped at the chance," says Orth. "The hiring process was as intense as any I'd been through as a nurse or case manager, but I made it through. I never want to work the floor again. My job with RTW lets me use my professional skills, contribute to the social good, add to the family income, and still be a good mom."

Orth specializes in workers' compensation case management with RTW, Inc. She feels the most important success factors for a telenurse are being self-directed and able to stay on task, being empathetic yet firm, and having good telephone and computer skills.

Major Employers

Telenursing and case management positions are available at McKesson Health Solutions; CorVel; Aleris; FONEMED; KP OnCall (a division of Kaiser Permanente); RTW, Inc.; Aetna; Mutual of Omaha; United-Health Group; and IntelliCare.

OB/Gyn and pediatric care specialists are particularly in demand. Exclusively RNs, based in Colorado Springs, Colorado, specializes in teletriage for expectant mothers.

Virtual Radiologic and StatRad offer nationwide home-based tele-radiology positions.

Links to these and other employers plus related resources are available at UndressForSuccessOnline.com

18

How to Navigate the Web in Search of E-work

Sorry to disappoint, but the naked truth is that finding e-work isn't any easier than finding a traditional job. In fact, in some ways, it's harder. After all, with few exceptions, there are fewer e-work jobs than people who want them.

Today's count of Google hits on a search for *telecommute job* yielded a whopping 1,190,000 entries (your mileage may vary—the Web is very dynamic and search results change by the minute). If you're not familiar with how Google and other search engines decide who winds up where in their search results, or which listings are actually ads, you'll be at a disadvantage as you navigate the Web in search of a way home. Take a moment to read about it before you move on.

Search Engine Optimization

Since the early days of the Web, search engines (e.g. Google, Yahoo, etc.) have tried to rank web sites so that search results are useful. Each search engine has its own proprietary approach, but the fundamentals are similar.

Early on, search engines relied on web page developers to accurately describe their work within the code that defines their web pages using so-called *metatags*. Page authors placed tags with keywords in the computer code (known as hypertext markup language, or HTML) that defines the page. That code is invisible to you when you look at a web page, but if you're curious you can see it in most web browsers by choosing the menu option called something such as "View source." Even the graphics and photos on a web page include tags to help search engines figure out what a page is really about.

But, as you might have guessed, relying on the honesty of web page authors didn't work out so well. The whole game in web page design and marketing is to land a spot on the first page of search results—preferably in the first handful of entries. So if I wanted to make sure a search engine gave my web page a high rank, I could pump up the content by using otherwise invisible words that would make the search engine think a site was all about work, work, work when it was really all about sex.

So the search engines decided to fight fire with brimstone, and set about like a nun convinced of her students' reprobate thoughts to actually scrutinize the content of the pages themselves.

Of course, no one at Google or Yahoo! could actually read the content of the 30 billion pages on the Web,[1] so they devised computer programs, known as *spiders*, to scurry around the Web to do it for them. Many of the spiders now look at every word on every page of every web site and, through secret algorithms, attempt to divine the true nature of a page. But where there is opportunity, there are opportunists, and before long web page designers were on to the game. All they had to do was pepper their sites with a healthy dose of invisible keywords and the coveted page one ranking was theirs.

So the search engine companies decided to bow to a higher authority. Metatags and keywords were all well and good, but the ones they should bless with high ranking, they decided, should be sites with links from other high-ranking sites, particularly those with the august *.edu* extension. If there are a lot of links to a site, the search engines assume the site must be worthy. These days, links from a few of the most popular sites can propel a low-ranking page into the number one or two spot. Not to be outwitted, web developers quickly devised techniques with nefarious names such as *link doping, link baiting, link farming,* and *incestuous linking* to bolster their inbound links.

And so the battle continues. The search engines continue to look for better ways to bring you meaningful results, and web page developers continue to look for ways to outwit them.

Pay-per-click Advertising

One legitimate way for web site owners to improve their visibility is to pay for it. Pay-per-click ads, or *sponsored ads*, as Google calls them, are the ones

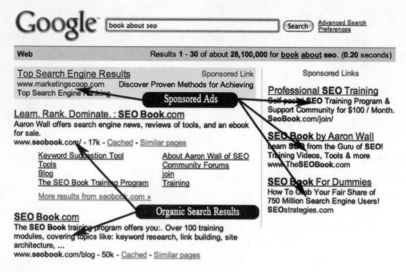

Figure 18.1 Pay-per-click Advertising

that appear across the top, bottom, sides, and even in the middle of your search results.

Let's say you want to learn more about search engine optimization (SEO). You might do a Google search for *book about seo*. The sponsored ads are shown across the top and right side of the page. (See Figure 18.1.) The owners of these ads bid for the right to have their ads appear when someone is searching for information about a book on SEO. If you click on their ad, they pay a fee to Google based on the amount they've bid. For the most part (though not entirely), the more the advertiser is willing to pay for a click-through, the higher its ad will appear in the list of ads.

Don't confuse the ads with the natural, or *organic*, search listings. The screenshot in Figure 18.1 shows that SEObook.com has the highest organic listing. The order of the organic listings is determined by that secret formula we referred to in the preceding section. Companies can't pay for top organic listings.

Developing, maintaining, and hosting a busy web site is costly. Web site owners offset their costs and try to make money by selling something or collecting membership or subscription fees. They can also make money by posting ads on their sites. If I had a site about cameras, for example, I could sign up for Google's AdSense program. Links to sites related to photography would then appear on my site, and I would receive a portion of the revenue every time someone on my site clicked on an ad. As the web page owner, I can specify where on the page the ads appear. Some site owners opt for a tasteful placement along one side or the bottom of a page. Others plaster them so haphazardly that it's impossible to find real content.

Other ads, including pop-overs, pop-unders, regular old display ads, and those pesky pulsing banners that are enough to induce a seizure, further litter the web pages you'll visit. They're particularly obnoxious on sites where the site owner is more interested in ad income than in offering any real information.

While web advertising can be annoying, many excellent sites wouldn't exist without it. But here's a problem you'll face. If I was running a web site about, say, how to find work you can do from home, who do you think would most want to advertise on it? That's right, the home-based opportunity shysters—and with few exceptions, a site owner who chooses to include ads can't control which ones appear. The ad wholesaler selects the ads that, based on the nature of the target web site and the keywords the advertiser provides, seem most relevant. So unless I'm willing to forego all pay-per-click ads, which are the richest and easiest source of ad income, I have to take the good with the bad. As a result, many of the web sites you'll visit, even legitimate ones, will be rife with ads that link to scams.

Googling for Dollars

With all this in mind, let's examine a little more closely the first page of those 1.1 million Google hits we found in our *telecommute job* search.

The first entry took us to a web site called Telecommuting Jobs. Based on our research, they're actually one of the good guys—you'll read more about them later.

The next listing belonged to Monster.com, one of the top traditional job search sites. When we clicked on it, it took us to a page with 687 listings that mention *telecommuting*, but some scary monsters lurked in the shadows.

First, some of the listings do include the word *telecommute*, but only in the context of "This is *not* a telecommute position." Second, since e-work can be done from anywhere, some employers repeat their listings in every city so the folks who do local searches will stumble across them. As a result, there may be dozens of listings for the same job. Nevertheless, there are lots of legitimate e-work posts to be found on Monster and the other behemoth job sites. We show you how to pare them down to size in Chapter 19.

★ "REVERSE FUNNEL SYSTEM" ONLINE.com $250K
Earn Your Annual Income in 1 Month, Home - Based Business
Not "MLM", No Selling, No Prospecting, No Inventory
*NO Selling *NO Prospecting *NO Cold Calling *$1,000.00 per SALE + Residuals!
FREE INFO HERE: Best kept "Secret" to Creating Your "Automated Wealth" from Home

Figure 18.2   Sucker Links

The third Google listing took us to a site claiming to specialize in legitimate work at home. They even offer a page about how to avoid scams, yet their site includes links like those shown in Figure 18.2.

Does the phrase "There's a sucker born every minute" come to mind? If it doesn't, you must have skipped Chapter 4 on scams.

The problem with this site and many other job boards where employers pay to post their jobs is that there's no incentive for the site host to evaluate the legitimacy of the offers. Thus, the floodgates are open to a deluge of scams. By providing some content about e-work, and using clever SEO techniques, sites like this can rise to the top of the search engines. Once they do, they can attract advertisers. Once they do that, they can attract more companies willing to pay for posts. All of this allows them to work at home in their jammies, but doesn't do much to help you find a way to work in yours.

The next two entries on page one of our Google search led to what are called *consolidator sites*. They sprinkle a bit of real content on their home pages, such as articles about how to avoid scams, e-work success stories, or self-assessment quizzes. But every one of their links takes you to a whole page of links to other sites—the great majority of which are either other consolidator sites or scams, too. Again, these guys are playing the keyword game to place high in the search engine rankings, which brings them eyeballs (yours), which brings them advertisers, which brings *them* the booty.

Finally, we came to a site that promises prescreened links to legitimate e-work. Click on a category such as transcription, and you'll be presented with a dozen or so job listings. Click on each of them and here's what you'll find: four links to what might have been legitimate jobs at one point, but have since expired; four active Craigslist job posts which you may or may not have been able to find by going to Craigslist directly (more on that later); two listings that came from other web-based job sites; and two that point directly to the job search section of employer web sites—but give no indication of how to tease out the e-work jobs. In other words, another roadblock on your journey home.

I wanted to believe the next site on the search page was one of the white knights. The home page was simple and not cluttered with ads. It offered some sage advice and useful links to legitimate opportunities. Still, something had my b.s. detector chirping. Sure enough, I clicked one of those promising links, and was whisked away to a page that looks like a swarm of click-through ads built a nest there. They're everywhere. They flash across the top of the page. They crowd both sides of the page, leaving a skinny aisle of space down the middle for real content—provided the sentences are no more than five words long. You're even invited to "GET PAID TO SHOP AND EAT IN FANCY RESTAURANTS" smack in the middle of a paragraph that warns about scams.

Alas, the final entry on our Google search page offered no salvation. It chastises the rotten apples and offers itself as the virgin fruit. Buy their "not-sold-in-stores" self-published book, and they'll deliver you from evil. Their epic 24-page pitch tries to seduce you into scrambling for your MasterCard. No kidding, 24 pages of "Buy now," "Limited time offer," and three postscripts with information they apparently weren't able to squeeze into of the body of the tome. Seriously, who buys this stuff after a pitch like that?

After all that clicking you may be ready for a nap, but you're no closer to finding a way to work in your jammies. That first page of search results pretty much sums up what you'll find in the rest of the 1.1 million entries. If you want any meaningful results, you'll need to refine your search technique.

Search Techniques

In Chapter 19 we cover how to look for e-work specifically using some of the top web-based job boards, but here are some basics you'll need to know about how to use them.

All of the major job search web sites allow you to limit your search to certain types of jobs (e.g., clerical, computer, customer service, etc.). You can further refine your search by adding keywords.

Keyword search routines are very persnickety. If you type *work at home* in a search box you'll get very different results than if you enter "work at home" with the quote marks. In most search engines (including Google), quotes around a phrase will deliver only listings that include that exact phrase, not just listings with the words *work* and *home* (words like *at* are ignored unless they're part of a phrase).

Some words and phrases work better than others in producing legitimate e-work results. The obvious ones—*work from home, work at home, work anywhere*, and *home-based* (with or without quotes)—produce lots of junk. The keywords *telecommuting, telecommute,* and *telework* will produce more useful results, but still a fair share of junk. The terms *virtual office, virtual worker, remote work*, and *remote worker* will also occasionally bear fruit. If it's freelance or contract work you're looking for, use the terms *freelance, contractor, 1099,* or *independent contractor*. As we've pointed out, some of your searches on these terms will include listings that mention those words, but only in the context of "No telecommuting" or "Not a freelance position."

Many sites support what's known as Boolean search. This allows you to put a whole string of words together and search them all at once. If you include an *AND* between search terms, you'll find only those listings that have both the first term and the second term—for example, *telecommute AND customer service*. The Boolean functions must be capitalized (AND, OR, NOT). If you include an *OR* between terms, your search results will include listings that have either one or the other term, but not necessarily both. The *NOT* function allows you to exclude terms from your search, which is handy when a single employer has multiple listings that you want to skip. So, as an example, you could might use *telecommute AND programmer NOT boeing* to a find a job as a programmer anywhere but at Boeing.

Some sites allow you to use an asterisk to do wildcard searches. For example, instead of searching on *telecommute OR telecommuting*, you can search on *telecommut** and capture both terms at once, along with telecommuter.

Most job boards offer an advanced search feature. If it's available, use it. The advanced page usually offers search boxes that take the place of Boolean searches. Such boxes will be labeled "Include all the words," "Include any of the words," or "Find the exact phrase." On some search sites, Boolean searches and wildcards only work on the advanced search page.

When using Boolean searches and wildcards, always test them against single-word searches to make sure you're getting the results you want. For example, if you do a search on *telecommut** and you get 70 hits, do one on *telecommute*, one on *telecommuting,* and one on *telecommuter* as well. If the combined search results yield substantially more than 70 hits, the wildcard search technique isn't available or isn't working. If the numbers are close, the difference may just be a few ads that use more than one of the search words.

When refining results, most sites offer the chance to change the criteria right on the results page. Often, however, these quick-change options either don't recognize Boolean/wildcard terms, or they forget some of the criteria you originally set.

As an example, we entered the following criteria on the advanced search page of a job search site: (1) keywords with at least one of these words: *telecommut* telewor**; (2) show jobs from employer sites only; (3) exclude staffing agencies; and (4) age of post less than 15 days old. That search produced 160 listings. If I now want to do a search on *work from home*, the obvious thing to do would be to stay on the results page and change the word *telecommut** to *work from home*. But no-o-o!

If we do that, it forgets that we wanted results from employer sites only, no staffing agencies, and listings less than 15 days old. In fact, even if we leave the original *telecommut** in the keyword box, and simply hit the "Find Jobs" button again, it will return 11,424 results instead of the 160 we found the first time because it resets the other criteria back to the default settings. Grrrr.

Chapter 19 will help you use the tools you learned here to search the top job boards for e-work.

19

Using the Job Boards to Find E-work

A zoo commissioned a sculptor to create a life-size statue of an elephant. When he was done, a reporter asked how he went about such a mammoth undertaking. The artist explained that he started with a big block of marble and then chiseled off everything that didn't look like an elephant.

That's been our strategy, too. We started with the 1.1 million Google hits from the search phrase *telecommute jobs* and then tried to hack off anything that didn't look like legitimate e-work. What was left were a handful of conventional jobs sites that offer some e-work, a collection of web sites that specialize in home-based jobs, and a few good sources of freelance work. Now we need to chip away some more.

While you'll find a lot of overlap among the sites we recommend, each offers some unique jobs. If you're just starting a job search, it's worth going to the trouble of entering your personal profile on each of the sites, and using their notification services to automatically deliver new jobs to your e-mail inbox.

The Web is constantly evolving, so be aware that how—and how well—sites work may change by the time you read this. At UndressForSuccessOnline.com you'll find e-work jobs that we hand-picked, links to some of the best e-work employers, and alerts to scams as we find them. In addition, our site offers links to the constantly changing list of our favorite job boards, and tools to help you connect with, optimize, and use them. You'll even find some discounts and special offers for products and services that support e-work.

Megasites

Job ads have traditionally been a significant source of income for newspapers but, according to Borrell Associates, by the end of 2006 online job ads exceeded those of any other medium, including newspapers. Borrell projects recruitment advertising will account for almost 10 percent of all online advertising in 2008. At over $6 billion a year, it's no surprise that the ownership of a number of online job boards includes names such as the *New York Times*, Rupert Murdoch, Gannett, and Tribune.[1]

The big job search sites such as Monster, CareerBuilder, Yahoo! HotJobs, and Craigslist include listings for all kinds of jobs. Most of their posts are for those conventional jobs where employers actually expect you to dress up and commute to an office. Still, some e-work is included on these sites, so you need to get to know them.

Each of these major job sites offers free searches for people looking for jobs. Employers pay around $400 to list a job for one month (except for Craigslist, which charges between nothing and $75 per post depending on the city or job category). CareerBuilder and HotJobs also make money from pay-per-click ads, so be careful to click on the listings, not the ads.

Table 19.1 offers a quick summary of how each of the major job boards performed on the following search: clerical or customer service jobs, with the keyword *telecommut** (or the Boolean equivalent), posted in the past 30 days.

Now for some details on each of these job boards. We realize that trying to describe web pages, and how to use them, is a little like trying to do a striptease on the radio: It loses something in the translation. As you

Table 19.1   Major Job Board E-work Search Summary

	Monster	CareerBuilder	HotJobs	Craigslist
Number of listings	44	73	8	*
Percent bad	10%	0%	55%	*
Ads present	Display ads	Sponsored and display	Sponsor and display	None
Shows number per company	No	Yes	Yes	No
Keyword technique	Boolean and wildcards	Boolean and wildcards	Separate terms, no wildcards	Check box
E-mail leads	Yes	Yes	Yes	No

*Does not offer nationwide search, so results are not comparable.

read the following descriptions of the major boards, you might want to follow along on the computer.

Monster

Monster.com is the oldest and largest job site on the Web. With the *New York Times* as a partner, their database of resumes includes over 70 million job candidates. Another 50,000 are added every day.[2]

To find the e-work positions, start on their home page and click on "Advanced Search"—it supports Boolean and wildcard searches. In the "Keyword" box, type: *telecommut** (as with the rest of the job boards, the phrases *work from home* and *work at home* produce mostly junk). Click on the occupations that interest you (or leave it blank); then in the "Locations" area, click on "NA" (not "US" or "Global") and scroll down past Canada and Mexico to "US" (for all United States). Now click "Search."

Once you've done your search on Monster it will allow you to refine your results by when the job was posted, educational requirements, years of experience, or career level (e.g., entry level, executive, etc.). Other click boxes allow you to exclude specific keywords (such as *no telecommuting*), companies, industries, or job types. Like all of the other mega job sites, Monster offers a host of other features that help you organize and save your searches, prepare a resume and cover letter, or upload them from a file. You can set up their Job Search Agent to e-mail you new jobs that match your criteria as they're posted.

If you're concerned that your current employer might stumble across the fact that you're looking for a job—not a good career move—you can make your resume private so no employers will be able to see it unless you send it to them. You can also use what Monster calls "Privacy Plus" to hide your information from the search results of up to 20 employers, or you can make your resume public but hide your contact information, current company, and references. That way, employers who find your background interesting can request the hidden information via a confidential e-mail to you.

CareerBuilder

CareerBuilder—jointly owned by Gannett, Tribune, McClatchy, and Microsoft—boasts 21 million users per month. The interface is straightforward and their "Advanced Search" allows you to specify keywords, job categories, and other criteria. It lets you save your search criteria and will e-mail job posts as they are added.

The keywords that yield the best results on this site are *telecommut** and *telewor**. Type both words in the keyword field.

Once you've performed your search, CareerBuilder makes it easy to spot companies that have multiple listings. For example, when we did a search for information technology jobs (using the keywords just mentioned), the "Company" field showed that 131 of them are with Lockheed Martin. It turns out that the word *telecommute* appears in all Lockheed's job listings because telecommuting is one of their employee benefits and is included as part of the description of each job. You can exclude them from your next search on the "Advanced Search" page.

In addition to keywords, CareerBuilder allows you to refine your search by all of the same categories as Monster plus the type of employment (full-time, contractor, part-time, seasonal, intern) and salary range. You can also exclude listings based on keywords, job title, company, those that don't offer salary information, and other criteria.

Yahoo! HotJobs

Yahoo!'s HotJobs functions much the same way as Monster. Through partnerships with over 350 newspapers, HotJobs reaches almost 12 million users.

Like Monster, HotJobs lets you enter keywords, pick a job category, and refine your search. It doesn't support wildcard or Boolean searches, so enter the words *telecommuting, telecommute, telecommuter,* and *telework* in the "Any of These Words" search box on the "Advanced Search" page. One useful feature of HotJobs is that it allows you to exclude staffing company listings.

That said, in our experience, you have to kiss more than the usual number of frogs on HotJobs. For example, while a search for customer service jobs that included the keyword *telecommute* produced 312 listings, 304 of them were from the same three companies that were offering questionable "business opportunities." The remaining eight were either similarly suspect or showed up because the listing included the phrase *no telecommuting.*

Craigslist

Craigslist is another seasoned citizen in the web-based job search business. It receives 2 million new job listings every month.[3] Though substantial, employment posts are only part of what Craigslist does: More than 40 million people view 10 billion pages of free classified ads, job posts, and service listings every month.

In spite of a one-quarter ownership stake purchased by eBay in 2004, Craigslist has maintained a cultlike aversion to corporate folderol and greed. Despite its reach, world headquarters is still a Victorian house in San Francisco—home to all 25 employees. Job listings are free except in seven of the largest cities. Even those paid listings are substantially below the cost of ads on other job sites.

Craigslist does not accept job posts for business opportunities, multilevel marketing, positions that require up-front fees, or referral marketing—which is not to say you won't find any on their site. No one polices every listing. If you find bad links on Craigslist (or elsewhere), be sure to report them to the webmaster so others won't have to suffer—it's kind of like picking up trash when you're out for a walk.

There is one serious drawback when it comes to looking for e-work on Craigslist. The web site is organized geographically, so if you're searching the San Francisco listings for an e-work job, you'll miss one that's posted in New York. This doesn't matter much when you're looking for a traditional job, but an e-work job could be based anywhere.

Still, there's e-work available on Craigslist, so here's how to go about your search. Go to the home page for whichever city you choose to search first, and click on the word "Jobs" in the list of categories.

The next screen you see will show you all the jobs listed, by order of posting date. Here Craigslist offers a leg up on the other job boards. Employers are given "Telecommuting is ok" as one of the parameters when they post a job. Click on the "Telecommuting" box, enter whatever other keywords you'd like, choose a job category, and hit the search button.

A word of caution: If you choose to use the keyword box, instead of using the clickable telecommute button on the jobs page, use the term *telecommut** or the search will not be valid. You can also perform this search from the home page by typing *telecommut** in the keyword box and selecting "jobs" from the pull-down menu just below it.

As with the other job search engines, some listings will appear because the employer shows telecommuting as an employee benefit rather than as a feature of the particular job.

There's also offers a section for "Gigs" on Craigslist. If you're seeking work as a freelancer or contractor, be sure to search there, too. You'll read more about looking for freelance work in Part 3.

Scrapers and Aggregators

Many job boards you'll run across are what are known as scrapers or aggregators. Their posts are culled from other job boards such as Career-Builder, Monster, HotJobs, and hundreds of smaller sites that include feeds provided by newspapers, associations, and even employer sites. As a result, the job listings you'll find on these sites will include some of the ones you've seen on the other job boards. Sorry to say, that includes the junk, as well.

The advantage of the scraper sites is that in addition to speeding your search (by aggregating the results from many sites), each offers its own special features, filters, and resources to help organize, refine, and improve your job search.

All of the sites that follow are free to users. Click-through and display ads abound, but they're the reason you don't have to pay to use the site, so just tiptoe around them.

Jobster

Jobster, Inc., is venture capital–funded job site that offers over 2.5 million active job posts. Ninety percent of them come from other sites. The other 10 percent are "Featured Jobs" that have been placed directly with Jobster. These show up first in the listings and are scrubbed by a proprietary algorithm that weeds out the junk. As a result, except for a few that slip in under the radar, the "Featured Listings" are top quality. The rest of the listings include the usual mix of legitimate jobs and junk.

To search for work-at-home jobs on Jobster, use *telecommut** as your search term on the main search page or refine your search using the "Advanced Search" option (place the term *telecommut** in the box that says "with at least one of the words"). Their filtering options are not as extensive or as intuitive as other job sites, but that may change. Some filtering is available on the "Advanced Search" page.

Jobster offers an extensive list of options for building your personal profile. It even allows you to import information from your LinkedIn or Facebook page (more about them later). "Using cutting-edge technologies, we make it easy for job candidates to put their best face forward, and we offer them a powerful networking tool to make sure it's seen," says Christian Anderson, Jobster's director of corporate communications.

Your profile can include links to your web page, blog, portfolio, or other web sites that pertain to you. You can embed a YouTube-based video resume or demo reel. You can set up e-mail job alerts, insert resume keyword tags to help employers find you, list your work and education history, include recommendations, and build your own social network by linking to other Jobster users.

SimplyHired

SimplyHired is another product of Silicon Valley's deep pockets. Among its investors is Rupert Murdoch's News Corporation. SimplyHired reports that it is the largest job search engine on the Web, with over 6 million jobs and counting.

SimplyHired's interface is very straightforward. It supports full Boolean search, but not wildcard searches, so use keywords *telecommuting OR telecommute OR telework* for the best results. The "Advanced Search" page allows you to avoid Boolean syntax and helps filter your search in the same ways as the other job boards we've covered. It also allows you to limit your search based on company size, company revenue, whether they're socially responsible or dog-friendly (although most home-based positions are), or whether they're recognized as one of *Fortune*'s Best Companies, *Working Mother*'s 100 Best, *Inc.*'s 500, and so on.

In March 2008, SimplyHired simplified its long-standing partnership with LinkedIn by integrating a feature that allows you to view any LinkedIn connections you have with the employers that appear in your job search results. If your cousin Rupert knows Brian, who knows Janine, who works for the mayor, you may have a foot in the door if you're looking for a city job.

In addition to the LinkedIn feature, Myspace, Facebook, Google, cell phone, e-mail and RSS connections are available to keep you constantly up-to-date with job posting activity.

SimplyHired offers some very useful salary and employment trend data to help you investigate prospective jobs. It also offers a forum where you can communicate with fellow job seekers, some of whom may work for the companies you've targeted in your search.

Indeed

Indeed.com is owned in part by the *New York Times* and other institutional investors. Its interface looks like a Google or Yahoo! search page, so no special technique is needed to do a search.

Indeed offers full Boolean and wildcard searches. The "Advanced Search" page offers all the usual refinement options.

Once you've performed the search, you can filter the results by salary, title, company, location, job type, and whether you want to see recruiter listings.

Job alerts can be delivered via RSS feeds, to a My Yahoo! account, or by installing any one of a number of browser and e-mail plug-ins from the "Tools" menu.

Similar to what you'll find at SimplyHired, Indeed offers useful trend and salary data. For example, type *transcription* in the search box, click on "Trends," and you'll see the percentage growth over the past two years for job posts that include that term. Use the "Salary" button, and you'll see the average nationwide or local salary for that type of job. If you want to know what it's like to work at FedEx, type it in the search box and click on "Forums" and you can ask people who work there.

E-work Specialty Sites

We looked at hundreds of job sites, hoping to find a few that were free (or low cost) and delivered quality job listings. Many claim to have eliminated the e-work scams, but only a few deliver the goods. Visit UndressForSuccessOnline.com for up-to-date links to our favorite e-work job sites.

MomCorps

Founded in 2005 by a Harvard MBA and working mother, Mom Corps (momcorps.com) is a home-based recruiting firm with over 30 e-working employees. Their focus is entirely on jobs that offer flexible working conditions.

The employers that Mom Corps represents range from Fortune 100 companies to small businesses. In spite of its name, Mom Corps represents both men and women looking for flexible work. According to the founder, Allison O'Kelly, the typical client is 30 to 44 years old, and 90 percent of them have college degrees (a third have graduate degrees). The positions they fill average $30 to $70 per hour.

Mom Corps earns its money from employers when they successfully place employees. As a result, the quality of their job posts is among the best we've seen. There are no fees for job candidates, who can either upload their resumes for consideration or apply for specific positions listed on the site.

With the telecommuting option clicked on, virtually all of the listings are for valid telecommuting positions, and you won't have to dance around click-through ads.

Dream Jobs Inc.

The business model for Dream Jobs Inc. (www.dreamjobsinc.com), like Mom Corps, is different than most of the other job sites. Rather than simply posting positions, they advise companies on how to develop flexible work strategies. Then they match the companies with highly qualified candidates who want those flexible positions. Though currently operating solely in Texas, their connections with Fortune 500 employers are fueling rapid expansion.

"Companies are feeling the pain [of the labor shortage]. When I walk into a boardroom and talk about how to retain and hire exceptional talent by offering flexible work, executives are eager to listen," says Dream Jobs Inc. CEO and founder Jenny Krengel.

Job candidates at Dream Jobs Inc. must have at least five years in their field and at least an undergraduate degree or 10 years of work experience in technology, finance and accounting, or other professional fields.

Companies pay to post jobs and review candidates' profiles. Job posts must be for professional positions that pay at least $35,000 per year (or the hourly equivalent).

The site contains no pay-per-click ads. There are no fees to job candidates, although their application process, which must be completed before you gain access to job posts, is rather extensive.

Telecommuting Jobs (Tjobs)

With over 12 years of experience in the field, Telecommuting Jobs (tjobs.com) editors are adept at weeding out listings that promote business opportunity schemes, require up-front payment, or involve selling products or services. They refuse all ads from companies that have outstanding complaints against them with the Better Business Bureau or RipoffReport.com. Because they do not charge employers for listings, they can stipulate who can and cannot be included. They also screen resumes to ensure that employers receive quality listings.

The site offers hundreds of e-work opportunities. Some come from other job boards, like Monster, but only if they represent real e-work. According to Sol Levine, publisher of Tjobs, 96 percent of listings are filled from applicants on their site. He and all his staff work from home.

Jobs categories include art, desktop publishing, photography, data entry, transcription, programming, sales, web design, writing, other skills, and freelance projects.

To help users develop connections, the site offers links to information about the latest in collaboration tools. It also offers a resume builder, and allows users to showcase their home offices for prospective employers.

Since Tjobs doesn't charge employers for listings and they don't litter their site with click-through ads, something has to pay the bills. There's no charge to look at a brief job listing, but for the full monty and to submit a resume, you need to register ($15 per year). Based on the listings we've seen, it's worth the investment.

Rat Race Rebellion

Chris Durst and Michael Haaren created RatRaceRebellion.com to help people simplify their lives by, among other ways, working from home. They handpick e-work jobs and employers who make that possible and post them on their site and in their free newsletter. They caution readers to conduct their own due diligence research on the listings, and they do try their best to weed out the scams. Nevertheless, Google ads help pay their bills, so you'll see Google's ads—and the scams they include—liberally scattered throughout the site.

Other Sites Offering Flexible Jobs

Other sites that focus on flexible work arrangements for working parents and caregivers include On-Ramps, Flexible Executives, Flexible Resources, FlexPaths, and FlexWork Connection. The Families and Work Institute site is a good place to look for additional flexible work resources. Links to these and other organizations are available on our web site.

Industry-Specific Sites

There are hundreds of sites that specialize in jobs within specific industries such as health care, transcription, information technology (ComuputerJobs.com is one we like), journalism (JournalismJobs.com is a good one), and others. Like the rest of the web universe, there are a few bright spots but mostly empty space, so keep your phasers on stun when you encounter a new one. As always, check our web site for other recommendations.

Industry Associations

Many industry associations are getting into the job posting game, so it's worth checking with those organizations that represent your industry to see if they're among the players. Some feature job posts from members and others utilize technology provided by companies such as Indeed, Jobster, and SimplyHired.

20

Your Digital Resume

While there are plenty of books about how to present yourself on paper, looking for virtual work requires a slightly different approach.

In the old days, you'd agonize over every word of your resume to make certain it effectively extolled your virtues. Then you'd craft an impassioned cover letter to shepherd your missive through the HR department into the hands of the person who makes the hiring decision. They would be so impressed by your presentation, you hoped, they'd want to hire you on the spot.

The gatekeepers are now computers, and they're indifferent to your elegant prose. Their job description is pretty monotonous: Scan resumes, look for keywords, catalog them, prioritize the ones that correlate most closely with the master's needs, and spit out the rejects. If applicant 25647's resume mentions MySQL, XML, and Python (the programming language, not the BBC comedy), and applicant 54329 only mentions MySQL, 54329 may be left pounding the virtual pavement.

Keywords

In large organizations, even paper resumes and cover letters are scanned and evaluated by computer. As a result, some resume experts suggest including a keyword section on your resume, and some even suggest that you put it at the very top of the page. This is becoming common in the technology fields but isn't a mainstream trend. In any event, you need to make the content of your resume and cover letter keyword rich and computer friendly.

Here is a list of tips on how to find and use keywords that will impress the cyborgs that will read your resume:

- Use the most important keywords and phrases early in your resume and use them as often as possible without seeming forced.
- Be sure your resume or online application includes all of the keywords and phrases that appear in the job post.
- When applying for e-work, be sure to use words such as *self-starter*, *independent*, *industrious*, *hardworking*, and *highly productive*—assuming you are—and include the names of any e-work technologies you're familiar with.
- Read your prospective employer's annual report, web content, official and unofficial blogs, and literature in search of buzz words, values, and philosophies.
- Parrot or at least paraphrase your target company's mission statement in your resume.
- Mine keywords from a dozen or so similar job posts.
- In your career objective statement, use keywords that appear in job postings a step or two higher than the job you're applying for.
- Use social networking sites to solicit advice from the people who already work for your target employer.
- Read trade magazines and industry web sites in search of keywords.
- Use free web-based keyword tools such as the ones available from Google AdWords or at SEOBook.com.
- Look at the metatags in the source code for the web site of your target company (in Safari and Firefox, go to the site and in the "View" menu select "View Source." The metatags will be near the top on a line that starts with *<meta name="keywords" content>*). These are the words the company holds most dear, and you should too.
- Unless acronyms are very well known, spell them out and include the acronym in parenthesis.
- Name-drop. If you worked on a NASA contract while employed at IronClad Solutions, be sure to include NASA in your resume.
- If you have any legitimate way of inserting the names of key competitors, that can be very useful as companies often like to hire from those ranks.

- Computers are even better at whacking knuckles for spelling and grammar errors than parochial school teachers, so mind your p's and q's.

E-resumes

Once you have 30 to 50 good keywords sprinkled throughout your resume, you'll need to work on formatting it for various audiences. Of course, you'll want one that looks nice on paper and can be distributed by snail mail, fax, or by hand. For this version, use bullets, italics, and bold text to make it attractive. But once you're happy with content and it's all checked and rechecked for spelling and grammar, you'll need to prepare a variety of electronic versions.

PDF

Because of the threat of viruses, many employers won't accept your resume as an e-mail attachment. If they do, the best way to transmit it is in PDF format because that will eliminate any missing fonts and other formatting issues between your computer and theirs. To create one, do a "Save As" using the "PDF" option, or select "Print" and use the "Print to PDF" option.

Plain Text

A plain text (also known as text-only or ASCII) version of your resume will be needed for job boards and employers who require you to submit information via their online forms. This will be a bare-bones version of your print resume that's devoid of any formatting niceties.

Start with your original resume. Set the page margins so that the text is 6.5 inches wide. Convert the whole document to Courier (12 point). Eliminate any non-text elements (such as lines, boxes, etc.), hard carriage returns, double spaces, italics, underlines, indents, unusual fonts, and formatting. If your original includes bullets, you can replace the bullet character with a regular dash but do not indent them. Do a "Save As" and change the format to plain text. Close the file, then reopen the plain text version and make sure everything looks as it should.

Scanner and E-mail Friendly

Next you'll need a scanner-friendly copy of your resume. This will be read by a machine using optical character recognition (OCR) that prefers plain vanilla text.

Back in your word processing program, open the plain text document and do a "Save As" using the "text with line breaks" option (rename the document so it doesn't overwrite the plain text version you saved earlier). Check it carefully for any errant spacing or formatting, and you now have a read-bot ready, albeit ugly, resume.

This version of your resume will also be useful if you need to e-mail it to a prospective employer who does not accept attachments. To create an e-mail version, simply paste the contents of this version into the body of your e-mail message. To avoid the dreaded ignosecond (that instant between when you hit "Send" and when you notice an ignorant and embarrassing error), give it a final read before you dispatch it as your personal job ambassador.

HTML

For those in talent-based fields, *show* is better than *tell*, and a web site or online portfolio is a must. Graphic artists, writers, architects, designers, and people in other similar professions are among those who should have samples of their work available online—in other words, walk the talk.

A number of freelance job boards that you'll read about later in this book (see Chapter 26) offer an easy way for job candidates to showcase their talents for prospective employers and clients.

Before you go whole hog with the multimedia resume thing, be aware that experts warn against overkill. As Mark Twain said, "Better to keep your mouth shut and be thought a fool than to open it and remove all doubt." Unless you're in a field where how you look or sound matters, skip the photo or video, and stick with convention.

One final caution: Most job boards, and many direct employers, will want you to use their job application form. Don't just refer them to your web site instead of filling out their form. If they want you to apply via their web form, do it their way. If a prospective employer is interested, you can bet they'll visit your site, but only after you've given them a reason to take the step.

MS Word

If you're asked to send your resume as a Microsoft Word (or other word processor) document, be sure to use a standard font such as Arial or Times New Roman to ensure that what you see is what they get. If you use some fancy font that the recipient doesn't have, all your efforts to make the spacing look nice may be wasted.

Old School

Finally, since an actual human will eventually read your resume and cover letter (we hope), don't forget all the usual advice about action verbs, writing style, clarity, and layout. If you're not familiar with the "situation, action, results" (SAR) approach to writing a resume, do an online search and read up on it.

Digital Skeletons

Remember the YouTube video your, um, friend posted on your behalf? The one where you were dancing the Macarena in Ugg® boots and a purple tutu that belonged to your little sister? Do you really think IBM's going to be impressed when they see it? Not so much.

Before you go job shopping, Google yourself and see what lurks in your virtual closet. As simple as that sounds, a study conducted by Execu-Net, the executive career and business networking organization, showed almost a quarter of executives have never done it. "For better or worse, the Internet provides recruiters and employers with a wealth of unfiltered information that's used to evaluate candidates," says Dave Opton, CEO and founder of ExecuNet. "From a candidate's perspective, there's no question that managing your reputation online is as important as it is offline." Their 2007 survey of over 130 independent and corporate recruiters revealed that over 80 percent use search engines to learn more about job candidates, and over 40 percent have rejected people based on what they found.[1]

Blog posts, web comments about prior employers, book or movie reviews, photo or video posts, revealing memberships, and unseemly nicknames or e-mail addresses (e.g., IHateToWork@nothere.com) all contribute to a prospective employer's decision about whether to hire you.

You might want to also take a look at the quantity of your online posts. If you're a prolific blogger with a full-time job that doesn't pay you to blog, a prospective boss might wonder whether you'll be blogging on company time.

In any event, you need to know what's out there so you can start planning your excuses—er, strategy for deflecting them.

Resume Resources

Three of our favorite online resources for job hunting and resume advice are: Job-Hunt.org, JobHuntersBible.com (the web site for *What Color is my Parachute*), and Weddles.com. Go to our web site for links to these and others.

21

Collaboration and Social Networking for E-work

It's said that if you were to link up all the people you know, with all the people they know, and they add all the people they know, within six iterations you'd have a connection with anyone in the world—six degrees of separation. Facebook offers an application named "Six Degrees" that calculates the degrees of separation between people. In the summer of 2008 there were about 132 million unique visitors to Facebook with an average separation of 5.73 degrees. And that's what social networking sites are all about: connectedness. Social networking started in the United States, and while its growth is tapering off here, it's exploding elsewhere. MySpace is still number two with over 100 million visitors, but has grown 100 percent in the past year, ahead of Friendster, Orkut, LinkedIn, Plaxo, Bebo, and Skyrock Network.[1]

If you haven't yet navigated the social web, you're missing an entire universe of networking opportunities. If you want to catch up in a hurry, read *The Virtual Handshake* by David Teton and Scott Allen. This book and their blog (thevirtualhandshake.com) offer some of the very best advice available on both face-to-face and virtual networking.

One very good reason to get linked, faced, and spaced is that job recruiters use the social networking powerhouses to troll for candidates. Over 200,000 corporate and independent search firms are themselves LinkedIn.[2]

Another good reason to belong to social networking sites is that search engines index most of them. This means that as a member, you'll show up in a Google search when someone searches on your name.

The line between social networking sites and job sites is starting to fade. The former are beginning to host job boards, the latter are starting to add social networks, and they're all learning to play well with others. LinkedIn and MySpace use SimplyHired's job search engine, and Facebook uses Jobster's.

While Facebook is the busiest social network on the Web and MySpace is second, LinkedIn is the most business-oriented of the three, though Plaxo is nipping at their heels. Aside from the time it takes to set your profile up, there's no harm in belonging to more than one social network to extend your reach. The more complete you make your profile, the more useful it will be, so don't cut corners.

All three of the following social networks are supported by ad revenue, so they are free to users. Here's a bit more about each.

LinkedIn

Venture-funded LinkedIn was established in 2003. Its main purpose is to allow users to create a network of businesspeople they know and trust, and to expand their reach by linking them through a series of connections. Because it was designed for business, it's the most powerful when it comes to career networking.

LinkedIn's job board is powered by SimplyHired, but not all the jobs are scraped. Some are LinkedIn's own listings—they're shown in a separate tab.

Once you've entered your professional information and are linked in, some very interesting features become available. Beside each company that appears in your job search, a link that says "Who do I know at XYZ Corp?" will appear. Click on that, and if any of your contacts (or their contacts) have a connection with XYZ Corp, they will appear. Shake hands, virtually, with your newest friend.

Another interesting feature on LinkedIn is that it allows you to sort your job search results by the number of degrees of separation contacts are from you. You can even customize your LinkedIn profile and give it a personal web address (e.g., linkedin.com/in/YourName).

There's a downloadable plug-in for your web browser (called the LinkedIn Toolbar) that allows connections from the LinkedIn network to show up when you navigate to other job sites.

Facebook

Facebook was launched in 2004 as a social network for college students. In 2006, it was opened to anyone over the age of 13. Funded with venture capital and a recent investment from Microsoft, Facebook has grown rapidly and continues to blaze new ground. In 2007, it added a job board powered by Jobster. It allows users to post resumes (including video), search for jobs, and use their Facebook connections to get a face in the door.

Since the career interface is hosted by Jobster, you'll find that it works the same way.

MySpace

MySpace is the largest online social network and one of the highest traffic sites on the Web. It was founded in 2003 to offer users a way to share personal profiles, photos, music, videos, blogs, and other content with people all over the world. Rupert Murdoch's News Corporation purchased MySpace and its parent company (eUniverse) in 2005 for $580 million.

The job network on MySpace is powered by SimplyHired, so the interface and the results are the same. So far, there is no integration between your MySpace contacts and job leads, but it's likely that this powerhouse will be a major player in the future job search market.

3

Freelance in Your Frillies

22

Who Freelances and What Do They Do?

The term *freelance* made its debut alongside Robin Hood, "king of outlaws, prince of good fellows," in Sir Walter Scott's *Ivanhoe*. Set in twelfth-century England, this 1819 novel dubbed a medieval mercenary—someone who would carry his lance into battle for a price— a *free lance*.

Today, the country's 10.3 million freelancers represent about 7 percent of the U.S. workforce.[1] They joust for work in a variety of fields such as writing, programming, graphic design, web development, marketing, sales, law, accounting, engineering, and art. The trend toward freelancing has grown steadily in the new millennium. CareerBuilder's "2008 Job Forecast" indicates the momentum will continue. "In the midst of economic uncertainties, employers are turning to freelance or contract workers to help support business initiatives," says the report. Almost a third of surveyed employers expect to work with freelancers in the coming year.[2]

Daniel Pink, author of *Free Agent Nation*, cites four factors that have fueled the growth of the freelance industry:[3]

1) The social contract of work—in which employees traded loyalty for security—crumbled.

In other words, when employers stopped being loyal to employees, no longer offering job security that would carry their workers from their first paycheck to their gold watch, employees stopped being loyal to employers.

2) Individuals needed a large company less, because the means of production—that is, the tools necessary to create wealth—went from expensive, huge, and difficult for one person to operate to cheap, houseable, and easy for one person to operate. . . . I call it Digital Marxism. In an age of inexpensive computers, wireless handheld devices, and ubiquitous low-cost connections to a global communications network, workers can now own the means to production. . . .

3) Widespread, long-term prosperity allowed people to think of work as a way not only to make money, but also to make meaning. . . .

4) The half-life of organizations began shrinking, assuring that the individuals will outlive any organization for which they work.[4]

Merger mania, now-you-see-'em-now-you-don't startups, and spectacular implosions at companies such as Enron, Bear Stearns, and Arthur Andersen demonstrate the tenuous nature of employment today.

Pink also points out that we now live in a society where 85 percent of the people were not around during the Depression. "The Great Depression profoundly and permanently affected the attitudes of the people who lived through it . . . that haunting economic fear—and the public attitudes it engendered—is no longer seared in the American consciousness," writes Pink.[5]

Fueling the demand side of the equation, companies both small and large turn to freelancers to:

- Lower costs by saving on benefits, employer share of taxes, offices, and other organizational overhead.
- Reduce their operating leverage—by trading the fixed cost of an employee for the variable cost of a freelancer.
- Increase their access to skilled workers and slow the baby boomer brain drain.
- Keep pace in an environment of accelerated change.
- Gain access to new ideas and perspectives.
- Increase accountability (freelancers being the ultimate pay-for-performance workers).
- Quickly ramp up or down in times of growth or decline.

A trend with many names—outsourcing, offshoring, homeshoring, subcontracting, on-demand working, whatever you want to call it—is a trend that's good news if you're a prospective freelancer.

Who's Freelancing

Collis Ta'eed, author of *How to Be a Freelance Rockstar* and Freelance-Switch.com—both essential reading for anyone who wants to earn a living as a business mercenary—conducts a periodic survey of readers. The finished report, the Freelance Statistics Report, like his book and web site, offers a wealth of information based on input from over 3,500 active freelancers. Table 22.1 gives some of the 2008 results.[6]

Table 22.1 2008 Freelance Survey Findings

- 85 percent work at home.
- 81 percent are male.
- 87 percent are between 18 and 37 years old.
- 65 percent had two or more years experience before they started freelancing.
- Web designers accounted for the largest percentage of freelancers at 41 percent.
- Graphic designers accounted for 25 percent, programmers 13 percent, writers 6 percent, and illustrators 4 percent.
- About 15 percent of freelancers do so part-time in hopes of making the transition to full-time.
- About half plan to expand beyond the sole operator.
- 54 percent do not feel secure as a freelancer.
- When asked why they decided to freelance, they answered:
  - For more flexibility (72 percent).
  - For more creative control (60 percent).
  - To work from home (58 percent).
  - To make more money (54 percent).
  - To grow a business (49 percent).
  - To work for myself (39 percent).
  - To spend more time with family (15 percent).
- 89 percent are happier since freelancing.
- The majority work between two and five hours for every hour they bill.

Best Bet Freelance Work

Freelancers are often sole operators, but many find that by adding staff or affiliating with other freelancers they can broaden their reach, improve their responsiveness, and increase their income. Of course,

Table 22.2   What Kinds of Work Do Home-Based Freelancers Do?

- Web services
  - Web programming.
  - Web site design.
  - E-commerce.
  - Applications.
  - SEO (Search Engine Optimization).
  - SEM (Search Engine Marketing).
  - Flash animation.
- Design/multimedia
  - Logo design.
  - Graphic design.
  - Banner design.
  - Illustration.
  - Animation.
  - Videography.
- Writing/translation
  - Article writing.
  - Web content.
  - Copywriting.
  - Technical writing.
  - Ghost writing.
  - Translation.
  - Editing/proofing.
- Administrative support
  - Virtual assistant.
  - Research.
  - Data entry.
  - Bulk mailing.
  - Transcription.
  - Mailing lists.
  - Word processing.
- Sales and marketing
  - Search and online advertising.
  - E-mail and direct lead generation.
  - Telemarketing.
  - Research/surveys.
- Finance and management
  - Accounting.
  - Bookkeeping.
  - Consulting.
  - Business planning.
  - Financial planning.
  - Budgeting and forecasting.
  - Recruiting.
- Legal
  - Patent and trademark.
  - Contracts.
  - Wills and trusts.
- Engineering and manufacturing
- Computer-aided design (CAD)
  - Manufacturing.
  - Architecture.
  - Electrical.
  - Industrial design.
  - Mechanical design.
  - Interior design.
- Other hardware/software
  - Enterprise solutions.
  - SAP integration.
  - Customer relations management.
  - Database customization.
  - Communications and network design.
  - Remote tech support.

along with added staff come added headaches—more about those in Part 4.

Not all freelance work can be done at home. Professional photographers need to work on location. Some consultants need to be seen and heard. Interior designers and landscape architects have to visit, survey, and schmooze their clients. Table 22.2 shows the kinds of freelance work that can largely be done both *from* home and *at* home.

Tips from Veteran Freelancers

There's no substitute for advice from the trenches. Table 22.3 lists some of the best advice we've gathered from our own experiences as well as those of veteran freelancers.

Pros and Cons of Freelancing

oDesk.com, a top freelance project web site covered in Chapter 26, asked its members what they felt was the hardest thing about freelancing. Amazingly, almost a quarter of them said, "It's all good." Freelancing offers varied work, flexible hours and location, and protection against layoffs or downturns (if you have multiple clients). It requires little

Table 22.3 Tips for Freelancers

Stay true to the reason you decided to freelance to begin with.
Underpromise and overdeliver.
Don't work with clients you don't like or trust. Life's too short.
Throw in an occasional freebie—it builds loyalty.
Do it right. Do it well. Deliver it on time.
Communicate with your clients—don't keep them in the dark.
Avoid surprises—unless they're good ones.
Don't overcommit.
Put it in writing.
Your reputation is your greatest asset.
Blow your own horn.
Never stop marketing.
Avoid price buyers.
Keep your overhead low.
Automate payment by having clients authorize you to charge their credit card or PayPal account, or by using an escrow service.
Pay attention to who owes you money. If possible, withhold final work until you're paid.

---

capital, and allows you to choose whom you want to work for and what you want to work on.

Naturally, as with everything else in life, you have to take the good with the bad. oDesk.com members said their top challenges were that there's no guarantee of payment, workload, and so on; you constantly have to find new work; workloads are inconsistent; loneliness; distractions; staying focused is tough; and keeping clients happy is often difficult. Other drawbacks include the reality that unless you add staff, when you stop, the money stops; lack of backup if you get too busy, and the lost opportunity costs of having to turn down work; competition from people who are willing to work for peanuts; nonbillable hours; and a lack of benefits.

23

Putting Your Best Slipper Forward

If you were a freelancer in the olden days—say 10 years ago—how you sounded, dressed, and presented yourself largely determined whether or not you landed a gig. As a virtual freelancer, what you do and how well you do it takes center stage. What's more, your online portfolio can be interviewing for new work while you're taking care of existing clients. It's your alter ego—what you use to convince clients of your talent, skills, and professionalism.

"It's amazing how often creative people sabotage themselves with a poorly designed, anemic portfolio," says Eric vanHamersveld, a freelance animator and former Disney Imagineer. He and his wife Sue, also a freelance designer, offer these thoughts on how to put your best slipper forward:

- Treat your portfolio as an advertisement, and remember you'll only have about seven seconds to catch someone's attention, so position your best work at center stage. Portfolios are a teaser for your skills. Overdoing it will appear amateurish. Give them the sizzle, not the steak.
- If you include a downloadable portfolio—and you should, so they can print it and take it to meetings—keep it simple. Samples of your work are the most important element. Your contact information should be in black type with a conventional typeface—nothing elaborate. Artists tend to use too much eye candy.
- Make your printed portfolio either 8″ × 10″ or 8″ × 14″ (legal size) so pages can be easily printed and photocopied. Make sure that your work looks decent when it's copied in black and white.

- Some companies will want to see *process*, how you arrived at the final artwork—sketches on a Starbucks napkin or Post-it note, a snapshot of a building, plus intermediate sketches, as well as the finished product. For computer projects, they'll want to know what programs you used.

Unbelievably, several recent surveys indicate that the majority of freelancers do not have web sites. Yet for less than the cost of a hundred business cards they could. Indeed, with tools such as WordPress, Blogger, and Apple's iWeb you can create a professional-looking site in a few hours for free.

If your web site is intended to serve as a virtual portfolio, be sure it effectively serves the purpose. Here are some tips from veteran freelancers:

- Make your work the centerpiece of the site. That's what your customers want to see. Don't make them dig for it.
- If your client will own the copyright to your completed work, be sure to secure the right to display their project in your portfolio.
- If you're new to the business, consider doing some volunteer projects to build your portfolio.
- Make sure your pages load quickly. Avoid Flash, JavaScript (unless they're your specialty), and HTML frames.
- If you're selling search engine optimization, public relations, or marketing services, be sure your web site is high in the rankings. This sounds obvious, but you'd be amazed at how many self-proclaimed experts don't make the grade. The same goes for ugly web designer sites, poorly written writer sites, malfunctioning web developer sites, and the like.
- Another "duh": avoid broken page links, spelling and grammar mistakes, political or religious commentary, or anything you wouldn't want your grandmother to see.
- Do not run ads on your portfolio pages—they're supposed to sell *you*, not printer ink, cell phones, or books (unless you wrote them, of course).
- Make sure your web page and keyword tags include all the terms that someone seeking your talents might use in their search.
- Include testimonials from satisfied customers. Remember to ask for them as you complete projects.

- List your credentials including education, work history, skills, talents, specialties, expertise, and any certifications you've received. If you've won any awards, accolades, or news mentions, this is the place to blow your horn.
- Ask for the business, and make sure it's easy for prospective clients to reach you.

24

What Am I Worth?

Some years back, I was hired by Eastman Kodak to deliver a six-hour program for independent photo lab owners across the United States and Canada. It was called "Money—Making It, Managing It, Keeping It, and Cashing Out." The industry's biggest problem, I soon discovered, was that many of the photo lab owners had very little understanding of their costs. Each lab tried to underbid the other without considering whether they could actually make money at the lower rate.

I've seen the same problem in dozens of industries, including freelancing. New professionals, hungry for work, are willing to undercut everyone else just to get the job. As a result, others undercut them and, in the end, no one makes money. If you want to succeed as a freelancer, you need to understand what your time is worth.

The fundamental approaches to pricing that apply to home-based solo freelancing include fully allocated pricing, marginal cost pricing, volume pricing, premium pricing, and competitive pricing. One more, suicidal pricing, though commonly practiced, is one you want to avoid.

Fully Allocated Pricing

Fully allocated pricing assumes that every hour you bill contributes an equal portion to your annual cost of doing business and to your take-home income needs. In other words, this is the average rate you need to charge to stay in business.

Table 24.1   Fully Allocated Pricing Example: Annual
Expenses

Office supplies	$1,500
Telephone/utilities	$2,000
Web hosting/access	$750
Software	$1,500
Equipment	$1,500
Accounting/legal	$2,000
Licenses/permits	$1,250
Marketing/travel	$1,500
Insurance	$1,000
Living expenses (including health care)	$45,000
Desired profit	$10,000
Total	**$68,000**

To calculate your fully allocated rate, take your projected annual costs (office supplies, utilities, software, equipment, personal expenses, taxes, permits, licenses, insurance, what you need to live on, and the profit you want to make) and divide by your number of annual billable hours. Table 24.1 gives an example of fully allocated pricing.

Using this example, in order to cover all your costs, both business and personal, and end the year with a $10,000 profit, you need to earn $68,000 per year. Now not every hour you work is going to be billable. Paying bills, working on your web site, marketing, and other administrative tasks will eat into your productivity. The ratio of billable hours to total hours worked will vary from one freelancer to the next, but a good rule of thumb is that you generally have to work two hours for every one that's billable. Here's the rest of the calculation:

HOURS WORKED PER YEAR	**1,920 (48 WEEKS, 40 HOURS A WEEK)**
Billable percentage	50 percent = 960 billable hours
Pretax hourly rate needed	$71/hour ($68,000/960)
After-tax hourly rate	$101/hour (Pretax/(1 − tax rate of 30 percent)

In this scenario, you'd need an hourly billing rate of $101 in order to make a $10,000 profit (or $86/hour if you're willing to forego the profit). FreelanceSwitch.com offers a neat online tool to help you calculate your minimum hourly rate.

Marginal Cost Pricing

Marginal cost pricing recognizes that, at least in the short run, not every billable hour has to contribute equally to covering your costs. Some of your costs are fixed. Your insurance, accounting, living expenses, and many other costs will be the same whether you do one project a year or a hundred. The concept suggests that all you really have to cover is the extra expenses that relate to a specific project (known as the variable costs).

Since your variable costs as a freelancer, aside from your time, are practically nil, you could drastically lower your hourly rate without going out-of-pocket. While this might be the right approach for a teaser project or one that adds significant credibility to your portfolio, if you price too many of your projects this way you'll soon be looking for a traditional job.

Volume Pricing

Some people subscribe to the theory that you can afford to charge less for big jobs or repeat work. This may be true, but only if those jobs allow you to either increase your percentage of billable hours, or reduce your costs.

For example, let's say a big company is willing to contract with you to do 10 small projects a month, but only if you lower your hourly rate. If those projects allow you to reduce the amount of time you spend marketing, and therefore give you more billable hours per month, a rate cut may be justified—but cutting back on your marketing is always risky. This is a classic freelancer conundrum. While a single large customer may look like a gravy train, you'll quickly go hungry if the engine derails.

Premium Pricing

Though it may not be possible when you're first starting out, premium pricing should be the ultimate goal of a freelancer. It's based on the reality that customers are willing to pay more when they *perceive* they are receiving a more valuable service—emphasis on *perceive*. People don't buy Gucci products because they last longer; they buy them because they associate them with status. How you market, package, and present your services can make a significant difference in what you are able to charge.

Premium pricers need to keep in mind that you can't offer low-quality service at a high price. As the old saying goes, you can't make a silk purse from a sow's ear. You have to earn the right to premium price.

Premium pricing can also be achieved by exploiting a niche where competition is low. Nick Dalton established himself as an iPhone expert by writing an e-book titled *101 iPhone Tips and Tricks* (iPhone-Incubator .com/blog). When Apple released its iPhone software development kit (SDK), Dalton already had both the credibility and the contacts to market his services. He picked up his first order the very afternoon the SDK was released. In less than a year, he became the person to know in iPhone application development. While it won't support him forever, that reputation gives him a significant head start and advantage over competitors. It allows him to consistently win bids without playing price games. Using Elance.com and a few other freelance job boards, Dalton has since added five employees on three continents.

Competitive Pricing

What your competitors charge obviously has to play a role in what you can charge. Having said that, if their prices are the business equivalent of jumping off a cliff, keep in mind there's no future in being a lemming.

Competitive pricing issues are particularly challenging in freelance industries where offshore providers are willing to work for a pittance. If this is the case in your industry, don't panic and try to match rates. Figure out what the low-price bidders are good at and what they aren't. Let them chase the pennies while you capture the dollars.

Also, keep in mind that while others may be bidding ridiculously low rates, they're not necessarily winning the bids. "When we first started to outsource projects I was intrigued enough to try a couple of the $2 an hour providers" says Ken, a Guru.com outsourcer. "I quickly found I got what I paid for. Now I just ignore the majority of the low-price offshore bids." We heard this repeatedly from users of freelance services.

Still, it's important to be aware of what others are charging. Some industries make it relatively easy to find competitive pricing information. In the writing industry, for example, *Writer's Market* (F&W Publishing) does a very thorough annual survey that includes low, average, and high hourly and project rates for over 100 types of writing projects.

Trade associations can also be a good source of benchmark pricing information. Freelance job boards such as oDesk.com, Guru.com, and

Elance.com are an excellent source of competitive information as well. Just do a search as if you were a client looking for the kind of work you do, and see what other domestic providers charge.

The best one-stop resource we've seen for freelance rate information is the Freelance Statistics Report that we mentioned in Chapter 22. The full report is available free to freelancers who participate in the survey; others can purchase it by making a donation to FreelanceSwitch.com. The report includes the average rates for software designers, web designers, graphic designers, programmers, writers, illustrators, videographers, project managers, 3D artists, and photographers. Rates are stratified by country, city, and experience level. As you might expect, more experience generally means more money. Surprisingly, rates vary significantly by the country where the work originated. In case you're wondering, the Greeks and Norwegians shell out the most euros and krona for web design services.

According to the survey, software designers get the big bucks, while writers—who seem particularly fond of suicidal pricing strategies—seem to prefer fame over fortune.

Suicidal Pricing

Suicidal pricing often occurs by default rather than by design. Any time you price your services below your costs, you're at the cliff's edge. If you're still not convinced, consider the tips in Tables 24.2 and 24.3.

Table 24.2   Eight Reasons Not to Cut Prices

As soon as you do, another client will call with a full-fare project that you won't be able to accept.

The lowest rate a client has paid in the past is the highest they'll expect to pay in the future.

Price buyers will be your worst customers.

Price buyers will tell other customers.

Price buyers are not loyal—they're always searching for a better deal.

Price buyers expect more than other customers.

It's always easier to lower your prices than to raise them. Keep them high and use discounts, coupons, and special offers to maintain the higher perceived value for your service.

If you're going to go out of business, why go out of business tired?

Table 24.3   You Know Your Prices Are Too Low When . . .

You have more work than you can handle.

No one ever complains that your prices are too high.

There's a stunned silence on the other end of the phone when you name your price,
   followed by immediate acceptance.

Competitors beg you to raise your prices.

Prospects are surprised at how well you speak English.

Clients regularly add an unsolicited bonus to your check.

Project versus Hourly Pricing

A little over half of freelancers surveyed by FreelanceSwitch.com offer their services based on estimates rather than fixed quotes. There are obvious risks in providing clients with fixed quotes. Unless the project is very straightforward, or you've done the same kind of thing enough times that you *know* how long it's going to take, it's easy for a freelancer to get burned with a fixed quote.

Even if you are confident of your own talents, there's the client to consider. New outsourcers may not be capable of explaining what they really want. They may change their mind once the project is under way. They may be hard to reach or unable to make decisions. They may quit in the middle of a project, forcing you to start over with their replacement. Programmers may find themselves having to untangle a rat's nest of someone else's code before they can get down to work. Organizational politics may even come into play.

For all these reasons, try to avoid fixed quotes. If the client insists, try to quote a range, rather than a single amount.

A good pricing strategy won't help you win the battle to make a freelance living unless you're able to collect what you're owed at the end of a project. Chapter 25 offers defensive tactics to help you avoid that skirmish.

25

Proposals and Contracts

If you've never had a client who tried to renege on payment, you probably haven't been freelancing very long. In a survey of over 3,500 freelancers conducted by About.com's Desktop Publishing editor, 65 percent said they'd been burned by not having a contract.[1] Yet there's a tendency, particularly among newer freelancers, to be very informal in their client relationships.

Some assume that e-mail and other informal communications are adequate. Some fear too much formality will put a prospective client off. Some simply don't know what they don't know about proposing or documenting work relationships, or they're intimidated by the legal lingo involved. Some don't give it much thought at all until they've been burned. In the end, using a written agreement to document your client relationships is simply good business. We can almost guarantee that the client who won't sign a work order or contract will be the same client such documents were designed to protect you from.

In a prior incarnation, I was a consultant who helped business owners find financing. At the start of a business relationship, the process of raising capital mystified them. Most had already been rejected by a number of lenders or investors. They were often desperate by the time they hired me and, since the majority of my fee was contingent on success, their downside was protected. Though I did use a contract to document my fees, collecting was often a problem because once funding was secured, my services no longer seemed as valuable as they did when the client was desperate.

Most freelancers solve problems for their clients. A web programmer might be engaged by an e-tailer who's desperate to fix a bug in her shopping cart. A search engine optimizer might be engaged by an author whose web site languishes on page 12 of a Google search. And they all have the same problem as Will, an animator who was hired to produce a demo reel for a Cartoon Network pitch. When the pitch failed, the client—who was originally thrilled with the animation—no longer felt it was worth the price. The same is true when the shopping cart is fixed, or the web site starts appearing on page one of the search results. While a contract or signed estimate won't guarantee payment, it will give you a leg to stand on if the worst happens.

Bidding and Proposals

All of your client communications should be in writing. You'll develop your project bid from your client's written spec and other written communications. Your bid should include the following information:

- An overview of the project.
- An explanation of your relevant skills and reference to portfolio samples that demonstrate success in similar projects.
- How you propose to complete the project.
- Your pricing, justification, and time estimates.
- A description of what is and isn't included in your estimate.
- How you would like the client to respond to your bid.

Figure 25.1 shows what a sample bid looks like, as provided by Guru.com's help center.

Project Plans and Milestones

Before you go to work on a project, you and the client should clearly understand what's included, when and how it will be delivered, and when and how you will be paid. Whenever possible, you should create checkpoints and milestones to make sure the customer is on board throughout the process. Often, particularly when you're working on a lengthy project, these milestones should trigger progress payments so that you don't have to wait until the end for your payment. On shorter projects, a 50 percent deposit is common. Figure 25.2 shows a project plan for the design of a brochure.

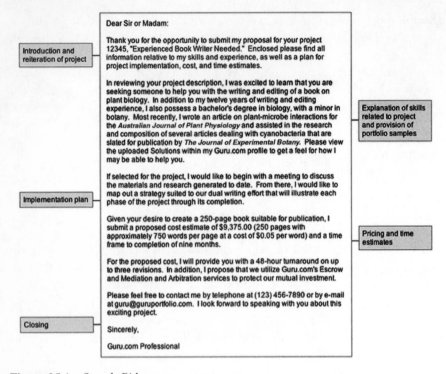

Dear Sir or Madam:

Thank you for the opportunity to submit my proposal for your project 12345, "Experienced Book Writer Needed." Enclosed please find all information relative to my skills and experience, as well as a plan for project implementation, cost, and time estimates.

In reviewing your project description, I was excited to learn that you are seeking someone to help you with the writing and editing of a book on plant biology. In addition to my twelve years of writing and editing experience, I also possess a bachelor's degree in biology, with a minor in botany. Most recently, I wrote an article on plant-microbe interactions for the *Australian Journal of Plant Physiology* and assisted in the research and composition of several articles dealing with cyanobacteria that are slated for publication by *The Journal of Experimental Botany*. Please view the uploaded Solutions within my Guru.com profile to get a feel for how I may be able to help you.

If selected for the project, I would like to begin with a meeting to discuss the materials and research generated to date. From there, I would like to map out a strategy suited to our dual writing effort that will illustrate each phase of the project through its completion.

Given your desire to create a 250-page book suitable for publication, I submit a proposed cost estimate of $9,375.00 (250 pages with approximately 750 words per page at a cost of $0.05 per word) and a time frame to completion of nine months.

For the proposed cost, I will provide you with a 48-hour turnaround on up to three revisions. In addition, I propose that we utilize Guru.com's Escrow and Mediation and Arbitration services to protect our mutual investment.

Please feel free to contact me by telephone at (123) 456-7890 or by e-mail at guru@guruportfolio.com. I look forward to speaking with you about this exciting project.

Sincerely,

Guru.com Professional

Labels: Introduction and reiteration of project; Explanation of skills related to project and provision of portfolio samples; Implementation plan; Pricing and time estimates; Closing

Figure 25.1   Sample Bid

Who	Milestone	Target Date	Hours	Method	Amount Due
Client	Sign off on project agreement	9-Jun		PayPal	$1,500
Client	Provide sample copy	10-Jun		Delivery by e-mail	
Client	Provide brochure photos (300 dpi)	10-Jun		Delivery by e-mail	
Both	Client / Contractor to discuss brochure	11-Jun	1	Phone—1 hour	
Contractor	3 mock-up brochure designs	17-Jun	15	Delivery by e-mail	
Client	Respond to mock-up designs / choose approach	19-Jun	1	Phone or e-mail	
Contractor	Refine and delivery full brochure mock-up	26-Jun	15	E-mail sign-off	
Client	Respond to brochure mock-up	28-Jun	1	E-mail sign-off / phone	
Contractor	Deliver low-resolution color proof	30-Jun	2	E-mail / Payment by PayPal	$1,500
Contractor	Deliver final art	on rcpt of pmt	1	E-mail	

Figure 25.2   Project Plan for Brochure

Contracts and Agreements

Agreements or contracts will vary by industry. It's always a good idea to have your standard agreement reviewed by an attorney. A sample project agreement and other useful forms are available at UndressForSuccessOnline.com.

At a minimum, your client agreement should include the following elements.

The Parties

The first paragraph names the parties to the agreement. It should set forth the fact that you are acting as an independent contractor. If you're dealing with a large organization, it should establish that the person signing has the authority to enter a contract on their company's behalf. The date of the agreement should be included here as well.

The Project

This section should include a description of the services you'll provide, with as much detail as possible. If you're to produce a six-panel, double-sided, full-color brochure, spell that out, rather than just saying "brochure development." Broad statements of work are of little use to either party.

Timeframe, Milestones, Payment

This section should answer the following questions:

- Payment: Are you quoting the project on an hourly, daily, or project rate? What is the rate or amount?
- How many revisions or iterations are included in the project? How are additional revisions to be authorized, billed, and paid? How will other overages be handled if the project exceeds the agreed-upon hours, days, or scope? If you're working on a fixed price, specify how changes or additions will be identified, billed, and paid.
- How will out-of-pocket expenses such as shipping, copying, and proofs be billed and paid? Is there sales tax?
- What are your terms of payment at milestones? when a certain number of hours is reached? when a certain dollar limit is reached? prior to release of final copy? on completion? 30 days after completion? What late fees are involved? When will they be triggered?
- Will the client be invoiced? What method of payment is acceptable—credit card, wire transfer, cashiers check, bank check, PayPal? To whom should payment be made?
- How will project changes be handled? Are they to be governed by this agreement or is additional documentation required? Does an e-mail from the client suffice as a change order?

The time frame and milestones we discussed in the previous section should be included within, or as an attachment to, this agreement.

Copyright and Ownership of Work

If a salaried employee creates something for his employer, the employer automatically owns that work. This is referred to as *work for hire* or *work made for hire* and is governed by the United States Copyright Act of 1976. With freelancers and contractors, it's just the opposite. In the absence of a specific written transfer of ownership, the freelancer owns the work.

If the work is not a work made for hire, the hiring party has no copyright ownership. For example, a movie producer uses many freelance artists. Without a work-for-hire agreement, any one of them could limit use of the entire film by denying permission to copy their contribution.

These are important issues for freelancers. A software developer, for example, may want to use some or all of the embedded software routines designed for a client on later projects, or may have already used some of the code in the past on other projects. If so, the designer needs to be careful about signing a work-for-hire agreement. A compromise approach would be to license the rights to some or all of the work to the client so they can use it without owning it.

We learned about work for hire the hard way. After we sold our flightseeing business, a contractor claimed that our license to the shopping cart he built did not transfer to a subsequent owner. At the peak of the holiday season, he threatened to shut down the company's web site (and did) using a back door that he'd built into the code. While we had several e-mails where the contractor stated the software was licensed to the company, without caveat, he claimed the license was to us personally, not our corporation. While there was no doubt in our, the new owner's, or our attorney's mind that we were right, it wasn't worth the hassle, cost, or potential lost sales to battle it out. The new owners created a new site and abandoned the $20,000 site we'd built. Live and learn.

Cancellation and Termination issues

This section of your contract should address what happens in the event the client (or you) wishes to cancel the agreement. Can they? If so, under what circumstances? How will you be protected for the work you've already done? What happens to payments you've received to date? What about unreimbursed out-of-pocket expenses? Will the work you've done so far be returned? Can they use it going forward? Who owns the work if the contract is terminated?

Dispute Resolution

What happens in the event of a dispute? Does it go to mediation? to court? In what city, by what state laws? Who pays the attorney and court costs?

26

Finding Freelance Work

Online freelancers find work in different ways depending on what kind of work they do. The FreelanceSwitch.com Freelance Statistics Report offers a breakdown by industry, but in general here's what they found: Referrals are the richest source of business—almost 90 percent of freelancers reported relying on word of mouth. Following that, the top sources of work were portfolio web site, 44 percent; Internet job sites, 36 percent; social networking sites, 22 percent; blog, 15 percent; advertising, 13 percent; and cold-calling, 13 percent.

When they do find work, thanks to the Internet, it comes from all over the world. "When I got started twenty years ago, every one of my clients fell within a fifty-mile radius of my home," says Cartoon Bob (aka Bob D'Amico at CartoonBob.com). "Thanks to the Web, my clientele now spans the globe. Having access to all those buyers allows me to pick and choose the work I enjoy most."

So how do you find all those people who want to buy your expertise? There are two basic models among the web-based freelance job boards. In the first model, project listings include direct links to employers. In the second model, the web site acts as an intermediary between employers and contractors.

Direct employer listings are typically found on large newspaper and specialty magazine sites, association web sites, Craigslist, the large job board and scraper sites we covered in Chapter 19, and specialty freelance sites.

Specialty sites such as 37Signals.com (IT and web design), Authentic-Jobs.com (IT and Web design), and FreelanceSwitch.com offer thumbnail summaries of the projects and a direct link to the employer or agency that's handling the listing. Like traditional job boards, these sites make their money from the companies and individuals who post jobs and from advertising, and they're free to people looking for work.

The intermediary sites offer the richest source of freelance work. The biggest among them are Guru.com, Elance.com, Rent-A-Coder.com, and oDesk.com. Each offers a unique suite of services that allow freelancers and outsourcers to find each other, bid and accept proposals, manage work, finalize payment, and rate each other's performance.

Guru.com

Inder Guglani, founder and CEO of Guru.com, was one of those smart guys who saw the rise of the freelance nation before most of the rest of the world. Working from his basement in 1998, he was looking for a way to bring employers and qualified freelancers together. "My goal was to build an efficient platform that would connect businesses with freelance professionals all over the world. More importantly, since the fact that someone has a master's degree offers no guarantee about how well they'll perform, I wanted to provide a way for employers to evaluate the competency of the freelancers." In 2000, when the economy tanked, suddenly there were thousands of dot-com techies out of work. Guglani seized the opportunity.

Today, Guru.com is the leading freelance job board with more than a million registered members. About 10 percent are actively bidding at any given time. Over 30,000 employers, including Viacom, Hewlett Packard, IBM, the National Geographic Society, and thousands of small companies, use Guru.com for their outsourced project needs. Of the over 93,000 projects that were posted in 2007, 80 percent originated in the United States and more than 50 percent were completed domestically. Annual growth is projected to exceed 50 percent a year.[1]

Guru.com has built a community where freelancers can build a profile, post work samples, display their feedback ratings and details about completed projects, post images, and even include a video resume. McKay Stewart, a web site designer, offers his profile overview page as an example of how he promotes his services on Guru.com.[2] (See Figure 26.1.)

Just as employers rate freelancers, freelancers rate employers. In addition to employers' ratings, freelancers can evaluate prospective clients based on the number and value of projects they've completed through Guru, total of invoices outstanding, and the time delay in payment. (See Figure 26.2.)

| Overview | Resume | Work Samples | Completed Projects |

Summary

Category rank:	1451 in Web site Design / Web site Marketing
Feedback:	✪✪✪✪✪ 9 reviews
Earnings (year):	$21,459.97
Earnings (all):	$34,429.22
Min. rate / hour:	$95.00
Min. project budget:	$2,000.00
Member since:	15 Dec 2004
Last sign in:	29 May 2008 11:19 AM ET
Work onsite:	No

Skills

Experience:	13 years
Highest degree:	Bachelor's Degree
Subcategories:	Flash for Web sites Web sites-Brochure (Standard HTML) Web sites-Database/Ecommerce (Dynamic)
Industries:	Hotels, Restaurants, Clubs, Other Leisure Media, Advertising, Publishing, Entertainment Consulting, Legal, Engineering, Accounting, Other Real Estate, Insurance Retail, Wholesale
Software skills:	Photoshop, Illustrator, FLASH, Shockwave, Maya 3D, 3DSMax, Final Cut
Additional skills:	PHP, MYSQL, MSSQL, CMS, JOOMLA/MAMBO, OSCOMMERCE, HTML, XML, JAVA, JAVASCRIPT, CSS, PHP, ASP, .NET, COLDFUSION, PERL, CGI, C/C++

Highlights

I manage and direct a team of highly skilled developers and designers. Each of these guys (and girls) has the skill sets necessary to deliver the highest quality and most original web sites on the Internet. Form meets function, complements it, in our creations. Cutting-edge, original designs work together with animation and web applications, shopping carts, etc. to make your web site POP and keep your clients coming back. This, combined with unprecedented value (our sites are typically worth 2-3 times what we charge), make THE WEB SAINT a company you will want to refer all your friends... Show all

Work Terms

I maintain a very high level of integrity and responsibility in all of my work and I expect the same from any client I choose to do business with. I typically develop all of my work on my own servers and once the client approves the work the client pays and then the work is transferred to the client's own server(s). This is an Internet standard for professionals.

Before work begins I have three (3) documents that the client must agree to and sign:

1. PROJECT SCOPE—This document details exactly the deliverables
2. INVOICE—This contains the budget and how it is broken down
3. TERMS AND CONDITIONS... Show all

Figure 26.1   Guru Freelancer's Profile

Employer Statistics

Feedback rating:	★★★★★
SafePay payments:	$9,465.00
Invoices paid:	24 More info
Invoices outstanding:	0
Pay time lag:	2 day(s) average
Employer location:	(hidden—may not view)

Figure 26.2   Guru Employer Statistics

Guru's Help section offers templates and advice for developing project plans, milestones, and agreements. The whole concept is that the freelance transactions can be bid, performed, managed, and paid from within Guru.com. By keeping all communications under one umbrella, both employers and freelancers are protected.

Guru.com offers three levels of membership. Basic users pay nothing for membership and receive limited access and features. Guru members (individuals) pay $60 to $200 per year depending on their skill category. Guru Vendor members (freelance organizations) pay $78 to $260 per year. In addition to the membership fees, Basic members pay 10 percent of the value of each completed project; Guru and Guru Vendor members pay 5 percent (project fees).

Guru's SafePay Escrow service assures freelancers that employers are able to pay for services by requiring them to place in escrow the funds they'll need for each project milestone. Guru.com's fee for use of this feature is 2 percent of the project value. While it does not guarantee payment, less than 3 percent of all SafePay Escrow projects go to mediation, and less than half of one percent go to arbitration.

PayPal and credit card transactions carry a fee of between 2.5 and 4 percent per transaction (the fees are passed through by Guru with no markup). To avoid these charges, you can specify that clients pay by check, e-check, or wire transfer. Of the three, wire transfer is the safest method of payment. With checks and e-checks, you run the risk of finding out the check is bad after you've released your work to the employer. Guru considers this an act of fraud and will ban an employer from the site should this occur, but that may be a day late and a dollar short as far as you're concerned.

If you plan to use Guru frequently, you will want to sign up for one of the premium membership accounts. The 5 percent difference in project fees means that annual projects totaling $1,200 and $4,000 (depending on your skill category) justify the upgrade to one of the higher membership categories (Guru or Guru Vendor), but other membership differences tip the scales in favor of the higher membership levels as well. As a Basic member, you are able to create a simple profile in up to five skill categories, but only one category can be active at a time. You can bid on up to 10 projects a month within your active skill category. Only about 20 percent of projects are available to Basic members.

Other benefits of the higher membership categories include the ability to offer package deals, a limit of 100 bids per month (with more available for purchase), up to 10 active profiles in different skill categories, priority placement of your vendor profiles, more storage space for work samples, the ability to post video profiles, expanded vendor descriptions, and full access to the Project Question Board and Private Discussion Board for communicating with employers.

The following categories of work are available to Guru.com freelancers:

- Web site design/web site marketing.
- Graphic design/presentations/multimedia.
- Illustration/cartooning/painting/sculpting.
- Photography/videography.
- Writing/editing/translation.
- Broadcasting.
- Fashion/interior/landscape/set design.
- Programming/software/database development.
- Networking/hardware/telephone systems.
- Enterprise resource planning (ERP).
- Customer relationship management (CRM).
- Sales/telemarketing (front-end).
- Administrative support (legal, medical, and accounting).
- Business consulting.
- Legal.
- Finance and accounting.
- Engineering/CAD/architecture.
- Marketing/advertising/sales/public relations.

As projects come up, freelancers can place blind bids on those within their skill category. Bidders are not privy to each other's quotes. Some employers choose to use "Invite-only" bidding so they can specify who can bid on their projects.

Guru offers a variety of resources to help build your bid, project plan, milestones, payment schedule, and project agreement. Once you begin working on a project, you upload your work-in-progress to a temporary "workroom" where employers can provide feedback. When the project is complete, or when payment milestones are met, Guru.com's SafePay^{TM} invoicing and SafePay Escrow^{TM} features help ensure that you are paid. In the event of a dispute, SafePay Escrow users receive mediation and arbitration services.

We asked McKay Stewart for his thoughts about working with Guru:

> It gets easier the more positive ratings and more money you make. You can become very adept at selecting which jobs to bid on. I would also say that the online marketplace doesn't quite take the place of good old-fashioned pavement-pounding, shaking bushes, and generally handing your business card to everyone you meet. But you can make a decent living just from clients acquired online at Guru.com. I relied almost entirely on clients and income from Guru for several years.

Elance.com

Elance got its start in the late 1990s just like Guru.com. While its creators' original intent was to build a marketplace where outsourcers and freelancers could connect, they soon found that large companies were interested in their expertise as a way to manage outsourced projects. Elance began to build enterprise software to help the likes of FedEx, American Express, Wells Fargo, and others track and manage their ad hoc workforce. In 2006, Elance sold off the enterprise portion of the business, and returned to their original plan of helping small businesses easily and efficiently hire freelance talent online.

As of May 2008, Elance had over 130,000 freelance service providers and 40,000 active buyers—an increase of 60 percent from the year prior. More than 4,000 projects—representing $2 million in business—are posted each week. The value of projects completed in 2007 exceeded $40 million. More than half of Elance's freelance service providers are based in the United States; 60 percent of projects originate in the United States and Canada, 25 percent come from Western Europe, and 15 percent come from the rest of the world.[3]

Elance's "Remote Work System" enables employers to track progress on their work through well-developed communication and collaboration tools that are designed to clearly establish requirements and milestones, while tracking progress toward completion. The system makes it easy for employers to give their providers feedback during the process, which leads to good results and high levels of satisfaction for both parties.

Elance's value-added services include portfolio hosting, proposal templates, service agreement templates, nondisclosure templates, project tracking, project invoicing and payments, escrow payments, email alerts, and satisfaction ratings for both freelancers and employers.

Elance offers four levels of provider membership.

- Basic membership is free and comes with three "Connects," the currency freelancers (Elance calls them *providers*) use to submit proposals. Providers can purchase additional Connects as needed for $.50 each. Unused Connects do not roll over to the next month. Basic members pay a transaction fee of 6 percent—that is, Elance receives 6 percent of project total.
- Individual membership is $9.95 per month and comes with 20 Connects per month; the transaction fee is 4 to 6 percent. More active providers pay lower fees: 4 percent for providers with six-month earnings over $40,000, 5 percent for providers with six-month earnings between $10,000 and $40,000, and 6 percent for providers with six-month earnings less than $10,000.
- Small Business membership is $19.95 per month and includes 40 Connects per month; the transaction fee is 4 to 6 percent.
- Large Business membership is $39.95 per month and includes 60 Connects per month; the transaction fee is 4 to 6 percent.

Membership comes with a choice of one service category (administrative support, design and multimedia, engineering and management, finance and management, legal, sales and marketing, writing and translation, or web and programming). Individual, small business, and large business members may add additional categories for $4.95, $9.95, or $19.95 per month per category, respectively. The payment processing fee for credit card or PayPal payments is 2.75 percent for all membership levels. Use of Elance's escrow service is free.

The idea behind Elance's Connect pricing is to give lower-budget projects lower proposal costs and higher-budget projects slightly higher proposal costs. For example, a $1,000 Standard (i.e., non-Featured) project requires a provider to use two Connects when submitting a proposal. If the provider chooses to submit a Sponsored bid, it will require four Connects. If it was a Featured project and the bid was Sponsored, it would require six Connects. At $1,001, the Connect requirements go to 4, 8, and 12 respectively.

The number of Connects required to bid on a project varies according to the value of the project (higher-budget projects require more Connects). The number of Connects required also varies by the

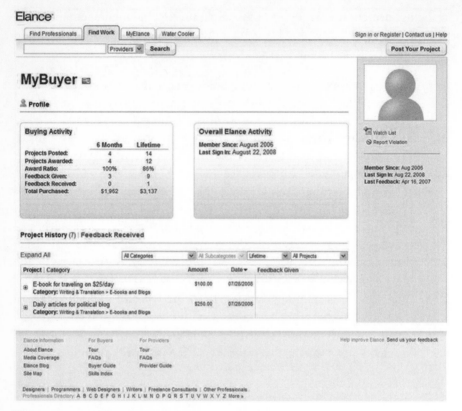

Figure 26.3   Elance Employer Profile

visibility employers and providers select for their job and proposal, respectively. Buyers who want better visibility can select the "Featured" option for their project. Featured projects are highlighted with a special seal that helps them stand out in the search results. Providers who submit proposals can elect to gain a leg up on the competition by using additional Connects to upgrade their bid to "Sponsored" status. This places their proposal at the top of the buyer's response list. The number of Connects a provider will use to submit a proposal on a Featured project depends on the dollar value of the project and whether the provider on the project has chosen the Standard or Sponsored proposal option.

Bob D'Amico (aka Cartoon Bob, creator of CartoonBob.com) has been a freelance cartoonist, photographer, and art director for over 20 years. He's been an Elance provider for four years. Like us, Bob found Elance's pricing methodology a bit confusing at first, but he uses Elance almost exclusively now because of it. "On some of the other job boards, my cartoon work competes with over a hundred other bidders. Not all of them are competent, but the volume of bids creates a great deal of noise for the buyer. When I bid on Elance's Featured projects, I'm typically up against only a handful of competent bidders. In those cases, what it comes down to is which cartoon style the buyer prefers. Being able to set myself apart from the mass of bidders is what makes the difference on Elance."

All membership levels include a collaborative workspace where providers track communications with clients, share documents, track their engagements and milestones, and leave feedback. Financial features at Elance include the ability to create, send, and manage invoices; accept payment by credit card, Paypal, direct deposit, check, or wire transfer; and take advantage of escrow billing with free mediation if needed. Arbitration services are available for an additional charge.

Freelancers can learn about a prospective client by viewing their employer profile. (See Figure 26.3.) In addition, providers can create their own unique profile on Elance to showcase their skills, portfolio, services offered, credentials, feedback, and business practices. Elance's membership sign-up process walks you through how to build your profile and portfolio. The interface is very user-friendly. (See Figure 26.4.)

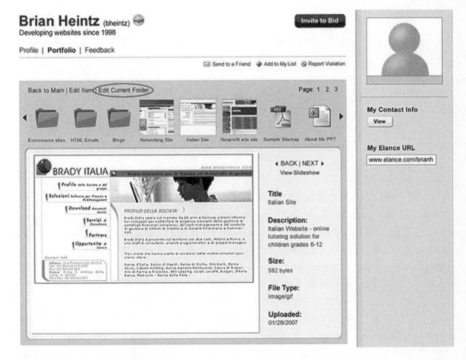

Figure 26.4   Elance Sign-up

Once you have your profile and portfolio set up, you can start to submit proposals for jobs. The filtering options allow you to prioritize the projects you see by whether they are fixed fee or hourly, how soon the bidding closes, when the job was posted, and other factors. E-mail alerts and RSS feeds can be set up to let you know when new projects in your categories of interest are posted.

Elance offers employers the ability to specify either sealed or open bidding. While sealed bidding is the most popular option, it's worth perusing a few open bids as a way of gathering information about other providers—of course, other providers will be doing the same on your open bids. Invite-only bidding allows buyers to invite specific providers to submit a proposal on a project.

Elance offers freelancers a testing service that allows them to certify their expertise in over 200 skills. Tests for all of the popular software and programming languages are available. Individual membership includes two free tests; small business membership includes four; large business membership includes eight. Additional tests are $4.00 each. They can be taken as many times as you like and you can choose whether your proficiency score shows in your profile. These tests offer a great way for freelancers to benchmark their skills and prove their expertise to prospective employers.

Elance's Water Cooler and Elance University offer a wealth of information about how to use the system and how to be a successful freelancer. There are even a number of downloadable samples, including a statement of work, change order, project agreement, and nondisclosure agreement. Direct links to these are available on our web site.

Rent A Coder

RentACoder.com was the brainchild of Ian Ippolito. As a freelance programmer, Ian was overwhelmed with requests for custom programming. Frustrated at having to turn away paying customers, in 2001 he conceived the Rent A Coder concept and went live the same year. One year later, the site was facilitating almost 1,500 software projects per month. In 2007, it was added to the prestigious *Inc. 5000* list of the fastest-growing software companies in the nation.

While software and firmware coding gave Rent A Coder its start, it now represents a broad range of freelancers, including software developers, hardware engineers, and web programmers; writers; administrative assistants; web marketers and researchers; computer-based graphic artists; and art and music designers.

Today its pool of talent has expanded to include over 200,000 professionals. Approximately 100,000 companies and individuals use Rent A Coder to hire freelancers. Over 7,000 projects are completed each month—a number that's been growing by nearly 50 percent a year. Over 90 percent of its business is from repeat customers.

The United States accounts for over half of all projects posted on Rent A Coder. The United Kingdom and Australia are the next largest customers with 11 percent and 9 percent, respectively. On the provider side, 20 percent of coders come from India, 13 percent from the United States, and 11 percent from Romania, so foreign competition for work is significant. Ian cautions American freelancers not to be discouraged when projects are inundated with cheap foreign bids. "The difficulty in enforcing copyright protection in foreign countries as well as security concerns often cause buyers to favor U.S. bidders," say Ippolito.

Membership on Rent A Coder is free. The project fee is 12.5 percent. Like the other freelance job boards, its PayPal or credit card processing fee (2.5 percent) can be avoided by specifying that buyers pay by check or wire transfer. Rent A Coder pioneered the freelance web site escrow and arbitration service and offers it at no charge, according to Ippolito. All buyers are required to escrow the entire project fee with Rent A Coder at the start of the project so that freelancers know the money will be there when the job is done. About 10 percent of the projects go to mediation or arbitration.

Rent A Coder allows freelancers to generate a profile, show completed Rent A Coder work along with buyer ratings, check out buyer histories, chat with buyers, submit status reports, upload completed work, and receive e-mail notifications on new projects. There is, however, no provision for showcasing work samples.

Professionals are encouraged to certify their skills by taking tests on ExpertRating.com. The results are automatically linked to your Rent A Coder profile but can be removed if you prefer. General office skill and programming tests run about $10. Some advanced tests cost $25 or more.

Rent A Coder's search interface allows users to be very specific about the kinds of projects they want to see. (See Figure 26.5.)

Bids are selected on an auction basis, and you can't see what others bid. Once the project is assigned, the winning bid and the last several losing bids are made public. Looking at competitors' historical bids is a great way to refine your own bid strategy.

Categories:
☑ All

Or choose individual categories:

☐ Software Related (Includes Websites) (more specific)   ☐ Marketing (more specific)

☐ Graphic Design / Art / Music (more specific)   ☐ Virtual Assistant (more specific)

☐ Writing (more specific)

☐ Other (more specific)

Show Bidding Expiration:

◉ Not yet expired   ○ All
(Choosing this option will slow down your search significantly)

Show Status of:

☑ Initial Posting by Software Buyer   ☑ Bid Request Activated   ☑ *Buyer Accepted A Bid

☑ *Buyer Deposit Escrowed   ☑ *Coder Deposit Made   ☑ *Coder Deposit Escrowed   ☑ *Programmer Finished Work

☑ *Final Work Accepted   ☑ *Programmer Credited With Escrow

* = To protect the privacy of site users, only the buyer (and selected coder) can search for their own bid requests that are in this status.

Show Project Type:

☑ Small Business Project: $100(USD) and above   ☑ Very Small Business Project: under $100(USD)   ☑ Personal Project / Homework Help   ☑ Unsure of Project Price or Beginner Assistance

☑ Medium Business Project: $500(USD) and above   ☑ Large Business Project: $5,000(USD) and above   ☑ Enterprise Business Project: $50,000(USD) and above   ☑ Very Large Business Project: $25,000(USD) and above

Pay Type:

☑ Pay for deliverables   ☑ Pay for time

Display In Order of:

○ Alphabetical order   ◉ Newest approved bid request first   ○ Oldest approved bid request first   ○ Most popular bid request first

Figure 26.5   Rent A Coder Job Search

Rent A Coder's Help section offers a wealth of advice as well as standard document templates. One template of particular interest to software professionals is a Test Plan Outline that helps manage the testing of new software.

Their legal pages contain important details about working as a Rent A Coder freelancer. Be sure to read them thoroughly.

oDesk.com

oDesk.com is a relative newbie, but with the help of $29 million in venture capital, it's not far behind the top three. Its site calculator shows 92,000 posted projects, 87,000 freelancers, and $34 million in total project values. The number of hours billed through oDesk has more than tripled in the past year. The majority of oDesk freelancers are U.S.–based. India and the Philippines represent the second and third largest group of providers.[4]

While oDesk does allow fixed-price jobs, its business model is designed for hourly billing, and their focus is on tracking hourly work. The average fixed-price post is valued at $687, while the average hourly rate project lasts 218 hours.

Membership in oDesk is free. The project fee is 10 percent and covers merchant processing, payment guarantee fees, dispute management, and other services. The majority of oDesk work is technical (programming and web development), but categories such as technical writing, product package design, administrative support, and marketing are gaining a foothold.

oDesk offers an extensive battery of tests and recommends which are appropriate for each skill category. Its tests are completely free, and you can choose whether the results appear in your profile. Tests can be taken more than once. You can also compare your results with those of others.

oDesk uses what it calls a Work Diary to track project activity, and this is where its model is radically different from the other freelance job boards. oDesk guarantees you payment for all the hours you spend on a project as long as you properly log your time on its Work Diary. (See Figure 26.6.)

When you start working on a project, you log on to the oDesk client server. From then until you log out, your work progress is recorded in the Work Diary. Some, though not many, clients even opt for oDesk's webcam feature that allows clients to view images of you working on their projects. (See Figure 26.7.) The green bar on the side of each photo indicates activity such as a mouse movement or keystroke. Summary data about your activity is available to employers by the hour, day, or week.

This may all seem a bit scary, but if you think about it, how different is it from having a boss looking over your shoulder (assuming you have

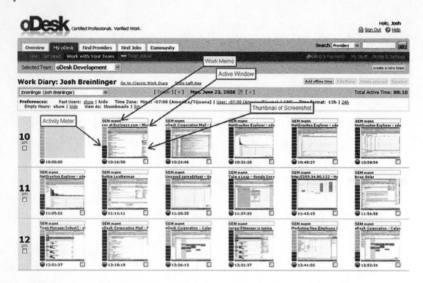

Figure 26.6 oDesk Work Diary

Figure 26.7 oDesk Work Diary Cam View

some clothes on)? If you really are working, what do you care who's watching? Consider, too, the single biggest reason employers don't allow telecommuting is that they don't trust their employees. If this kind of oversight technology is what it takes to convince more companies to outsource work, those of us who really want to work from home should embrace it. Our guess is that we'll see a lot more of this kind of interface in the future of e-work.

oDesk offers a well-designed, easy to use web site for showcasing your talents, managing your projects, and making sure you get paid. It offers video tutorials and extensive documentation about how to use its interface and succeed as a freelancer. It regularly conducts interesting user polls on topics that range from freelancer's beverage of choice to a freelancer's biggest worries.

In addition to being a great project and relationship management site, oDesk beats all of the other large freelance sites when it comes to providing information. It offers statistics on just about everything that happens through the site. Want to know what freelance skills are most in demand and which ones are on the way out? Who the top Joomla programmers are? Where they live? How many hours they've logged? Their hourly rate? It's all available at oDesk.

Other Freelance Sites

While the four freelance job boards we covered here are the largest, they are by no means the only good ones. On our web site you'll find links to others we like, including GetAFreelancer.com, Net-Temps.com, and many more.

4

Bedroom Businesses

27

Who's Running Home Businesses and What Do They Do?

In spite of the fact that in any given year, more people are starting home businesses than exchanging wedding rings or having babies, useful information about the nature of home-based business is difficult to come by.[1]

You would think that the U.S. Small Business Administration (SBA) would offer some insight, but most of its data relates to the *entire* small business population—one they define as companies with fewer than 500 employees. That includes over 99 percent of all U.S. businesses!

The Bureau of Labor Statistics (BLS) also gathers information about businesses, and they do slice it in ways that offer a glimpse of the home-based portion of the population. However, their data lumps full-time and hobby businesses together, and it omits information about home-based corporations and partnerships.

The IRS has a wealth of information available too, but because tax minimization is the goal of every taxpayer, it's hard to rely too heavily on what's reported.

The Census Bureau has some of the best information available, but its more than 1,500-page survey of small businesses hasn't been updated since 2002, a time when remote work technologies were just becoming mainstream.

Most of the independent research on the topic uses a mash-up of all this data. Private studies of entrepreneurship tend to focus on the fastest-growing small companies that don't typify the average home-based business.

Regardless of the source, the other problem with most of the available data is—as we've mentioned elsewhere—that just because a business is home-based doesn't mean it will allow you to undress for success. Working *from* home and working *at* home are two different things.

In spite of all these flaws in the available data, we were able to piece together some interesting information about the nature of small and home-based businesses.

Who's Doing What

Small businesses are the backbone of the U. S. economy. They contribute half of our private gross domestic product, create most of the nation's net new jobs, foster innovation, and represent almost 98 percent of all employers. At any given time, 7 percent of the population is starting a small business—most of them at home.[2]

Over half of all businesses began at home, including household names like Microsoft, Apple, Hewlett-Packard, and Dell. Home-based businesses account for nearly half of all U.S. businesses.[3] While they come in all shapes and sizes, here are some facts about them:[4]

- Most home business owners are solo operators with no employees. Of those that have staff, only about 1 in 10 employ more than 10 people.
- Women are slightly more likely than men to operate a home business.
- Like grapes, entrepreneurs take time to ripen.
  - Less than 2 percent are younger than 25.
  - 12 percent are 25 to 34.
  - 24 percent are 35 to 44.
  - 32 percent are 45 to 54.
  - 19 percent are 55 to 65.
  - 11 percent are over 65 years old.
- While the majority have some college education, a quarter do not.
- Over half work more than 48 hours per week.
- Only 3 percent of home-based businesses are franchises. Even fewer are purchased from someone else.
- Most are organized as sole proprietorships. Only 4 percent are partnerships, and 5 percent are Subchapter S corporations.[5]
- Seventy-five percent of home businesses are operated part-time.[6]

- On average, home businesses earn less than non-home-based firms in terms of both gross income and profit, but they enjoy higher profit margins.[7]
- Profitable non-home-based businesses earned three times the gross income of home-based businesses, but only twice the net income, reflecting the lower costs of home offices.[8]
- Home-based businesses contribute over $100 billion per year to the U.S. economy.[9]

According to Census Bureau data, the following industries account for the largest share of home businesses (see Figure 27.1):

- Professional and technical services, including lawyers, accountants, bookkeepers, payroll specialists, architects, designers, computer services, consulting, researchers, photographers, translation, and other specialty service providers.
- Construction, including general contractors, construction managers, plumbers, electricians, masons, and so on.
- Retail, including non-store retailers such as those that sell through the Internet, infomercials, direct mail, catalog, in-home demos, portable stalls, and vending machines.

Industries with the Most Home-Based Firms: 2002
Total: 8,250,294

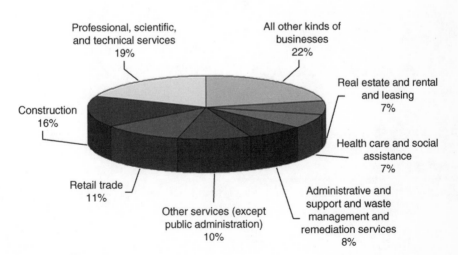

Figure 27.1   Industries with Home-Based Firms

- Other services such as equipment and machinery repair, dry cleaning, personal care, pet care, dating, and photofinishing.

It's interesting to see the kinds of businesses that are run from home, but this book is about how to make a living *at* home. While landscapers may answer calls and do administrative work in their jammies, unless they hire other people to plant and prune, the majority of their income is made when they leave the house. The same is true of many other operations that wear the home-based label.

While most home-based businesses will require you to leave the house occasionally, the ones we've picked for Part 4 are ones we consider the best fit for our from-home, at-home criteria.

28

The Right Fit

Entrepreneurs are notorious for a "ready, fire, aim" approach to business. As a result, they often end up misfits in their own ventures when the business matures. Take, for example, Steve Wozniak, one the founders of Apple, who found himself running a company when what he really liked to do was twiddle bits. Or Famous Amos, the cookie maven who was booted out of his own company, and stripped of even the right to use his own name.

Choosing a business that matches your motivations, personality, talents, and resources will save you a lot of heartache down the road.

Motivations

We started a flightseeing business because (1) we were sick of the rat race, (2) we wanted to spend our days together, not just our nights, and (3) we wanted to do something we loved.

One year into the business, for most of our working hours we were separated by 1,500 feet: Tom in the air, me on the ground. So three years into the business we started adding airplanes and pilots. Suddenly *they* were the ones doing what they loved while we worked at home. Sixteen years into the business the passion was gone—sapped by the day-to-day drill of accounting, advertising, regulatory compliance, and management. Who'd have thought a cool little flying business would become *work*?

In our own defense, we had no choice but to grow. The business was capital intensive, and our customer acquisition costs were high. When the

Travel Channel, *USA Today*, or AAA ran a story about us, we needed to be able to handle the volume. That meant adding planes and pilots—that part was fun, admittedly—but it also meant more paperwork, bills, and other things that weren't much fun.

Sure, we could have hired people to do those things, but one of the things we understand about ourselves is that we're lousy managers—leaders maybe, but not managers. Our management style was about mutual admiration, friendships, and making people happy—a style that fortunately worked very well for us, but generally not a good way to grow a company.

The point of this self-incrimination is to point out how easy it is to forget your motivations, and be caught up in the momentum of a business.

Table 28.1 lists the factors that motivated the owners of *Inc.* magazine's 5,000 fastest-growing businesses to strike out on their own.[1]

What's your motivation? Are you looking for a more flexible lifestyle? If so, be careful to choose a business that will allow you to maintain that flexibility even as it grows. Are you out to make your mark on the world? If so, understand that that may not be compatible with your desire to work from home. Are you hoping to make a living doing what you love? Don't forget about all the administrative tasks you won't love. Are you hoping to build a business you can sell in five years? If so, you'll need to build it in such a way that someone else can easily fill your slippers.

Personality

The business you choose also needs to fit your personality. Researchers have tried for years to figure out what makes entrepreneurs tick. They've studied the successes and failures. They've tried to correlate whether a childhood paper route or lemonade stand sowed the seed, or whether entrepreneurial parents planted it even earlier.

Table 28.1 Inc. 5000 Motivations

44 percent	The challenge of starting a business
30 percent	Best route to financial independence
25 percent	Demand for product/service
24 percent	Creating a high-growth company
20 percent	Wanting to work independently
20 percent	Unhappy working for someone else
3 percent	Unemployment

While almost 40 percent of the founders of Inc. 5000 companies grew up in entrepreneurial families, genetic researchers haven't located a gene that codes for business greatness.

I've never really found an entrepreneurial personality test I like. Perhaps that's because, in spite of having run three successful businesses, I've never found one I score well on. We considered creating one of our own, but have concluded that the paths to entrepreneurship are so varied, it's silly to think there's a single defining personality test value that will be predictive. What it takes to be a solo freelancer is entirely different from what it takes to build an Inc. 5000 company. For that matter, a successful bricks-and-mortar retailer needs a completely different personality and skill set than a successful e-tailer.

Whether people succeed or fail in business has more to do with whether the kind of business they choose to start fits their particular mix of motivations, personality traits, talents, and resources. No one factor can be considered in a vacuum.

A terrific salesperson should choose a business that leverages that talent and should probably have someone else run the administrative and production side of things. An introvert won't do well in sales. An inventor isn't going to be happy managing people.

The following is a summary of the personality traits that studies suggest are common to entrepreneurs. As you look through them, ask yourself how you rate. The point here isn't to determine whether you'll succeed or fail as a business owner—it's to assess what kind of business best fits your personality, and what parts you'll be better off jobbing out to others.

Passion

Running a business is hard work. A healthy dose of passion for what you do will sustain you in the long hours. The most successful business owners genuinely enjoy what they do, they like to work, and they ooze energy. If you're considering a work-at-home business because you think it will be easy, think again.

Resourcefulness

Running a business is full of unknowns. You just never know what problems or opportunities each day will bring. Small business owners don't have an IT department to call when the broadband router won't connect. They don't have a legal department to crank out a work-for-hire agreement. They don't have a staff that can research the cost-effectiveness of a new Google Ad campaign. Successful owners are inventive enough to quickly and effectively deal with whatever comes their way.

Time Management and Ability to Prioritize

Some days it feels like everything and everyone is screaming for your attention. You're trying to make the FedEx deadline, and your web site is down. An important client calls with a quick question that isn't. Three dozen new e-mails litter your inbox. You haven't posted today's blog yet. The cat just puked on your printer.

For a business owner, every moment can be a struggle to stay focused on what's important, instead of what's urgent. Kitty puke notwithstanding, most of what seems urgent really isn't.

Flexibility

One of the advantages a small business has over a large one is its ability to adapt—it's agility. Good entrepreneurs are light on their feet and able to shift gears when conditions require it. They like dynamic environments. However, this is an asset that can easily become a liability. Entrepreneurs are easily bored, and that makes it difficult for some to stay on course.

Self-direction and Independence

Tom knows that if he wants me to do something, telling me I *have* to is the worst possible approach. Business owners don't like or want to be told what to do, either. Their fire comes from within, not from other people. They're leaders, not followers.

Deliberateness

The best business owners are constantly planning, setting goals, and evaluating results. They're able to contain their "ready, fire, aim" urges in favor of a more considered, businesslike approach.

Persistence

Business owners don't give up easily. They're not easily pulled from the chase once they have a kill in sight. Here again, this tendency can be their undoing—many persist in endeavors far longer than they should because of an undying devotion to their beliefs. Working harder and harder on something you shouldn't be doing at all isn't the path to success—or happiness.

Impatience

If there's one universal characteristic of entrepreneurs, it's the constant urge to get on with it. They don't suffer fools lightly. They go around obstacles instead of through them. You won't find many of them in the football stands—they're players, not spectators.

Self-awareness

Good business owners play to their strengths. They either avoid situations that exploit their weaknesses, or find ways to outsource the things they're not good at. Timothy Ferriss, author of *The Four Hour Workweek* is the guru in this area. His book is essential reading for freelancers and small business owners.

Confidence

A fellow aviation enthusiast once described a gathering of air show pilots as an event "where egos soar." She could have just as easily been talking about entrepreneurs. It takes a healthy dose of confidence to succeed in business—"damn the naysayers, full speed ahead." Self-assuredness, or at least the ability to act the part, is particularly important when you're selling your own skills. When you're the business and the business is you, being able to convince people of how good you are is a crucial skill.

Visionariness

Being able to notice subtle cues, see the big picture, and anticipate trends offers business owners a leg up on the competition. The most successful entrepreneurs are constantly looking forward. They're voracious readers. They're eager to learn new things, and not afraid to experiment.

Organized

As a commercial lender and later as a consultant, I've toured hundreds of company facilities and offices. Some looked like they'd been hit by a tornado, others were the picture of calm. While I've seen both types succeed, from a lender's or investor's point of view, neatness counts—and there's a reason for that. All that clutter is distracting.

As you start your business, try to put systems in place to keep things organized, particularly if this doesn't come naturally to you. Set up a computer database for your contacts. Make your accounting system as painless and automated as possible. Set up computer and paper files so things are easy to find. If you wait too long to lay the groundwork for keeping things organized, it may be impossible to catch up once the business takes off.

Sociability/Extroversion

While many business owners describe themselves as loners, the successful ones are able to push themselves into the limelight when they need to. It helps to be able to blow your own horn.

Support Systems

A small business owner doesn't need people constantly asking why she doesn't just go find a *real* job. Having a family and friends who are supportive and who know what you're going through is a big help as you build a business.

Talents

Michael Gerber, renowned author of *The E-Myth*, calls that moment when people decide they just have to start their own business an "Entrepreneurial Seizure."

> Once stricken . . . there is no relief . . . . In the throes of your Entrepreneurial Seizure, you fall victim to the most disastrous assumption anyone can make about going into business. It is an assumption made by all technicians who go into business for themselves, one that charts the course of a business—from Grand Opening to Liquidation—the moment it is made. That Fatal Assumption is: *if you understand the technical work of a business, you understand a business that does the technical work.*

In other words, just because someone is a great web designer, photographer, medical transcriptionist, or virtual assistant, they think they know all they need to know about how to run a business that does that. In fact, Gerber asserts, "rather than being [the business owner's] greatest single asset, knowing the technical work of their business becomes their greatest single liability."[2]

A small business owner wears many hats. One minute you're the marketing department, the next you're operations. Recognizing where your talents lie, or, more specifically where they don't, is crucial to success. Just as with personality issues, a small business owner has to play to his strengths and shore up his weaknesses. This is *not* a time or place for wishful thinking. A good grasp on reality will help you succeed more than anything else.

Resources

While time is a business owner's most critical resource, depending on the kind of business you start, money and people will be important as well.

Money

Unless you're lucky enough to be launching a business that will make money right out of the starting gate, or you have a secondary source of income, you need to have some savings that will allow you to pay the bills until the business can support you. How much of a nest egg you need depends on the kind of business you intend to start, your personal monthly expenses, and how long you figure it will take to secure an income if your business doesn't pan out. In other words, don't quit your day job just yet. Build your business while someone else pays your bills.

Every business is different in terms of how long it will take to make money. Some businesses take years to turn a profit while others, particularly those with low expenses and high demand, may be profitable from the get-go. As a cushion, most experts agree that you should have squirreled away enough to carry you six months longer than you think it will take your business to start producing enough profit to cover your personal expenses. If you need $3,000 a month to live and the business isn't likely to make that kind of profit for 10 months, you should have $48,000 on hand before you start ($3,000 × 10 months plus $3,000 × 6 months).

One of the fundamental mistakes business owners make is underestimating how much money they'll need to start and grow a business. If you're no good with the numbers end of things, enlist the help of someone who is. You'll find some resources on this subject on our web site.

Table 28.2 2007 Inc. 5000 Start-up Funding Sources

Self-financed	82 percent
Loans from friends, family, business associates	22 percent
Bank loans	18 percent
Lines of credit	18 percent
Venture capital	8 percent
SBA or other government funds	4 percent

You may be surprised to learn that few businesses obtain outside capital to fund their start-up costs. In fact, most home businesses start with less than $10,000 in capital.[3] Even the fastest-growing businesses in the country are overwhelmingly self-funded at start-up, as shown in Table 28.2.

Take a lesson from their success. Have a nest egg. Start small. Stay lean. Don't burden yourself with debt if you don't need to. When it does come time to look for money, plan ahead. Don't wait until you're desperate for capital—it doesn't play well with lenders or investors.

We wouldn't be very good entrepreneurs if we didn't mention a terrific book on the subject: *Finding Money—Secrets of a Former Banker, Confessions of an Entrepreneur*. We know it's good because we wrote it. The fully updated version is available as an eBook at UndressForSuccessOnline.com.

People

Even if you are a sole proprietor, other people can make a difference in your business. The formal advisers you choose, the contractors you select, and your informal support network will all have an impact on your success.

When choosing an accountant or lawyer, ask other business owners for references, and be sure to pick someone who has experience working with businesses of your size and preferably in your industry. You don't want to spend your time or money to educate them about what you do. In other words, don't hire someone who will borrow your watch to tell you what time it is. Make sure you can work with them—you don't have to like them, but you have to trust them and you certainly can't dread meeting with them. Make sure the person who sells you on the relationship isn't going to pawn your work off on an underling.

If you decide to hire help, try before you buy. Start out with a few small projects, then bigger ones. Do the same with contractors and freelancers. Check references. If possible, use one of the freelance services we covered in Chapter 26 to protect yourself from nonperformance issues.

Use caution when hiring friends or family. If things don't work out, it's tough to fire your mother.

29

Designing the Perfect Business

Have you ever run across a business that made you think, "Wow, that is *the* perfect way to earn a living"? Based on what our customers told us, our flightseeing operation was it. Not a week went by that someone didn't say something like, "You have the perfect business. It must be so nice to spend all day, every day, doing what you love." In the beginning, they were right. It was a fun business. We loved the old planes, we loved the pilots who shared our passion, and we loved sharing the fun with our customers.

But take our word for it: It doesn't matter what business you're in, it's still a business, and we're here to tell you the owner isn't in a continual state of entrepreneurial bliss. Having said that, you can stack the deck in your favor by choosing a fun business that's low on risk, low on hassle, and high on potential. As Warren Buffett put it, "I don't try to jump over seven-foot bars; I look around for one-foot bars that I can step over."[1]

While you may not ever find *the* perfect business, one that incorporates the following traits will fall near the mark.

Low Costs, High Prices

Aside from the obvious benefit of higher profitability, the combination of high prices and low costs makes it easier to ride out economic downturns, survive competitive attacks, and respond to changing markets. Look for the highest gross profit margin (revenue minus direct costs, as a percentage of revenue) you can find. "Buy low, sell high" should be your mantra.

Don't even think about selling a $100 techno-gadget unless you can buy or produce it for $40—and $10 would be ever so much sweeter.

A Large But Not Huge Market

Huge markets are usually dominated by huge players. On the flip side, a market that's too small won't sustain a business. The trick is to find that Goldilocks' "just right" niche.

Customers That Are Easy to Identify and Easy to Reach

If you want to market a bookkeeping service that specializes in small companies, you might identify as your prospects readers of small business magazines. Then what? Place an ad in their magazine or on their web site? That would cost thousands of dollars and you'd be competing against advertisers with pockets much deeper than your own.

Let's say, instead, your target audience was Wisconsin farmers. You could run inexpensive Google local click-through ads on relevant web pages. You could offer to contribute articles to the Wisconsin Farm Center newsletter. You could offer to do Alice in Dairyland's taxes for free—she's the state's most recognizable spokesperson. You could offer to contribute content to *Got Moo-la*, the state's annual business assistance directory (no, we didn't make that or Alice in Dairyland up). You could butter up the locals by posting thoughtful comments on local farm blogs. You could make sure a herd of reporters are there when you dress up as a cow covered in dollar signs to mail the last tax returns on April 15. (Okay, maybe that's an udderly cheesy idea and milks the concept a bit too much, but you see our point.)

Low Pre- and Post-sale Handling

Businesses where customers require a lot of hand-holding before and/or after the sale are difficult to scale up. If you need to spend huge amounts of time with each prospective customer, you won't have time for other sales and marketing. At the end of the day, or week, or month, the prospect you've worked so hard to land might choose your competitor, and leave you with nothing to show for your efforts.

Businesses with warranty, support, and other time-consuming post-sale issues are troublesome too. If you have to spend the majority of your time with existing customers, your growth will suffer.

No Huge Competitors

Trying to compete with IBM, the saying goes, is like trying to make love with an elephant. Instead of thinking of pleasure, you have worry about whether it's going to roll over on you.

There are exceptions, however. While everyone assumes Starbucks ran all over mom-and-pop coffee shops, there's plenty of evidence to suggest that they actually stimulated our taste for good coffee and increased the business of nearby independents.

Some Barrier to Entry of New Competitors

In the olden days, opening a new store meant plunking down big bucks for furniture, fixtures, equipment, inventory, and the like. That made it difficult for new retailers to casually enter the market. Web stores, by contrast, are cheap and easy to build. So if you find a profitable niche, someone else will quickly be nipping at your heels. Copycats can snag a fair piece of business; that can be good or bad for you depending on whether you're copying or being copied.

When choosing a business, try to find one that not just anyone could operate, one where you have special knowledge or abilities.

Some Real Advantage over the Competition

One of the fundamentals of sustainability is being able to ward off or beat out competitors. While most entrepreneurs think the most prized competitive advantage is a patented product, that's not the case. Patents are expensive to obtain, difficult to enforce, and make your trade secrets public. Small businesses are better off with a competitive advantage that comes from (a) a strong reputation or following, an extensive customer list, or broad subscription base; (b) a significant development jump on competitors; (c) a lower cost structure; or (d) higher quality, better distribution, better service, greater flexibility/customization, or more value-added.

Product or Services That Are Well Established

Unless you're very well funded, leave the exploring to the big boys. Remember, it was the pioneers who took the arrows.

Stable Technologies

Think about the video rental business. DVDs came along and required the whole industry to change. Rental stores suddenly found themselves having to double their inventory to accommodate DVDs as well as VHS tapes (never mind Beta). No sooner were they over that when TiVo, DVRs, and Netflix tossed them new headaches. Now it's downloadable, on-demand movies. Try to choose a business that isn't subject to radical shifts in technology.

A Business Model That Is Scalable

If you have to work just as hard to obtain and satisfy your thousandth customer as you did your hundredth, the business is never going to become any easier, and growing it will be difficult. The ideal scalable business is one where (1) you make one and sell many; (2) your unit costs go down as volume goes up; (3) new customers are easier and cheaper to reach as you grow; and (4) growth isn't predicated on large investments.

High Repeat Business

A business with lots of repeat customers has significantly lower customer acquisition costs for subsequent sales. Try to choose a business that offers a variety of products and services that you can cross-sell to a loyal customer base.

No Employees (Or Many)

Have you ever had to fire someone, or tell them they needed to work on their anger management, language, or even hygiene? If that kind of thing doesn't appeal to you, pick a business that doesn't require employees.

The financial and emotional overhead of having a staff is substantial. Employment-related expenses add 20 to 30 percent over salary costs. And unless the employees are completely self-directed, managing them will eat into your productivity.

Then there's time and financial cost of compliance with the myriad of ever-changing federal, state, and local employment regulations make it very difficult to be a small employer. With one or two employees, the services of a payroll and employee management service can be cost prohibitive.

The bottom line is that unless you have the skills, experience, and desire to manage people, aim to expand through outsourcing rather than hiring.

Low Start-up Capital Needs

The lowest-risk businesses are ones that don't require you to drain your savings (or someone else's) on up-front costs. Don't make it harder on yourself than it has to be by choosing a business where most of the money you make goes to pay off debt.

Easy to Test

Businesses that lend themselves to small-scale testing and phased growth are the best choice for small operators. You don't want to invest significant time and money in your great business idea only to find out that the market doesn't share your enthusiasm. Choose a business that allows you to dip your toe in the entrepreneurial waters rather than plunging in over your head. And by the way, asking your mom and friends if they like the idea isn't good enough. Even strangers will respond differently when cold hard cash, not just an opinion, is involved.

Nonseasonal

We started our open-cockpit biplane ride business in Philadelphia. One cold November morning a shivering nine-year-old passenger climbed out of the plane and pointed out the flaw in our business strategy when she suggested the ride would have been nicer if we'd had an airplane with a roof. The following year we moved the business to Sunny Diego in Southern California. We doubled our income the first year. It's tough enough to make a living as a small business owner—don't make it even harder by picking a business that limits your income to part of the year.

Limited Factors beyond Your Control

You can't protect yourself from everything, but try to choose a business that isn't likely to suffer when it rains, pours, blows, heats up, or cools down. Likewise, avoid those where your profits could be consumed by biologic, pathologic, pharmacologic, or bureaucratic forces.

No Significant Cycles or Trends

Choose a business that's likely to do well in both good times and bad, and is not subject to trends. Avoid industries, such as real estate, that are known to be cyclical. Big companies can ride the "troughs of demand;" small businesses are often sunk by them.

Diverse Customers and Suppliers

Businesses with too few customers or those where the customers are concentrated in one industry are risky. The loss of one big customer or industry could take you down.

The same is true for businesses that rely on too few vendors. If the one company that supplies your raw materials or products goes down the tubes, you may be sucked down right behind them.

30

The Business Model

As a small business owner, you have to be particularly vigilant to maximize the efficient use of your principle resources—time and money. To do that, it's best to choose a business model that minimizes risk and maximizes potential.

Igor Ansoff is famous for a matrix that he developed in 1957 to show the relative risk of different forms of diversification. With a little modification, his model can be applied to business start-ups as well. (See Figure 30.1.)

	Known Product / Service	New Product / Service
Established Market / Customer	**Lowest Risk**	**Low Risk**
New Market / Customer	**High Risk**	**Highest Risk**

Figure 30.1 Start-up Product/Market Matrix

The riskiest business model is one where you have to create both the product or service and the market—selling a new product to a market that doesn't exist. Many eager entrepreneurs are so enamored with their own ideas that they convince themselves, "If we build it, they will come." The first risk lies in the ability to build it. The second lies in the ability to identify and convince people they need it. Neither is a task for the faint of budget.

Selling established products to new customers is still a high-risk approach, but it eliminates or at least minimizes the product risk. A company that makes hospital bed liners sells the rejects with minor flaws as cat box liners. This approach can still be costly because you still have to find new customers, but at least you already have a known product.

A business that provides new products to existing customers doesn't have to beat the bushes for customers. "You like strawberry jam? Wait till you taste our strawberry mustard!" There's already an audience hungry for things sweet, red, and gooey.

The least risky kind of business is one that sells an established product or service to an established market. This is where small businesses can shine, particularly by focusing on what Chris Anderson, editor in chief of *Wired* magazine, dubbed the "long tail" of the market.

In his book *The Long Tail*, Anderson talks about why the future of business is selling less of more. Referring to how the Internet has transformed the music, book, and movie rental industries, Anderson writes, "We still obsess over hits, but they are not quite the economic force they once were. Where are those fickle consumers going instead? No single place. They are scattered to the winds as markets fragment into a thousand niches."[1]

An Amazon employee put it this way: "We sold more books today that didn't sell at all yesterday than we sold today of all the books that did sell yesterday."[2] *American Yodeling 1911–1946* may not be a chart-topping LP record, but One-Click® and it can be yours from Amazon. Best of all for the long tail marketers, low demand doesn't mean they have to give it away for a song, either. *American Yodeling* is priced higher today than it was when it made its debut. One Amazon reviewer was so delighted, he ordered two copies.

New technologies are changing the nature of how products are made and delivered. Short production runs are no longer cost prohibitive. Inventory management systems eliminate the need for huge warehouses by manufacturing products as they're needed. What we used to buy off a shelf we now download off the Web. First it was music, then books and video, then software. Now education and training are taking their place on the information highway, too. Perhaps virtual cruises will follow. Electronic creation and delivery slashes costs—though, fortunately for the e-marketer, not the price.

Instead of trying to eke out an existence by grabbing a tiny piece of a huge market, small businesses can succeed by serving niche markets where higher profits, less price sensitivity, and less competition favor small operators. Niches often represent market segments that big companies don't care about or can't serve effectively. Happily, their customers are easy to identify and easy to reach, by definition, and practically any product or service can be aimed at a niche.

A web designer might specialize in environmentally friendly businesses, thus leveraging the time and investment they've already made in understanding that market. Through the many blogs, web sites, associations, social networks, and organizations that green businesses share, a hypothetical How Green Is Your Web Site, Inc., could easily reach prospective customers. The prospects will appreciate not having to educate yet another consultant about their values, concerns, and market, and they'll love the fact that you're one of them.

A public relations wiz might specialize in promoting children's book authors so that she can leverage her industry contacts in that area. Her unique selling advantage is that she knows all the important book reviewers in the business. Her e-mails to them are actually read, not junked. She can easily identify prospective clients by combing the forthcoming book lists or schmoozing with the children's book publishers. Unlike a PR generalist whose testimonials might include Joe's Fish Shack, Thanks A Latte Coffee Emporium, and Bananas'R'Us, her recommendations will come from other successful children's book authors.

An Internet retailer might focus on products for:

- Personal characteristics such as height, weight, age, skin color, hair type, or hair color.
- Location.
- Occupation.
- Hobbies.
- Education.
- Ailments or afflictions.
- Phobias.

What kinds of things might you sell to people who live in places with exceptionally long days or nights (such as Alaskans)? How about blackout curtains? Once you've conquered that market, what other products could you add that might appeal to the same audience? Seasonal affective disorder (SAD syndrome) cures? Weight gain products? Travel services? Contraceptives?

What products would left-handed cooks want? What do arthritic golfers need? How about people with big feet, and those who are bonus size? The long tail offers endless possibilities for the clever entrepreneur.

31

Best-Bet Businesses

The Census Bureau provides data on over 400 types of nonincorporated small businesses. Using that data, we sifted out those that could be done both *from* home and *at* home. In broad terms, they include:

- Businesses selling to other businesses, and businesses selling to consumers (B2B and B2C non-store retail).
- Consumers selling to consumers (C2C nonretail sales).
- Businesses selling services to other businesses (B2B services).
- Businesses providing services to consumers (B2C services).
- Business wholesalers, distributors, and manufacturers.

B2B and B2C Non-store Retailers

Retail businesses represent about 11 percent of home-based businesses. But many failed to make our list because their money is made outside the home through sales in either vending machines, home parties, street fairs, or farmers markets. The best truly home-based retail businesses today are Internet-based.

According to a global survey conducted by The Nielsen Company, over 85 percent of the world's online population has used the Internet to make a purchase, up from just 40 percent two years ago.[1] But we were shocked to learn that even given behemoths such as Amazon, Dell, Office Depot, and Staples, e-commerce only accounts for 3.3 percent of U.S. retail sales.[2]

For the first quarter of 2008, e-commerce sales totaled almost $34 billion. According to Nielsen, the top online purchases were of:[3]

- Books.
- Clothing.
- Videos, DVDs, and games.
- Airline tickets and reservations.
- Electronic equipment.
- Music.
- Cosmetics and nutrition supplies.
- Computer hardware.
- Tours and hotel reservations.
- Event tickets.
- Computer software.
- Groceries.
- Toys/dolls.
- Sporting goods.
- Automobiles and parts.
- Sports memorabilia.

The fastest-growing segment of the market is fashion items (particularly in South Korea, China, Portugal, and France). The cosmetics/nutrition supply and grocery categories are also expanding.

According to Jonathan Carson, president, International, Nielsen Online, "Some of the biggest buyers of books on the Internet are from developing countries—China, Brazil, Vietnam, and Egypt—indicating massive growth potential for online retailers that can specifically target these fast growing markets."[4]

With over 96 percent of retail sales still taking place the old-fashioned way, there are plenty of opportunities for clever entrepreneurs to cash in on e-commerce. Take a look at the preceding list and think about how you might create a niche market in one of those categories.

C2C Nonretail Sales

Before the Web came along, consumer-to-consumer sales of handmade items, collectibles, art, photography, and the like were mostly conducted at street fairs, flea markets, and through word of mouth. Distribution was limited to how far proprietors were willing to travel to peddle their wares. Income was limited to how much time it took to produce each item. And profits were limited by prices that were based on what local markets would bear. Unlike the "make one, sell many" model we recommended earlier, C2C sales used to be typified by a "make one, sell one" approach.

The Web has changed all that. Now, with a little web savvy, local artists, craftsmen, and collectors can tap world markets. PayPal, Google, and others have eliminated the risk of nonpayment. Amazon, eBay, and others have provided the access. And on-demand production is evolving to reduce the costs.

In the late 1990s United Parcel Service ran a commercial that showed a scuba fin, trombone, water bottle, and football being *printed* on a desktop printer. While the funny ad suggested that UPS was the next best thing to instantaneous delivery, the joke may soon be on them. Cornell University's Computational Synthesis Lab recently announced its Fab@Home personal fabrication device (PFD), or fabber. For $3,000 you can assemble one of your very own, but eventually Cornell hopes to create a PFD that can replicate itself.

Known as personal fabrication, rapid prototyping, desktop manufacturing, digital fabrication, freeform fabrication, on-demand manufacturing, and a host of other names, once this technology is diffused into the marketplace, the long tail of just about everything that's made will grow longer. Imagine being able to produce on demand personalized iPhone cases, over-the-ear microphones that actually fit, or triple-E width shoes that don't cramp your style or your toes.

Companies are already off and running with made-to-order products. JuJups.com offers custom picture frames. Figureprints.com lets you order 3D World of Warcraft characters. Fabjectory.com helps bring your SecondLife avatar or SketchUp design to life. Zazzle.com, Qoop.com, and CafePress.com allow you to design your own T-shirts, mugs, and other novelties. ImageKind.com, DeviantArt.com, and iStockPhoto.com allow you to market your greeting cards and other photographic products. And Lulu.com lets you print your own books.

At the same time, virtual stores have become easy to start and more widely accepted by consumers.

Trendwatching.com reports that, according to a 2005 survey conducted by eBay, almost three-quarters of a million Americans consider eBay their primary or secondary source of income. In addition to the professional eBay sellers, another 1.5 million individuals say they supplement their income by selling on eBay.[5] More recent but unconfirmed sources suggest the number has doubled since then.

Google AdSense, the leading source of click-through ad income on the Web, paid almost $1.7 billion to its participant web sites in 2007, up 40 percent from the year prior.[6]

If you have a consumer-to-consumer business idea, the easiest approach to reaching a web-based audience is to set up a store on eBay, Yahoo!, and Amazon.

If you choose to also develop your own web site, you'll need a domain name, web hosting, and payment mechanism. Links to our favorite providers of these services and other resources are on our web site at UndressForSuccessOnline.com.

B2B and B2C Services

Because it's easy to parlay your skills or talents into an income with little or no start-up cost, companies that provide services to businesses or consumers represent over half of all home-based businesses. Based on tax return data, professional, scientific, and technical services earn the highest profit margins of all home-based businesses—almost 30 percent.[7] But, in this category too, we've had to eliminate most of the jobs in construction, health, social service, and retail because they don't meet our from-home/at-home criteria.

We looked at a number of home-based service businesses for "solopreneurs" in Part 3. For those with more ambitious business goals, and the skills to pull it off, the freelance model can be expanded to include employees, subcontractors, or a network of symbiotic providers. This broader business model solves some of the issues inherent in the freelance approach—particularly the "when you stop, the income stops" problem—but it adds its own issues as well. Primarily these include the time, energy, and cost of managing people, quality control issues, and the threat of your customers going direct to one of your associates.

Take another look at the freelance business categories in Table 22.2 (see Chapter 22) for some ideas about the kinds of businesses that fit the B2B and B2C service model.

B2B Wholesalers and Manufacturers

Wholesalers buy and resell in bulk, but less than 3 percent of home businesses engage in wholesale trade. Those that do typically either warehouse their purchases or utilize drop-shipping and just-in-time inventory strategies to avoid rental and real estate costs. Most home-based wholesalers are agents—brokers involved in the sale of nondurable goods such as machinery, wood and metal products, and electronics.[8]

Home-based manufacturing accounts for only 2 percent of home businesses. Metalwork, furniture, and apparel manufacturing account for most of home-based manufacturing. Food, printing, and other categories barely show up in the numbers.

32

Business Planning

You've looked at your motivations, personality, and talents. You've seen what kinds of home-based businesses are most successful. By this point, you probably have a good idea of what kind of business you want to start. Now it's time to put together a course of action that will turn your home-based business dream into a reality. For that you need a plan.

In my two decades helping business owners grapple with growth and survival issues—first as a bank lender and later as a business consultant—I've seen firsthand that businesses that fail to plan, plan to fail.

A business plan, whether formal or informal, allows you to dry-run your business concept. It forces you to think things through. It walks you through all of the parts of a business before your living is on the line. Better to do the research before you commit than to fumble around for solutions once you're engrossed in the day-to-day running of the business.

Unless you're trying to raise money from lenders or investors, the format for your business plan doesn't really matter. In fact, it doesn't even have to be a formal business plan at all.

Whole books are devoted to how to write a business plan, so we're not going to try to show you how to do that in a few pages. Instead, what follows is an overview of the kinds of questions you should be able to answer before you act on your entrepreneurial seizure.

Marketing

The single best piece of advice we could offer a business owner is this: Financial success comes from *marketing* what you do, not from *doing* what you do. You can have the best dang product or service in the world, but if no one knows that it exists, you'll fail. It's not an exaggeration to say that a well-defined marketing plan with a fuzzy product concept is far more likely to succeed than a well-defined product with a fuzzy market concept. The world's greatest golf gadget will be permanently stuck in the rough if you don't know how to reach the pros.

Your marketing plan is *the* pivotal section of your overall business plan. If you don't clearly understand your market and have a specific strategy for how you're going to generate sales, the rest of your plan will be meaningless.

Entrepreneurial wannabes are famous for back-of-an-envelope marketing plans that go something like this: "The market for our whiz-bang bicycle accessory (which they describe *ad nauseum*) includes 1.3 billion Chinese. Since, as everyone knows, they all ride bicycles, we've conservatively projected a 1 percent market share or 13 million units in year one." Sorry, but it just doesn't work that way.

Here are the questions you should be able to answer about the market for your business:

The Product/Market
- What are your primary and secondary products or services?
- How is your market segmented, and what segment will you go after?
- How will you test the market?
- How many customers are there?
- How many of those customers can you realistically reach and how quickly?

Your Customers
- Who exactly are your potential customers?
- What are their demographics?
- What do they read?
- What do they buy?

Your Competition
- Who are your competitors, direct and indirect?
- What are their strengths and weaknesses?
- What market advantage do they have over you?

- What competitive advantage do you have over them?
- What's to keep others from copying you?
- Why will customers choose you over the competition? (Price? Service? Quality? Customization? Personal Attention?)

Pricing
- How will you determine your prices?
- What profit margin will those prices provide?
- How will your prices compare to those of your competition?
- How sensitive is the market to price?
- What will happen if you have to cut prices?

Advertising and Promotion
- How will you identify/reach prospective customers?
- Where will you advertise?
- How will you promote the product or service?
- What will it cost to market your product or service?
- How will you measure the results of your promotional efforts?

The Sales Process
- What difficulties are you likely to encounter in converting potential customers into buyers?
- How long will it take to convert each prospect into a buyer?

Distribution
- How will you deliver your product or service?
- How will you scale up if you get busy?
- How will you handle customer support, returns, guarantees, complaints?

Operations

Think through how you're going to handle the day-to-day running of the business. Who will answer the phone, create invoices and receipts, pack and ship your product, or deliver your service? If the answer is you, what happens when you're at the grocery store or sick in bed?

Organization

- Will you be organized as a sole proprietorship, partnership, or corporation?
- Who can you enlist as formal and informal advisers? What do they bring to the talent pool that is missing?
- If you plan to have employees, what are their job descriptions? How will you recruit them? What will you pay them? How will you manage them remotely?
- What expenses will you have prior to start-up?

Licensing and Insurance

- What licenses or permits do you need and how will you obtain them?
- What insurance is needed/available? What will it cost?
- Are there any regulatory issues to consider?

Vendors, Suppliers, Contractors

- From whom will you buy, or whom will you hire as subcontractors?
- What alternatives are available if they don't work out?
- What will your suppliers/subcontractors cost?
- What are their terms of sale? (COD? Payment in 30 days?)
- How will you deal with cost increases?
- Could you and your vendors/contractors handle a sudden large order?

Financial

Based on the information from your marketing and operations research, you ought to be able to develop a start-up budget as well as monthly sales and expense projections. Doing *monthly* projections is essential. The timing of when you're going to pay that insurance premium, when you'll actually collect from that big sale, when you're going to have to shell out money for ads, and so forth, is what will determine how red the ink in the checking account may get. Without that knowledge and a plan for how to deal with start-up and early unprofitable operations, you'll be in trouble before you start. Even if the business is successful, you can quickly find yourself "growing broke" if you can't finance the cash gap that occurs between the time you spend money on supplies or raw materials and when you collect money from sales.

Here are some of the financial questions you should be able to answer:

- How much money do you need to cover start-up expenses?
- How much more might you need to finance the period between when you have to pay your bills and when your customers will pay you?
- Will there be any seasonality in your income?
- What is your gross profit margin?
- What are your fixed monthly expenses?
- At what point do you break even (where gross profits cover fixed expenses)?
- What will the financial impact be if it takes longer?
- How will a best-case and a worst-case scenario affect your cash flow?

There's simply no excuse for blindly launching a business without nailing down exactly what your costs are going to be. Everything you have to do to figure those out is something you'll have to do once you're in business, anyway. Why wait until it's too late to learn what you need to know? Projecting your income, by contrast, is more art than science, and that's why you need to look at high and low scenarios.

A word of caution here: *Spreadsheetitis* is a common ailment among business start-ups. By tweaking the spreadsheet, it's easy to produce any result you want. Once it's on paper, it's easy to start to believe it's real, even though you know the results are based on unsubstantiated assumptions. You're only kidding yourself if you allow yourself to fall into this trap. Spreadsheets don't go bankrupt—entrepreneurs do.

If you've written your plan down, have a few trusted advisers read it. It's amazing how often a novice—say, a nine-year-old—can spot the fatal flaws that elude those who have fallen victim to the entrepreneurial seizure.

33

Naked Truths about Home Biz

Running a small business isn't the bowl of cherries some might wish to believe. The National Federation of Independent Businesses regularly polls its members about what keeps them up at night. (See Table 33.1.)[1]

Many are self-explanatory, but here are our thoughts on some of the things that tend to sour the entrepreneurial experience.

Health Coverage

According to the National Federation for Independent Business survey, health insurance costs were a critical issue for almost two-thirds of respondents.[2]

As an employee, your employer paid some of your health care costs. For some, replacing health care coverage is so difficult and/or costly that it bursts their entrepreneurial bubble altogether. In some states, such as California, pre-existing conditions can preclude you from getting individual coverage at all. Individual or even group health coverage (such as one offered by an association or other membership organization) will likely cost significantly more than what your employer paid.

In addition to the owner's health care woes, the cost of health care limits their ability to grow and attract good employees.

Taxes

The IRS requires that business owners pay themselves a salary. On that salary, you'll owe *both* the employer and the employee share of taxes. On

Table 33.1   Small Business Owners' Top
Concerns

Cost of health insurance (56%)
Fuel costs (42%)
Business taxes (25%)
Property taxes (25%)
Workers' compensation costs (24%)
Tax complexity (23%)
Unreasonable government regulations (21%)
State taxes (21%)
Cash flow (21%)
Locating qualified workers (20%)
Death taxes (20%)
Cost and availability of liability insurance (19%)
Finding and keeping skilled employees (18%)
Poor profits (17%)
Cost of supplies/inventories (17%)
Electricity costs (16%)
Frequent changes in federal tax laws/rules (15%)
High fixed costs (13%)
Social Security taxes (13%)
Controlling my time (13%)

the employer side, this includes Social Security taxes (7.5 percent) and a handful of other federal, state, and local levies.

But the tax burden doesn't stop on page two of your tax return. The tax system is so complex that it's practically impossible for small business owners to prepare their own tax returns—that adds another $500 to $2,000 to your cost of compliance.

Extra Paperwork

Uncle Sam and most states don't like to wait for tax income from business owners. As a result, you'll need to file and pay quarterly estimated taxes. If you sell products that are subject to sales tax, you'll be responsible for monthly, quarterly, or annual payments of those, as well. If you have employees, the paper pushing never ceases.

Workers' Compensation

As the owner, you can exempt yourself from workers' compensation, but if you have employees it's another story. Here in California, workers' compensation rates are a weird nightmare. The nightmare part is the high rate. The weird part is how they're determined. In our flying business, the rate for pilots was 12 percent—so we paid 12 cents to the California Division of Workers' Compensation over and above every dollar of pilot salary. The rate for ground crew, the kids who swept floors and helped people into the airplanes, was *18* percent, 50 percent higher. Go figure. And if that wasn't bad enough, if one of our office staff *ever* helped in the hangar, the workers' compensation rate would go from 3 to 18 percent for that job, regardless of who held the position or how often they did it.

No Sick Days, Paid Holidays, or Paid Vacation

Can you imagine taking a job that offered no time off, no sick days, no paid holidays, no vacation? The average employee receives a month of pay each year for time they don't work. As a small business owner, you'll find the boss far less generous.

No Benefits

Your new employer (you) won't offer a 401(k), retirement plan, or gym membership, either.

The Buck Stops Here

We all make mistakes. Some are bigger than others. As an employee, regardless of how big the mistake you make, someone else pays to clean it up. As a business owner, your screwups are your problem. We once spent $5,000 on an ad that produced zero calls, never mind any sales. Ouch.

No Safety Net

For most business owners, there's no unemployment insurance, workers' compensation, disability insurance, or other safety net to break the fall.

Lawsuits Lurk at Every Corner

We probably don't have to pontificate on how lawsuit-happy the world has become, but for a business owner, lawsuits are a sad reality. In our flying business, we required our passengers to sign a four-page "we didn't mean it, you can't sue us" release of liability. Still, we feared the day when someone would trip over their own feet and sue us for their clumsiness. It never happened, and we never had to fall back on the waiver, but it's sad to have to run your business based on thinking that runs from the courtroom back.

Liability insurance to protect your business, if you can find it, is expensive. While it isn't noted in the list of concerns in Table 33.1, 1 in 10 business owners consider the cost and availability of liability insurance a critical problem.

So Much to Do, So Little Time

Small business owners stretch themselves pretty thin. There's always more to do. The only way to clear your to-do list is to close the business, sell it, or die. For some people, being constantly busy is a good thing. For others, especially those who tend to get lost in the minutiae, it can be a real problem.

The Home Business Stigma

Though attitudes are changing, there are still people who will dismiss your business as a hobby because you choose to forego the commute, save gas, reduce pollution, and spend more time with your family and friends.

Regulation

Even with the best of intentions, it's easy to run afoul of some federal, state, county, city, or even homeowner association regulation.

Here's one we encountered. A pilot can earn a license at age 16 (14 in a glider or sailplane). But according to the job police they can't earn money to pay for lessons, by rubbing grease off planes or sweeping the hangar floor, until they're 18. In spite of our honest efforts to comply with every rule the government threw at us, this was one of those little nuances we weren't aware of until we'd been in business for 12 years.

In another situation, we bought a lovely old Studebaker pickup, in tip-top shape, to advertise the business. The first night we parked it outside our condo, the homeowners association notified us that we couldn't keep it there. Apparently, vehicles with signage were considered a neighborhood eyesore. Oddly, they didn't seem to have a problem with the realtor's Cadillac with company information on their car door panels.

Before you embark on a business, be sure to do a thorough search of the rules and regulations that might affect you. Find a small business association that puts out alerts to changes, or use a Google Alert to clue you in to any changes that might impact your business. Violations, even unintentional ones, can be costly. Home-based businesses should be particularly careful of local or homeowner association rules that may limit their activities.

Effect on Personal Credit

If you've never been self-employed, you probably haven't noticed the little box on all credit applications that says, "Check here if self-employed." It might as well say, "Check here and you can be sure it will be harder for you to get a loan." Here's why it's harder for small business owners to obtain personal credit: (a) business use of personal credit cards affects your credit score; (b) personal guarantees on business loans (which are universally required for small businesses) may appear as contingent liabilities on your credit report; and (c) consumer lenders are used to dealing with 1099 and W-2 income. Since a small business owner's primary income comes from the net profit of their business (which is not reported on a 1099 or W-2), their tax returns look different from those of a typical consumer. The fact that business owners do their best to minimize their taxable income (and some risk takers try to hide it altogether) doesn't help, either.

5

Does It Come with Batteries?

34

Home-Based Technology

As recent as a century ago, the majority of work depended on muscle: A shovel and a pick and a dynamite stick, and—heigh-ho, heigh-ho—it's off to work you'd go. Not any more. Today the majority of work depends on brains, not brawn, and the tools of the trade are information technologies.

This chapter will help you understand the tools you'll need for communications, collaboration, and security. Some types of e-work require more technology than others. As writers, we sit five feet from each other and our needs are simple—a computer and an Internet connection and we're good to go. Setting up a meeting requires just a slight turn of our heads. Other e-work is more technology-intense and may require a whole host of tools such as virtual private networks, teleconferencing, real-time file sharing, and more.

As we scouted the Web for information about the best e-work technologies, we ran across a blog called GeekDoctor (GeekDoctor .blogspot.com). It's written by John D. Halamka, M.D., M.S., who is, among other things, the chief information officer and dean of technology at Harvard Medical School. What drew us to him, aside from his credentials, is that he wasn't always a supporter of e-work.

"I used to believe that productivity was optimized when everyone met and worked in close physical proximity. I didn't think telecommuting was right for information technology departments," wrote Halamka. He's since done an about-face, but has learned that giving people access to the right technologies is key to a successful work-at-home program.

With his help, we put together this summary of the naked truth about e-work technology.

As always, you'll find updates and links to all of our favorite technologies at UndressForSuccessOnline.com.

Your Office

While not technology per se, your office is the backbone of your e-work program. It needs to be a dedicated space where you can isolate yourself from distractions. Having a sense of mental separation is important.

Comfort counts, too. I used to think ergonometrically designed desks, chairs, keyboards, and the like were a sham. That was before my hand started to go numb and my back, shoulders, and neck started to spasm. What I've paid in doctor and physical therapy visits could have paid for a top-of-the-line desk chair many times over. All of which is to say, if you're going to be spending a third of your life (or more) in front of a computer, don't scrimp on the accommodations.

Telephone

You'll probably want a separate phone line for your office. When *USA Today* calls for an interview, you don't want to accidentally answer, "Hey, what's up?" A separate line will also help track your expenses come tax time.

To avoid the hassle and expense of installing a separate landline, a cellular phone might do, but many virtual employers require a separate landline. If you do install a new phone line, it's far cheaper to set it up as a personal line (don't tell the phone company you read that here). However, if you're running a home business and want your company listed in the white or yellow pages, you'll have to install a business line.

If incoming calls are the issue, you can avoid installing another physical phone line by adding what's called a remote-call forwarding (RCF) line. It's a phone number that doesn't have a physical location. You simply use call-forwarding to program where the phone rings—for example, into your home phone line or your cell phone. If the "distinct ring" feature is available in your area, you can set up your regular phone to play a different ring tone when a business call comes in to that line—personally, we liked the cash register *ka-ching* tone. Caller ID can also help distinguish business calls from personal calls.

The problem with all of these options is that they rely on you to program and unprogram them as you move from place to place. If you're like me, you'll forget more times than you remember, particularly when you're expecting an important call. After years of struggling for a solution to answering the phones in our flightseeing business, we found a company called FreedomVoice that offered a simple, elegant, and inexpensive solution to the problem.

We routed our phone lines to them and, through an easy online interface, we set up an elaborate hierarchy to manage how calls were routed and what customers heard when they called. The computer, a virtual operator, offered callers the option of receiving voice or fax information about our airplane rides or reaching a real live human. Depending on what they wanted—a reservation, weather update, gift certificate, or just to talk—their call was routed to the appropriate recording or person. As staff schedules changed, a few computer clicks was all it took to update the routing. If we were in the car, the technology would hunt though our phone lines until it found us.

We hate voice mail and endless menus as much as anybody, but FreedomVoice offered a professional solution and allowed us to inject some fun into the mix. We added engine sounds, honky-tonk music, and even some on-hold humor: "We're busier than a one-armed wing walker with a wedgie, but hang on, and we'll be right with you." We actually had folks complain if someone answered a call too quickly because they were enjoying the on-hold entertainment.

In the off-hours, the system recorded caller messages and forwarded them (as either a sound or text file) to our e-mail, fax, or iPhone. This is starting to sound like a commercial for FreedomVoice, but the naked truth is we didn't find anything else that worked as well.

Your Computer

If you plan to earn a living working at home, you'll need your own dedicated computer—sharing it with the family Guitar Hero fan just won't cut it. We happen to be Apple lovers, finding Macs more intuitive, user-friendly, and reliable than any PC we've worked with. Aside from the odd game or flight simulator, every business program we've ever needed is available for the Mac.

Of course, your choice of technology is your own, unless your employer specifies the kind of computer you use—sadly, that will probably be a PC.

Regardless of your choice, size matters. Buy the biggest hard drive and the most memory you can afford.

File Sharing

Sharing and transferring large files with clients and collaborators may require something more than e-mail (which will only handle up to about 10 megabytes). File transfer protocol (FTP) is one solution, but it's complicated to configure. If you're using Elance, Guru, or one of the other large freelance job sites, file transfer mechanisms are built into the work management systems. If not, you'll probably want to sign up with a company that supports file transfers up to a couple of gigabytes. Services such as these allow you to upload your file to a secure web site and then e-mail a user name and password to your collaborators so they can then access and download it.

Communicating

Communication may be the single most important element in a work-at-home arrangement. It doesn't matter if you're telecommuting, free-lancing, or running a small business from your home, your capability (and ability) to communicate what you're doing and what you're thinking will be pivotal. Technology has added lots of choices for the virtual equivalent of popping your head over the cubicle.

E-mail

E-mail is by far the most widely used method of virtual communications. We recommend you choose a service that offers remote access to your e-mail from anywhere and to any device. We use Apple's Mail application to access our Google Gmail accounts. Since we also have a few non-Gmail accounts, we forward the others to Gmail so that all our e-mail is available in one account. Other e-mail applications accomplish much the same thing but, in our opinion, with less panache than Apple Mail.

Instant Messaging (IM)

Many companies have developed an instant messaging (IM) culture for communications. One of the frustrations with IM, Halamka found, is that no one has yet done a good job of providing a system that works across all platforms (Linux, Mac, and Windows), or that allows users of different IM services to easily connect with each other. That means you have to pretty much have an account with each of the major providers to effectively use IM with a broad audience. One solution Halamka found recently is a company called Trillian that can bring together most of the major IM networks.

The major IM services are Google Talk, AOL, MSN Messenger, AIM Triton, Yahoo! Messenger, Skype, and ICQ.

Personal Digital Assistants (PDAs)

Halamka, who reviews over 700 e-mails a day, lives by his Blackberry. He's tried Treo, the early iPhones, and a number of Windows-based mobile devices, but for high-volume e-mail management, he prefers Blackberry. Second-generation iPhones, however, are already giving Blackberry a run for their messages.

Audio and Video Teleconferencing

As we've discussed, e-mail and instant messaging often fail to deliver the intended message because of their low bandwidth. For important communications, particularly those that involve multiple parties, higher fidelity may be needed. By adding tone of voice cues, a simple telephone call can communicate far better than the written word. For those times when body language really matters, videoconferencing offers the next best thing to being there.

Teleconferencing

We're not avid teleconferencing users, but Halamka's a big fan. "It works well, is low cost, and the technology is mature. I don't need an engineer to set it up, and I can use any mobile or landline phone I wish," says Halamka.

If you're tired of trying to set up a multiperson call on your regular phone, or if you need to create a teleconference for a large number of people, check out *free* conference calling with a company such as Freeconference.com or Instantconference.com. You can choose to have participants call in via an 800 line (you pay the charges), or save money by making it a toll call.

Voice over Internet Protocol (VoIP)

VoIP telephone service is becoming a mainstream competitor to POTS (plain old telephone service—we didn't make that up, that's what it's called). Companies such as Google, Microsoft, Yahoo!, and Skype offer free software and free computer-to-computer calls anywhere in the world over the Internet. Companies such as Time Warner and Cox offer VoIP phone service as part of their broadband packages. FreedomVoice offers an innovative and very cost-effective VoIP option as well.

While we often use VoIP to save calling costs, we haven't yet abandoned our landline or mobile phones. Availability and voice quality just isn't yet up to par with POTS, and not being able to make a call when the Internet is down, which still happens occasionally, is a real disadvantage.

Video Conferencing

Sometimes a picture is worth a thousand words, but full-on video conferencing can be expensive and quirky. If you need video conferencing, for the small business budget, Halamka found Mac's iChat (OS X with QuickTime 7) to be the only usable desktop solution.

Blogs

Blogging is a good way for freelance and entrepreneurial e-workers to connect with customers and prospects.

Blogger, WordPress, and TypePad are the leading blog platforms. We've used all three, but WordPress is our favorite for ease of use, available plug-ins, and easy integration of advertising options. Keep in mind however, that just having a blog won't do you much good. To be an effective business tool it needs to have useful and dynamic content, and you need to let the world know it exists.

Social Networking Sites

We looked at the job search details of social networking in Chapter 21, but they're also becoming a mainstream communications, work management, and collaboration tool. Networking sites such as Facebook, LinkedIn, Plaxo, SecondLife, and others encourage users to interact through chat, messaging, e-mail, video, voice chat, file sharing, blogging, discussion groups, and more.

One leading-edge company, Home2Office, has built an entire e-work management program around a social networking platform. It combines information technology, facilities, human resources management, and performance measurement systems; tracks employer cost savings and productivity increases; and even measures the greenhouse gases saved by program participants. As we go to print, the State of California is considering the Home2Office program for management of office-based and e-work staff. The program is priced to serve companies both large and small.

Remote Access to Your Computer and Desktop Sharing

There are two types of remote access. One allows someone else (or you) to log on to your computer and operate it remotely—if someone is in front of it to approve the access. The other allows you to access your computer from another computer or web-based device without the aid of someone sitting at the other end. The former is great for remote tech support. The latter is especially handy if you're on the road and realize you need a file from your home computer.

Built-in operating system tools that allow this include Apple's File Sharing and, in the Windows environment, Offline Files and Folders and the Windows Briefcase.

For $19.99 a month, web-based platform GoToMyPC® allows you to remotely access, transfer, and sync files on your Mac or PC from any web browser.

Presentation and Desktop-Sharing Tools

Presentation and desktop-sharing tools seem to offer the most promise for virtual collaboration. This class of tools enables a presenter to deliver content over the Web. "Remote presentation tools enable me to assemble virtual teams, convey ideas, seek feedback, and avoid commuting," says Halamka.

The most affordable of this class of tools is GotoMeeting® by Citrix. This web-based product works on Windows and Mac. It costs $39.00 per month for up to 15 users, and includes an integrated voice conference service. It allows presenters to draw, highlight, and point to items on participants' computer screens and allows them to collaborate on documents in real time.

Backup and Storage

Having a backup of the important information on your computer is an absolute must. Fire, flood, earthquake, or burglary can cripple you. One month before our deadline for the delivery of this book, we had two hard drives die on two different computers. Thanks to Apple's phenomenal customer service, we sent ours in and received new hard drives within 48 hours. Using our backups, we recovered all the lost information in a couple of hours.

For on-site backup, the best choices for individual files are DVDs and memory sticks. If you have large amounts of data to back up, you'll need an external hard drive. For off-site backup, you could drop DVDs at a neighbor's house, but that's not an automated process. A better solution is to buy web-based remote storage and schedule your computer to perform daily or even hourly backups automatically.

For $99 per year, you can receive 20 gigabytes of storage with Apple's MobileMe. Other good choices include Mozy and Carbonite.

Automatic though they may be, check your backups frequently to make sure they're doing what they're supposed to, and that the backup files are usable.

Security Issues

Firewalls, antivirus and malware software, and intrusion detection programs to protect you from network infiltration are essential e-work tools. Many of these are built into your computer's operating system, but they're only as good as the person using them. Be sure they're set up properly and kept up-to-date as new versions are released.

If you'll be accessing company data from your home office, you'll probably do so through what's called a virtual private network (VPN). You log on to the VPN through your Windows, Mac, or Linux platform by entering a security code. Some systems authenticate users with a so-called *dongle* or security token—essentially a constantly changing electronic key that you plug into a USB port on your computer. In a VPN environment, the central computer maintains the operating system (Vista® updates, for example), delivers any necessary application patches, and ensures the antivirus software on your machine is up-to-date. Once that's done, you're granted access to the company's applications, files, and network through a web browser.

Human error is to blame for a large number of security breaches—a memory stick left on the table at the Coffee Bean, a password that's easily guessed or accessible, unencrypted file transfers or e-mails, or unsecured Wi-Fi networks.

Keep security and privacy in mind as you undress for success.

6

What If Everybody Did It?

35

Let's All Undress

As we've shown, e-work offers a new way to work—a new model for employers and new opportunities for freelancers and entrepreneurs. But the impact of e-work goes well beyond individual or corporate benefits; it will impact our nation and the world.

"We keep trying to solve energy and environmental problems with transportation solutions. Likewise, we keep trying to improve economic, educational, and wellness conditions through traditional employment solutions. Empowering individuals through e-work is the solution," says Jack Heacock, co-founder of the Telework Coalition.[1]

A strong national e-work program can dramatically reduce our fossil fuel dependence and slow global warming. It can increase productivity. It can provide new employment opportunities for at-home caregivers, the disabled, and the un- and underemployed. It can offer rural and economically disadvantaged populations access to better jobs. It can improve family life and emancipate latchkey kids. It can bolster pandemic and disaster preparedness. It can reduce traffic jams and the carnage on our highways. It can alleviate the strain on our crumbling transportation infrastructure. It can help reclaim many of the jobs that have been lost to offshoring. And the billions of dollars saved by companies and individuals could fuel economic growth and bolster retirement savings.[2]

Almost 50 million Americans hold jobs that are suitable for e-work, yet they still drive to an office each workday. If they e-worked just half the time (the national e-work average) it would reduce our dependence on Persian Gulf oil imports by almost 60 percent[3] and lower greenhouse gas emissions by an amount equivalent to the fossil fuel burn for transportation in New York State.[4] At the same time, because home offices use a third less electricity than traditional work places, the new e-workers would save enough electricity to power all the homes in Idaho, New Hampshire, and Maine.[5]

The size of the new at-home workforce would also reduce the need for new office space. The greenhouse gas savings from less construction would have the same effect as taking 5 million cars off the road.[6] But the potential of e-work goes even further than that.

Traffic congestion alone robs the U.S. economy of $80 billion in productivity each year.[7] Over 4 billion hours per year are wasted in traffic—the same as 2 million workers sitting around doing nothing from 9 to 5.[8] Those hypothetical slackers are pissed off and stressed out, too; 40 percent of drivers admit they retaliate against other drivers for perceived impositions, and 70 percent have flipped someone off or tailgated to get even.[9] And just to make things worse, half of all nonrecurring congestion is caused by gawkers and lane closures caused by accidents.[10] Our new e-workers would save more than 2,000 lives, prevent almost 150,000 injuries, and save $23 billion a year in associated costs.[11]

What's more, according to John Edwards, chairman and founder of the Telework Coalition, for every 1 percent reduction in cars there's a 3 percent reduction in congestion,[12] meaning our new e-workers could eliminate traffic jams in many parts of the country, and reduce them by almost 50 percent overall.[13] Good thing, too, because over the past two decades our road capacity has already fallen so far behind that roadway expansion would have to double just to catch up.[14] By 2025, we'll need an additional 104,000 lane-miles of capacity to handle the projected load. Funding those improvements would effectively turn $525 billion tax dollars to stone.[15]

The Reason Foundation predicts that if traffic continues to grow at the current pace, over the next couple of decades, drivers in Atlanta, Baltimore, Chicago, Denver, Las Vegas, Miami, Minneapolis-St. Paul, Portland, San Francisco-Oakland, Seattle-Tacoma, and Washington, D.C., will be sitting in daily traffic jams worse than the infamous traffic jams that plague Los Angeles eight hours a day.[16] Commutes will take almost twice as long, and you'll have to leave even earlier to allow for traffic jams if you have to arrive someplace at a specific time, producing a further reduction to our national productivity.[17]

Four big-city mayors told Congress in 2008 they were overwhelmed by infrastructure needs and can't maintain their water systems, roads, and rail networks without more federal help.[18] But do bipartisan Congressional measures that address the critical needs of our nation's major infrastructure systems even mention telecommunications or e-work? Nope.

Yet cheap communications has been the catalyst for change throughout man's history, according to Tom Malone in *The Future of Work*. Until the 1800s, he points out, businesses were small and local—in many ways, bands of hunters and gatherers. "But by the 1900s," he says, "new communication technologies like the telegraph, the telephone, the typewriter, and carbon paper finally provided enough communication capacity to allow businesses to grow and centralize on a large scale, as governments had begun to do many millennia earlier."[19]

Now broadband technologies have put communications into the hands of individuals and allowed them to become (job) hunters and (information) gatherers. Still, there's a lot of room for improvement.

U.S. broadband services come in fourteenth slowest in speed and eighteenth highest in price compared to European and Asian countries. The average U.S. broadband download speed is more than 10 times slower and more than 20 times more expensive than in Japan, which has the fastest and cheapest Internet service in the world.[20] For all its technological might, as of 2008 the U.S. ranked fifteenth in the world in terms of broadband Internet access for its population.[21] Broadband access is not even available to a quarter of Americans—rural and low-income populations are the most underserved.[22]

Nevertheless, people are starting to notice that e-work can make a difference.

Since the mid-1990s e-work has been an important part of federal disaster-preparedness planning. In 2007, both the House and Senate approved legislation to encourage e-work for federal workers, and in 2008 new measures were introduced to help promote e-work as the default rather than the exception. Pending legislation would increase e-work eligibility and participation for federal employees, improve training, and require results measurement. Meanwhile, the Small Business Administration (SBA) has been charged with helping to promote e-work to corporate America with educational materials and outreach programs.

Arizona, California, Connecticut, Maryland, Oregon, Texas, Virginia, and Washington have active e-work programs, including some that encourage businesses to adopt e-work with financial incentives and free assistance. Representatives from the state of Hawaii and the Canadian provinces of British Columbia, Quebec, and Prince Edward Island recently asked for our help in evaluating their e-work potential.

The Positively Broadband Campaign—a coalition of companies and trade associations committed to fostering demand for broadband services—suggested way back in 2002 that just as

> . . . government subsidizes commuter use of mass transit [they] should consider comparable subsidies for e-work. Governments should also assist small and mid-sized companies' transition to e-work through education and consulting services that help establish e-work programs [and] should also promote e-work case studies and model programs.[23]

"Many companies in the private sector have utilized e-work with great success to enhance productivity for workers and improve work-life balance. It's time the government capitalized on those same benefits," said Harris N. Miller, president of the Information Technology Association of America (ITAA), a member of the Positively Broadband Campaign. "We believe that by taking steps to evaluate, plan for, and implement e-work policies, the government will be doing a great service to taxpayers, federal workers, and the economy by spurring broadband adoption," Miller added.

Rep. Frank Wolf, a champion of telework within Congress, greeted the coalition's efforts, noting:

> Federal agencies must lead by example. At the moment, telework is a great idea waiting to happen. As we proceed with business as usual, our roads have become badly congested, frequent ozone alerts have become a rite of summer, and workers are bearing the brunt of management practices well behind the technology curve. We agree that broadband can be a major enabler of telework and telecommuting. We welcome the useful ideas and suggestions of the Positively Broadband Campaign for creating telework incentives within the federal government as well as the private sector.[24]

With the cost per lane-mile of urban highway at almost $4 million[25] and the cost per mile of information superhighway at a mere $20,000,[26] this investment in America's future must be a national priority. Without it, the Americans who need it most will not have access to e-work.

There are many other steps that should be taken to encourage individuals, companies, and communities to support e-work:

- The Internet access tax moratorium, currently in effect until 2014, needs to be made permanent so that companies can plan their Internet futures.
- State and local taxing authorities need to abolish policies that double-tax home-based workers. For example, if you telecommute from your Connecticut home and your company office is in New York City, the Big Apple feels you owe them taxes on all your work, and so does Connecticut.
- Local zoning laws need to be relaxed to accommodate home-based work. Home office tax credits should be allowed for part-time e-workers, and employed e-workers should be able to deduct their home office equipment costs.
- Health insurance should be made available and affordable for small businesses and solopreneurs.
- Business leaders must learn the benefits of, invest in, and develop corporate cultures that fully support e-work.

Finally, for you, it's time to find your way home. If that means convincing your employer to let you e-work, head to our web site and we'll help you develop your proposal. If it means finding a new job, check out our links to e-work employers and useful job search sites. If you're ready to freelance in your frillies or follow your entrepreneurial dream, stop by our site for updates on the latest resources that will help you on your way.

Make the road less traveled your way to work.

Resources Available at UndressForSuccessOnline.com

We promised our publisher 60,000 words, but we actually wrote almost double that. In the interest of saving face, and trees, we've made the rest of our thoughts available to you as bonus material, virtually, on our web site. As a book buyer, you'll also gain access to discounts on our services and publications, including an e-book titled *Finding Money—Secrets of a Former Banker, Confessions of an Entrepreneur*.

To access the bonus information, you'll need to enter a special book-buyer code that's buried in the text of this book. You'll find a pirate's treasure map on our web site that will lead you to it.

Anti-Scam Resources

- New scams as we find them.
- What to do if you've been scammed.

Pajama Job Resources

- Our e-work proposal template and links to others.
- Links to sample e-work agreements.
- Links to the best e-work job boards and specialty sites.
- Links to e-work jobs and employers.
- Lists of e-work-friendly companies.
- Links to free job training resources for disabled persons and military spouses.
- Links to free and low-cost technical skills testing.

Freelance In Your Frillies Resources

- Links to sample statement of work, change order, project agreement, and nondisclosure agreements.
- Links to sources of freelance work.

Bedroom Business Resources

- Links to our favorite entrepreneurial assistance sites.

Other Resources

- Our favorite technology picks.
- Links to all our favorite books, web sites, blogs, services, and products.
- Information about federal, state, and local e-work initiatives.
- Links to organizations that support work-life balance.
- Links to other e-work resources.

Notes

Introduction

1. Alvin Toffler, *Future Shock* (Bantam Books, 1970).
2. WorldatWork 2006 Telework Trendlines™ commissioned from the Dieringer Research Group, http://www.workingfromanywhere.org/.
3. Society for Human Resource Management, 2006 Benefits Survey Report, p. 1.

Chapter 1 Who eWorks and What Do They Do?

1. Thomas W. Malone, *The Future of Work* (Harvard Business School Press, 2004), front matter.
2. According to the U.S. SBA Office of Advocacy, *Frequently Asked Questions*, 2007, 52 percent of the nation's 26.8 million small businesses are home-based. http://www.sba.gov/advo/stats/sbfaq.pdf.
3. U.S. Census Bureau, *2006 American Community Survey*, Table B08301—people who reported that their principal mode of travel to work was "work at home."
4. WorldatWork, Trendlines—referring to employees who work remotely at least one day per month during regular working hours.
5. Ibid.
6. Ibid.
7. Ibid.
8. Kenexa Research Institute, *2007 WorkTrends*™ survey of over 10,000 U.S. workers drawn to match the latest U.S. census and thus characteristic of the population as a whole.
9. WorldatWork, Trendlines.
10. Kenexa, *WorkTrends*.
11. Georgetown University, *Workplace Flexibility 2010, Flexible Work Arrangements: The Fact Sheet*, www.workplaceflexibility2010.org.
12. Kenexa, *WorkTrends*.
13. Ibid.

Chapter 2 What's in It for Me?

1. CDW 2007 Telework Report, p. 6.
2. Ibid., p. 11.
3. U.S. Census Bureau, *2002 American Community Survey*, Ranking Tables 2002. Average Travel Time to Work of Workers 16 Years and Over Who Did

Not Work at Home. Based on a 76-minute commute. (Minutes) http://www.census.gov/acs/www/Products/Ranking/2002/R04T160.htm.
4. U.S. Department of Transportation, Bureau of Transportation Statistics, *Omnibus Household Survey 2003*. Based on average commute of 26 minutes, one way.
5. University of Connecticut and Rutgers University, Center for Survey Research and Analysis and John J. Heldrich Center for Workforce Development; *Work and Family: How Employers and Workers Can Strike the Balance*. New Brunswick, NJ: 1999.
6. Ibid.
7. CDW 2008 Telework Report, page 22. Of federal teleworkers, 52 percent report being more productive at home, 43 percent report being equally productive. Of private sector teleworkers, 39 percent report being more productive at home, 51 percent report being equally productive.
8. Transportation figure based on Bureau of Transportation Statistics (BTS) *Omnibus Household Survey* that found average commute is 15 miles each way. Cost based on GSA March 2008 reimbursement rate of $.505/mile. Wardrobe figure based on U.S. Bureau of Labor Statistics 2005 Consumer Spending Report: Table 7, measuring relative spending of one earner versus two earners; the difference was $695 or $2.78/day, and that figure was used for Office Average. Table 12 measured average of manager/professional ($2,703) versus retired ($1,047). The difference was $1,656 or $6.24/day (50 weeks/year).
9. Assumes 25 percent down, 30-year term, 7 percent fixed.
10. *Safety & Heath Practitioner*, May 2008, p. 71.
11. October 2000, Public Law 106-346 Ï 359; January 2004, Public Law 108-199, Division B, Ï 627.
12. CDW 2007 Telework Report.
13. National Council on Compensation Insurance Inc., *Traffic Accidents—A Growing Contributor to Workers' Compensation Losses* (December 2006).
14. Ibid.

Chapter 3 Expose Yourself—Are You Right For E-work?

1. InnoVisions Canada, http://www.ivc.ca/bumperstickers.html.
2. Phil Plait, BadAstronomy Blog, http://blogs.discovermagazine.com/badastronomy/.
3. CDW 2008 Telework Report, p. 21.
4. Ibid., p. 8.

Chapter 4 Dirty Underwear—Uncovering the Scams

1. http://www.ftc.gov/opa/2006/12/falsehopes.shtm.
2. Ibid.
3. http://www.ftc.gov/bcp/edu/pubs/consumer/invest/inv14.shtm.

Chapter 5 Who's Paid to Work at Home and What Do They Do?

1. U.S. Census Bureau, *2006 American Community Survey*, Table B08301.
2. CDW 2008 Telework Report, p. 9. Among private sector employees, 11 percent e-work only occasionally, 9 percent less than one day a week, 15 percent one day a

week, 14 percent two days a week, 12 percent three days a week, 9 percent four days a week, 30 percent five days a week.

3. H. Scott Williams and Eric Matthews, "Telework Adoption and Energy Use in Building and Transportation Sector in the United States and Japan," *Journal of Infrastructure Systems*, vol. 11, issue 1 (March 2005), pp. 21–30. Estimated that information workers who could have the potential to telecommute represent 53 million Americans (which at the time was 40 percent of the workforce). That percentage was applied to *2006 American Community Survey* data. The number of people already working at home (U.S. Census Bureau survey, Table B08301) was subtracted before arriving at the number who could work from home.

4. WorldatWork, Trendlines.

Chapter 6 Take Your Job and Love It

1. Telework Exchange, *2007 Face to Face with Management Reality*, http://www.teleworkexchange.com/managementstudy/.
2. CDW 2008 Telework Report, p. 10.
3. Federal Managers Association and Telework Exchange survey of 214 federal managers (November 2006).

Chapter 7 The Naked Truth about Your Boss

1. Telephone interview with Jack Nilles.
2. Federal Managers and Telework Exchange survey.
3. Management-Issues.com, "Managers Still Suspicious of Home Working" (July 20 2007), quoting City and Guilds survey, http://www.management-issues.com/2007/7/30/research/managers-still-suspicious-of-homeWorking.asp.
4. Cali Ressler, Jodi Thompson, *Why Work Sucks and How to Fix It* (Portfolio Harcover, 2008), front matter.
5. Telework Exchange, *Face to Face*.
6. June Langhoff, "A Telemanager's Index: The Definitive Roundup of Telecommuting Statistics," *Home Office* magazine (April 1999).
7. U.S. General Services Administration, "Current Telework Costs" (January 23, 2006), PowerPoint presentation, p. 35.
8. U.S. Office of Personnel Management, *Status of Telework in the Federal Government—Report to Congress* (June 2006) p. 13.
9. Telework Exchange, *Remote Control Federal CISOs Dish on Mobility, Telework, and Data Security* (2007), http://www.teleworkexchange.com/cisostudy/.

Chapter 8 What's in It for Your Employer?

1. James Ware, Judith Gebauer, Amir Hartman, Malu Roldan, *The Search for Digital Excellence* (McGraw-Hill, April 1998).
2. Futurestep, Trends@Work Quiz, "61% of Executives Surveyed Believe Telecommuters are Less Likely to Advance in Comparison to Employees Working in Traditional Office Settings," news release, January 16, 2007.
3. Intranet DASHBOARD, *Telecommuting Survey: Results of 390 Person Survey of U.S. Executives*, July 26, 2007, http://www.intranetdashboard.com/press/db_press.aspx.

4. Information Technology Association of America, *Anytime, Anyplace, Anywhere Report* (July 2002).

5. Dice Holdings, Inc., *The Dice Report* (June 2008)—survey of over 1,500 tech professionals.

6. Manpower, Inc., *Talent Shortage Survey Report* (2007); survey of 33,000 employers in 23 countries. http://www.manpowerprofessional.com.hk/pdf/talent_shortage.pdf.

7. CareerBuilder.com, *Job Forecast 2008* (December 2007); survey of over 3,000 employers.

8. *Work Trends—Americans' Attitudes about Work, Employers and Government, Second Wind: Workers, Retirement and Social Security.* A joint project of the John J. Heldrich Center for Workforce Development at Rutgers, the State University of New Jersey, and the Center for Survey Research at the University of Connecticut.

9. Robert Grossman, "The Truth About the Coming Labor Shortage," Society for Human Resource Management (March 2005), http://www.shrm.org/hrmagazine/articles/0305/0305covstory.asp.

10. *Work Trends.*

11. BusinessWeek Research and TransitCenter, *The Impact of Commuting on Employees* (February 2008); survey of 1,048 employees.

12. U.S. Bureau of Labor Statistics, Table A-1 and A-5 (July 2008) show that 34 percent of 154 million working-age Americans are not working, 19 million for noneconomic reasons and 5.5 million because they couldn't find full-time work or because of slack work or business conditions.

13. U.S. Bureau of Labor Statistics, *Monthly Labor Review* vol. 130, no. 11 (November 2007), p. 40.

14. U.S. Bureau of Labor Statistics, Table 20, employed persons by full- and part-time status and sex, 1970–2006 annual averages; Table 7, employment status of women by presence and age of youngest child, March 1975–2006.

15. AccessibleSociety.org, "Economics and People with Disabilities," http://www.accessiblesociety.org/topics/economics-employment/.

16. Jonathan Spira, Joshua Feintuch, *The Cost of Not Paying Attention: How Interruptions Impact Knowledge Worker Productivity* (Basex, Inc., 2005), http://lib.store.yahoo.net/lib/bsx/basexcostpayes.pdf.

17. Testimony of Ann Bamesberger, vice president of Open Work Services Group, Sun Microsystems, "Telework—Breaking New Ground," November 2007, U.S. House of Representatives.

18. Ressler and Thompson, *Why Work Sucks.*

19. The Telework Coalition, "Telework Facts," http://www.telcoa.org/id33.htm.

20. June Langhoff, "A Telemanager's Index: The Definitive Roundup of Telecommuting Statistics," *Home Office* magazine (April 1999).

21. WorldatWork, *ITAC 2006 Trendlines Report*, p. 5.

22. Telework Coalition, "Telework Facts."

23. Ibid.

24. Ann Bamesberger, *Flex Your Force: Building the Virtual Office*, Sun Executive Boardroom (August '07) Sun Microsystems, http://www.sun.com/emrkt/boardroom/newsletter/0807leadingvision.html.

25. Telephone interview with Linda Casey, McKesson Corporation, August 17, 2007.

26. Telework Coalition, "Telework Facts."

27. Ibid.

28. Ibid.
29. Ibid.
30. United States Equal Employment Opportunity Commission, *Work At Home/ Telework as a Reasonable Accommodation*, http://www.eeoc.gov/facts/telework.html.
31. CDW 2007 Telework Report, p. 13.
32. TalentKeepers, *Employee Turnover Trends: Survey Report*, April 2004.
33. Linda Casey, McKesson Health Solutions, "Tapping into the Hidden Workforce: Military Spouses, Disabled, Rural, Returning Veterans, Retired Workers, and Stay-at-Home Spouses Telecomm Cost Benefit," PowerPoint presentation, June 2007.
34. WorldatWork, *Member Survey: Attraction and Retention Practices*, October 2007; 46 percent report e-work has had a high impact on employee retention.
35. CCH, *CCH Survey Finds Most Employees Call in "Sick" for Reasons Other Than Illness*, CCH Unscheduled Absence Survey (October 2007). The study was conducted by Harris Interactive and included 317 human resources executives.
36. Ibid.
37. Hewitt LCG, "Uncover the Reasons Why People Are Absent. Fix Those Reasons, and You Could Recover Millions" (2003), http://www.nucleussolutions.com/pdfs/ Nucleus-Absence-Overview.pdf.
38. Ibid.
39. Joseph G. Grzywacz, Patrick R. Casey, "Workplace Flexibility Associated with Reduced Absences and Improved Job Commitment," Wake Forest University School of Medicine (April 2008); survey of 3,193 employees of a large multi-national pharmaceutical company, http://www1.wfubmc.edu/News/NewsArticle .htm?ArticleID=2355.
40. BusinessWeek Research, *Impact of Commuting*.

Chapter 9 Making Your E-work Pitch

1. Author interview with Cali Williams Yost, August 19, 2008.
2. CDW 2008 Telework Report, p. 7. Among organizations that allow e-work, 65 percent of private companies and 68 percent of federal agencies have a written policy to govern the practice.

Chaper 10 Best-Bet E-work Employers

1. Marcia Rhodes, WorldatWork, e-mail, August 19, 2008.
2. Public Law (PL) 106-346 section 359, October 2000.
3. CDW 2008 Telework Report.
4. Ibid.
5. WorldatWork, *Trendlines*.
6. CDW 2008 Telework Report.
7. Ibid, p. 9. Among federal employees, 24 percent e-work only occasionally, 30 percent less than one day a week, 24 percent one day a week, 11 percent two days a week, 2 percent three days a week, 2 percent four days a week, 6 percent five days a week.
8. U.S. Personnel Management, *Status of TeleWork*.
9. WorldatWork, "Attraction and Retention Practices" (October 2007).
10. CareerBuilder.com, *Job Forecast 2008*.

11. CNNMoney.com, *Fortune 100 Best Companies to Work For 2008*, http://money.cnn .com/magazines/fortune/bestcompanies/2008/benefits/telecommuting.html.
12. CDW 2008 Telework Report, p. 9. Among private sector employees, 11 percent e-work only occasionally, 9 percent less than one day a week, 15 percent one day a week, 14 percent two days a week, 12 percent three days a week, 9 percent four days a week, 30 percent five days a week.

Chapter 11 Work as a Call Center Agent

1. The Taylor Research Group, Inc., "Call Center Industry Statistics Related to PREDICTIONS" (sic), quoting unreferenced Yankee Group report, http://www.thetaylorreachgroup.com/industryStats.php?related=Predictions.
2. IDC Worldwide Contact Center Services, Vendor Profiles: Customer Care in Volatile Times—U.S. Home-Based Agent 2007–2011 Forecast: The Irony of Homeshoring's Rising Value Amid a U.S. Housing Bust (2008), http://www.idc.com/getdoc.jsp?containerId=208501.
3. A Yankee Group survey of 350 U.S. and Canadian call centers found that 24 percent of domestic agents (672,000 workers) are now home-based. Quoted in http://www.shrm.org/hrmagazine/articles/0107/0107fraseblunt.asp.
4. Ibid. IDC's latest research estimates that there are 112,000 home-based agents in the United States today; by 2010 that number could reach more than 300,000.
5. U.S. Department of Labor, Bureau of Labor Statistics, "2008–09 Occupational Outlook," http://www.bls.gov/OCO/.

Chapter 12 Work as a Virtual Assistant

1. U.S. Department of Labor, "Occupational Outlook."
2. Ibid.

Chapter 13 Work as a Medical Transcriptionist

1. Bentley College, *2007 Survey of Medical Transcriptionists: Preliminary Findings.* Prepared by the Healthcare Documentation Production Project for the AHDI/ MTIA Advocacy Summit, May 15–17, 2008.
2. FinancialWire.net, "Offshoring Of Medical Transcription Poised For Growth," June 13, 2008, http://www.tradingmarkets.com/.site/news/Stock%20News/1682552/.
3. Ibid.
4. Ibid.
5. Ibid.
6. Ibid.

Chapter 14 Work as a Teacher or Tutor

1. Lee S. Shulman, "It's All About Time!" *Perspectives*, Carnegie Foundation for the Advancement of Teaching, December 11, 2007, http://www.carnegiefoundation .org/perspectives/sub.asp?key=245&subkey=2483.

2. Susan McLester, "Ten Top Tech Trends," TechLearning.com, January 15, 2008, http://www.techlearning.com/story/showArticle.php?articleID=196604927&page=3.
3. Vicky Phillips, "Are Online Degrees Really as Good as their Campus Counterparts?" http://www.geteducated.com/surveys/publicacct.asp.
4. The Sloan Consortium, *K-12 Online Learning: A Survey of U.S. School District Administrators* (referring to the 2005–2006 academic year), http://www.sloan-c .org/publications/survey/K-12_06.
5. Evergreen Consulting Associates, *Keeping Pace with K-12 Online Learning—A Review of State-Level Policy and Practice* (2006).
6. July 2008 numbers, provided by Jodie Pozo-Alono, Sequoia Public Relations.
7. The North American Council for Online Learning and the Partnership for 21st Century Skills, *Virtual Schools and 21st Century Skills*, November 2006.
8. Sloan Foundation, Babson Survey Research Group, *Making the Grade* (2006); survey of 4,491 institutions.
9. Ibid.
10. Ibid.
11. Ibid.
12. American Association of University Professors, *Annual Report of the Economic Status of the Profession 2007–2008*, http://www.aaup.org/AAUP/comm/rep/Z/ecstatreport2007-08/.
13. ThinkEquity Partners, *Emerging Trends in Post-Secondary Education: The View to 2012*, December 9, 2002, http://www.usdla.org/ppt/THINKEQUITY.ppt.
14. Ibid.
15. Sloan Consortium, *K-12 Online Learning*.
16. Florida Virtual School web site: "FLVS Instructors—The Real Story," http://www .flvs.net/general/Employment.php.
17. Kerry Rice and Lisa Dawley, *Going Virtual—The Status of Professional Development for K-12 Online Teachers* (Boise State University, November 2007).
18. Evergreen Consulting, *Keeping Pace*.
19. Danielle Babb and Jim Mirabella, *Make Money Teaching Online* (John Wiley & Sons, 2007).
20. Suzanne B. Clery and Barry L. Christopher, "Faculty Salaries: 2006–2007," in National Education Association, *The NEA 2008 Almanac of Higher Education*.
21. Patricia Deubel, "What's Full-Time for K-12 Online Teaching?—A Dilemma," *T.H.E. Journal* (January 2007).

Chapter 16 Work as a Writer

1. U.S. Bureau of Labor Statistics, *2008–2009 U.S. Occupational Outlook Handbook*.
2. Ibid.
3. Ibid.
4. Marshall Brain, "Lesson 1a: Calibrating Alexa," http://webkew.blogspot.com/2005/ 04/lesson-1a-calibrating-alexa.html.

Chapter 17 Work in Telemedicine

1. R. Wooten, M. Loane, F. Mair, A. Allen, G. Doolittle, M. Begley, A. McLernan, M. Moutray, and S. Harrisson, "A Joint US–UK Study of Home Telenursing,"

Journal of Telemedicine and Telecare vol. 4, issue 1 (1998), 83–85. The study included an analysis of over 1,700 patient care cases.

Chapter 18 How to Navigate the Web in Search of E-work

1. Boutell.com: Based on an estimated 108 million web sites (Netcraft Web Server Survey, February 2007) and an average of 273 pages per site (derived from the last publicized count of pages by Yahoo in 2005: 19.2 billion pages); http://www.boutell.com/newfaq/misc/sizeofweb.html.

Chapter 19 Using the Job Boards to Find eWork

1. Borrell Associates, *Recruitment Outlook* (January 2007), and August 14, 2008, e-mail exchange with Peter Conti Jr., senior vice president of Borrell Associates.
2. E-mail from Lauren McDonald of Weber Shandwick, public relations liaison for Monster.com.
3. http://www.craigslist.org/about/factsheet.html.

Chapter 20 Your Digital Resume

1. ExecuNet, "Digital Dirt Derails More Job Searches as Recruiters' Use of Search Engines Increases," press release, August 16, 2007.

Chapter 21 Collaboration and Social Networking for E-work

1. ComScore, "Social Networking Explodes Worldwide as Sites Increase Their Focus on Cultural Relevance," press release, August 12, 2008, http://www.comscore.com/press/release.asp?press=2396.
2. Sarah Needleman, "Job Seekers: Put Your Web Savvy to Work," *Wall Street Journal*, September 9, 2007, http://online.wsj.com/article/SB118929136825921709.html?mod=googlenews_wsj.

Chapter 22 Who Freelances and What Do They Do?

1. U.S. Department of Labor, Bureau of Labor Statistics, *Current Population Survey*, February 2005 supplement: 10.3 million independent contractors represent 7.4 percent of the workforce.
2. CareerBuilder.com, *Job Forecast 2008*.
3. Daniel Pink, *Free Agent Nation* (Warner Books, 2001).
4. Ibid.
5. Ibid.
6. FreelanceSwitch.com, Freelance Statistics Report (2008).

Chapter 25 Proposals and Contracts

1. About.com, Desktop Publishing, http://desktoppub.about.com/od/contracts/&poll_id=2532325153.

Chapter 26 Finding Freelance Work

1. Data provided by Guru.com.
2. McKay Stewart, Guru.com freelancer and owner of TheWebSaint.com.
3. Interview and data provided by Cathy Siciliano, Elance Director of Marketing, July 2, 2008.
4. oDesk.com web site (June 2008), www.odesk.com.

Chapter 27 Who's Running Home Businesses and What Do They Do?

1. The University of Michigan, *Panel Study of Entrepreneurial Dynamics (PSED)*. Continuing study of nascent entrepreneurs since 1996.
2. U.S. Census Bureau, *2002 Survey of Business Owners—Owner Characteristics* (2006).
3. United States Small Business Administration, Office of Advocacy, *The Small Business Economy 2007—A Report to the President*.
4. U.S. Census Bureau, 2002 Survey.
5. Joanne H. Pratt, U.S. Small Business Administration, Office of Advocacy, "The Impact of Location on Net Income" (May 2006).
6. Ibid.
7. Ibid.
8. Ibid.
9. Ibid.

Chapter 28 The Right Fit

1. *Inc.* magazine, "2007 Inc. 5000 Entrepreneurial America: A Comprehensive Look at Today's Fastest-Growing Private Companies." http://www.inc.com/inc5000/2007/index.html.
2. Michael E. Gerber, *The E-Myth Revisited: Why Most Small Businesses Don't Work and What to Do About It* (Harper Collins, 1995).
3. National Federation of Independent Businesses (NFIB), "Small Business Resource Guide for the 110th Congress."

Chapter 29 Designing the Perfect Business

1. Mary Buffett and David Clark, *The Tao of Warren Buffet* (Scribner, 2006), p. 15.

Chapter 30 The Business Model

1. Chris Anderson, *The Long Tail* (Hyperion, 2006).
2. The Long Tail blog: "Definitions—Final Round," January 9, 2005, http://longtail.typepad.com/the_long_tail/2005/01/definitions_fin.html.

Chapter 31 Best-Bet Business

1. The Nielsen Company, Global Online Shopping Report (February 2008).
2. U.S. Census Bureau, Quarterly Retail E-commerce Sales, Second Quarter 2008.

3. The Nielsen Company, Global Online Shopping Report (February 2008).
4. Ibid.
5. TrendWatching.com, "Minipreneurs" (September 2005), http://trendwatching .com/trends/minipreneurs.htm.
6. Google, Inc., "Google Announces Fourth Quarter and Fiscal Year 2007 Results," http://investor.google.com/releases/2007Q4.html. Total acquisition costs, the portion of ad revenue shared with Google's partners, averaged 30 percent in the fourth quarter of 2007. That percentage was applied to partner revenue of 5.8 billion for all of 2007.
7. Pratt, "Impact of Location."
8. Ibid.

Chapter 33 Naked Truths about Home Biz

1. National Federation of Independent Business, *Small Business Problems & Priorities* (June 2008).
2. Ibid.

Chapter 35 Let's All Undress

1. Jack Heacock, e-mail, August 26, 2008.
2. UndressForSuccessOnline.com proprietary model based on data from the American Community Survey, EPA, Bureau of Transportation Statistics, the Reason Foundation, and others.
3. CO_2 savings calculated using UndressForSuccessOnline.com proprietary model based on data from the 2006 American Community Survey, EPA, Bureau of Transportation Statistics, the Reason Foundation, and others.
4. EPA State CO_2 emissions from fossil fuel by state (2005), http://www.epa.gov/ climatechange/emissions/state_energyco2inv.html. CO_2 from fossil fuel in transportation in New York was 72 million tons in 2005. E-work savings are based on UndressForSuccessOnline.com proprietary model showing a savings of 78 million tons for the 50 million new e-workers.
5. Joseph Romm, Center for Energy and Climate Solutions, Global Environment and Technology Foundation, *The Internet and the New Energy Economy* (2002), 141. New e-worker savings is calculated as 50 million e-workers $\times.5$ (for half-time e-work) $\times 1,400$ kWh/person/year $= 35$ billion kWh/year, our own assumption of 50 percent that are "lights out" when not being used $= 17.5$ billion kWh/year. U.S. Department of Energy, Energy Information Administration, Household Electricity Reports, United States, Table US-1 (2001). Average household energy use: 10,656 kWh/year so savings is enough to power 1.64 million households for a year. National Energy Information Center, U.S. Department of Energy (2003), www.eia .doe.gov/cneaf/electricity/page/at_a_glance/sales_tabs.html. The number of homes in Idaho, New Hampshire, and Maine are 532,000, 497,000, and 542,000 respectively.
6. American Consumer Institute, "Broadband Services: Economic and Environmental Benefits" (2007), p. 3. Telecommuting will reduce greenhouse gas emissions by 28.1 million tons due to reduced office construction. Equivalent in cars is based on Environmental Defense Fund Paper Calculator (the average car produces 11,013 pounds of greenhouse gases per year). For more information, visit http://www.papercalculator.org.
7. Texas Transportation Institute at Texas A&M University, *2007 Urban Mobility Report*, http://mobility.tamu.edu.
8. Ibid. 4 billion hours/1,920 work hours per year $= 2$ million man years.

9. RoadRagers.com, *Results: Analyze Your Driving Style* (2004) composite statistics from 11,120 quiz responses by drivers.

10. American Automobile Association, "Crashes vs. Congestion: What's the Cost to Society?" (February 28, 2008).

11. The 50 million new e-workers would avoid 180 billion miles of driving. Traffic Safety Facts NHSTA.gov 2007 shows traffic fatalities occur at a rate of 1.4 per 100 million vehicle miles traveled (vmt), and injuries occur at a rate of 83 per 100 million vmt. CommuterSolutions.org, "The True Cost of Driving" reports that traffic accidents cost individuals 8.1 cents per mile in personal costs of injury and property damage, and 4.6 cents a mile in government-paid cleanup, lost economic activity, and so on. http://www.commutesolutions.org/calc.htm.

12. John Edwards (chairman and founder), Telework Coalition, "It All Adds Up to Cleaner Air," quarterly newsletter (Winter 2006).

13. According to the U.S. Census Bureaus 2007 American Community Survey report SO802 "Means of Transportation to Work," the U.S. employs about 139.3 million workers. About 6.8 million use public transportation to get to work. About 5.7 million people already work at home roughly half the time, representing 2.7 million cars/day. So about 129.7 million people (139 – 6.8 – 2.7) commute every day and 105.9 million of them (81.7%) drive solo. So 50 million new e-workers would reduce the number of cars on the road by 20.4 million per day (50 million × 81.7% × 50% for half time e-work). That represents 15.8 percent of daily commuters. Using John Edwards' estimate of 3 percent reduction in congestion for every 1 percent reduction in vehicles, the new e-workers would reduce traffic congestion by almost half (47.4%).

14. Texas Transportation Institute, The *2007 Urban Mobility Report*. David Schrank and Tim Lomax. http://tti.tamu.edu/documents/mobility_report_2007_wappx.pdf.

15. The Reason Foundation, *Building Roads to Reduce Traffic Congestion in America's Cities: How Much and at What Cost?* (August 2006), http://www.reason.org/ps346.pdf. David T. Hartgen and M. Gregory Fields

16. Ibid, p. 7

17. The Reason Foundation, op. cit., p. 6, "For large areas over 3 million in population, congestion is predicted to increase from an average of 1.46 to 1.76 over the next 25 year. " *op. cit.*

18. U.S. Senate, Committee on Banking, Housing and Urban Affairs, *Condition of our Nation's Infrastructure: Local Perspectives from Mayors* (6/12/08), http://banking.senate.gov/public/index.cfm?Fuseaction=Hearings. Detail&HearingID=5a20ef0c-bf1c-41c7-bac2-98ba54f4ab7c.

19. Malone, *Future of Work*.

20. Organisation for Economic Co-operation and Development, OECD Broadband Portal, oecd.org/sti/ict/broadband.

21. Information Technology & Innovation Foundation, "2008 ITIF Broadband Rankings." http://www.itif.org/index.php?id=143.

22. Ibid.

23. Positively Broadband Campaign, *Anytime, Anyplace, Anywhere: Broadband and the Changing Face of Work*, industry whitepaper (June 2002).

24. Ibid.

25. Hartgen and Fields, p. 9.

26. Vermont Department of Public Services, *Understanding Broadband Deployment in Vermont*, p. 13. The cost for cable line extensions is approximately $20,000/mile based on data reported in Adelphia's 2005 Annual Report.

Index